Workshop on Computational Approaches to Language Data Pseudonymization (CALD-pseudo 2024)

St. Julian's, Malta
21 March 2024

ISBN: 978-1-7138-9448-3

Printed from e-media with permission by:

Curran Associates, Inc.
57 Morehouse Lane
Red Hook, NY 12571

Some format issues inherent in the e-media version may also appear in this print version.

Association for Computational Linguistics
209 N. Eighth Street
Stroudsburg, Pennsylvania 18360

Phone: 1-570-476-8006
Fax: 1-570-476-0860

acl@aclweb.org

Additional copies of this publication are available from:

Curran Associates, Inc.
57 Morehouse Lane
Red Hook, NY 12571 USA
Phone: 845-758-0400
Fax: 845-758-2633
Email: curran@proceedings.com
Web: www.proceedings.com

CALD-pseudo 2024

Workshop on Computational Approaches to Language Data Pseudonymization (CALD-pseudo)

Proceedings of the Workshop

March 21, 2024

Association for Computational Linguistics (ACL)
209 N. Eighth Street
Stroudsburg, PA 18360
USA
Tel: +1-570-476-8006
Fax: +1-570-476-0860
acl@aclweb.org

Introduction

We are excited to offer you the first proceedings from the workshop on Computational Approaches to Language Data Pseudonymization, CALD-pseudo 2024[1]!
We have accepted 10 high-quality papers representing a wide geographic diversity, namely co-authors with affiliations in the Basque Country, Canada, Finland, France, Germany, Japan, Norway, Spain, Sweden, and the USA.
In this volume, you can read papers that deal with the topic of personal or sensitive information, and the subsequent question of accessibility of research data. Accessibility of research data is critical for advances in many research fields but textual data often cannot be shared due to the personal and sensitive information it contains, e.g. names, political opinions, sensitive personal information, and medical data. General Data Protection Regulation, GDPR (EU Commission, 2016), suggests pseudonymization as a solution to secure open access to research data but we need to learn more about pseudonymization as an approach before adopting it for the manipulation of research data (Volodina et al., 2023). The main challenge is how to effectively pseudonymize data so that such individuals cannot be identified, while at the same time keeping the data usable for research (e.g. in computational linguistics, linguistics) and natural language processing tasks for which it was collected.
This workshop has invited a broad community of researchers in all concerned cross-disciplinary fields to jointly discuss challenges within pseudonymization, such as

- automatic approaches to detection and labelling of personal information in unstructured language data, including events and other context-dependent cues revealing a person;
- developing context-sensitive algorithms for replacement of personal information in unstructured data;
- studies into the effects of pseudonymization on unstructured data, e.g. applicability of pseudonymised data for the intended research questions, readability of pseudonymised data, or addition of unwelcome biases through pseudonymization;
- effectiveness of pseudonymization as a way of protecting writer identity;
- reidentification studies, e.g. adversarial learning techniques that attempt to breach the privacy protections of pseudonymized data;
- constructing datasets for automatic pseudonymization, including methodological and ethical aspects of those;
- approaches to the evaluation of automatic pseudonymization both in concealing the private information and preserving the semantics of the non-personal data;
- pseudonymization tools and software: evaluating the available tools and software for pseudonymization in different languages, and their ease of use, scalability, and performance;
- and numerous other open questions.

The workshop was one full day and included two invited talks - by Ildikó Pilán and Anders Søgaard.
We would kindly like to thank our program committee for their valuable (and enthusiastic!) contribution to the success of the workshop:

- Lars Ahrenberg, Linköping University, Sweden
- Terhi Ainiala, University of Helsinki, Finland

[1] https://mormor-karl.github.io/events/CALD-pseudo/

- Emilia Aldrin, Halmstad University, Sweden
- Špela Arhar Holdt, University of Ljubljana, Slovenia
- Andrew Caines, University of Cambridge, United Kingdom
- Hercules Dalianis, Stockholm University, Sweden
- Dana Dannélls, University of Gothenburg, Sweden
- Simon Dobnik, University of Gothenburg, Sweden
- Cyril Grouin, LIMSI, CNRS, Université Paris-Saclay, France
- Lasse Hämäläinen, University of Helsinki, Finland
- Aron Henriksson, Stockholm University, Sweden
- Dimitrios Kokkinakis, University of Gothenburg, Sweden
- Jannika Lassus, University of Helsinki, Finland
- Therese Lindström Tiedemann, University of Helsinki, Finland
- Pierre Lison, Norwegian Computing Center, Norway
- Krister Lindén, University of Helsinki, Finland
- Peter Ljunglöf, Chalmers University of Technology / University of Gothenburg, Sweden
- Ricardo Muñoz Sánchez, University of Gothenburg, Sweden
- Boel Nelson, Aarhus University, Denmark
- Lieselott Nordman, University of Helsinki, Finland
- Ildikó Pilán, Norwegian Computing Center, Norway
- Vipul Raheja, Grammarly, USA
- Tatjana Scheffler, Ruhr University Bochum, Germany
- Vicenc Torra, Umeå University, Sweden
- Thomas Vakili, Stockholm University, Sweden
- VG Vinod Vydiswaran, University of Michigan, USA
- Elena Volodina, University of Gothenburg, Sweden
- Xuan-Son Vu, Umeå University, Sweden

Our further thanks go to the generous support from the *Swedish Research Council*[2] through its funding to the research environment project *Grandma Karl is 27 years old*[3].

[2] https://www.vr.se/english/swecris.html#/project/2022-02311_VR
[3] https://mormor-karl.github.io/

Organizing Committee

General Chair

Elena Volodina, University of Gothenburg, Sweden

General Co-chairs

Simon Dobnik, University of Gothenburg, Sweden
Therese Lindström Tiedemann, University of Helsinki, Finland
Xuan-Son Vu, Umeå University, Sweden

Organizing Co-chairs

David Alfter, University of Gothenburg, Sweden
Ricardo Muñoz Sánchez, University of Gothenburg, Sweden
Maria Irena Szawerna, University of Gothenburg, Sweden

Program Committee

Program Committee

Lars Ahrenberg, Linköping University, Sweden
Terhi Ainiala, University of Helsinki, Finland
Emilia Aldrin, Halmstad University, Sweden
Špela Arhar Holdt, University of Ljubljana, Slovenia
Andrew Caines, University of Cambridge, United Kingdom
Hercules Dalianis, Stockholm University, Sweden
Dana Dannélls, University of Gothenburg, Sweden
Simon Dobnik, University of Gothenburg, Sweden
Cyril Grouin, LIMSI, CNRS, Université Paris-Saclay, France
Lasse Hämäläinen, University of Helsinki, Finland
Aron Henriksson, Stockholm University, Sweden
Dimitrios Kokkinakis, University of Gothenburg, Sweden
Jannika Lassus, University of Helsinki, Finland
Therese Lindström Tiedemann, University of Helsinki, Finland
Krister Lindén, University of Helsinki, Finland
Peter Ljunglöf, Chalmers University of Technology / University of Gothenburg, Sweden
Ricardo Muñoz Sánchez, University of Gothenburg, Sweden
Boel Nelson, Aarhus University, Denmark
Lieselott Nordman, University of Helsinki, Finland
Ildikó Pilán, Norwegian Computing Center, Norway
Vipul Raheja, Grammarly, USA
Tatjana Scheffler, Ruhr University Bochum, Germany
Vicenc Torra, Umeå University, Sweden
Thomas Vakili, Stockholm University, Sweden
VG Vinod Vydiswaran, University of Michigan, USA
Elena Volodina, University of Gothenburg, Sweden
Xuan-Son Vu, Umeå University, Sweden

Keynote Talk: NLP is Dead - Now What?

Anders Søgaard
University of Copenhagen, Denmark

2024-03-21 09:10:00 – Room: **Corinthia hotel, Gardjola 3 (virtual talk)**

Abstract: For decades, the NLP community was on a mission to get computers to understand language. To the extent the goal of the mission was defined, our mission is complete. Now what? There are still a ton of open problems, of course. Pseudonymization is one of them. Others include bias mitigation, performance parity, or getting things to run on-device. None of these problems are NLP problems, but they are all inter-dependent. Does their locus leave room for a raison d'être for the remnants of NLP?

Bio: Anders Søgaard is Full Professor in Natural Language Processing and Machine Learning, Dpt. of Computer Science, University of Copenhagen. He is also affiliated with the Pioneer Centre for Artificial Intelligence, Dpt. of Philosophy, and Center for Social Data Science. He was previously at University of Potsdam, Amazon and Google Research. He has won eight best paper awards and several prestigious grants.

Keynote Talk: Pseudonymisation and related techniques: a quest for determining what personal information to rewrite and how

Ildikó Pilán
The Norwegian Computing Center, Norway
2024-03-21 13:00:00 – Room: **Corinthia hotel, Gardjola 3**

Abstract: In this talk, we will walk through the different steps involved in the process of concealing personal information. We will start by looking at methods for which pieces of personal information to detect and how. We will then discuss strategies for rewriting these and, finally, we will look at approaches proposed for evaluating the resulting redacted text in terms of privacy protection and utility preservation. We will discuss previous work inspired by Named Entity Recognition as well as more recent approaches employing Large Language Models. We will also explore the differences between pseudonymization and anonymization highlighting the remaining challenges in performing these automatically.

Bio: Ildikó Pilán is a Senior Research Scientist at the Norwegian Computing Center, Norway. Her most impactful research comes from linguistic complexity studies within the domain of language learning, and recently from the area of anonymization and pseudonymization where she has been actively working on preparing datasets, benchmarks and models for automatic anonymization and pseudonymization of Norwegian and English data in the project Cleanup (e.g. Lison et al., 2021; Pilán et al., 2022). Her fields of expertise include Natural Language Processing, Machine Learning, privacy protection, data privacy, medical text processing and Intelligent Computer-Assisted Language Learning.

Table of Contents

Handling Name Errors of a BERT-Based De-Identification System: Insights from Stratified Sampling and Markov-based Pseudonymization
Dalton Simancek and VG Vinod Vydiswaran 1

Assessing Authenticity and Anonymity of Synthetic User-generated Content in the Medical Domain
Tomohiro Nishiyama, Lisa Raithel, Roland Roller, Pierre Zweigenbaum and Eiji Aramaki 8

Automatic Detection and Labelling of Personal Data in Case Reports from the ECHR in Spanish: Evaluation of Two Different Annotation Approaches
Maria Sierro, Begoña Altuna and Itziar Gonzalez-Dios 18

PSILENCE: A Pseudonymization Tool for International Law
Luis Adrián Cabrera-Diego and Akshita Gheewala 25

Deidentifying a Norwegian Clinical Corpus - an Effort to Create a Privacy-preserving Norwegian Large Clinical Language Model
Phuong Ngo, Miguel Tejedor, Therese Olsen Svenning, Taridzo Chomutare, Andrius Budrionis and Hercules Dalianis 37

Extending Off-the-shelf NER Systems to Personal Information Detection in Dialogues with a Virtual Agent: Findings from a Real-Life Use Case
Mario Mina, Carlos Rodríguez, Aitor Gonzalez-Agirre and Marta Villegas 44

Detecting Personal Identifiable Information in Swedish Learner Essays
Maria Irena Szawerna, Simon Dobnik, Ricardo Muñoz Sánchez, Therese Lindström Tiedemann and Elena Volodina 54

Data Anonymization for Privacy-Preserving Large Language Model Fine-Tuning on Call Transcripts
Shayna Gardiner, Tania Habib, Kevin Humphreys, Masha Azizi, Frederic Mailhot, Anne Paling, Preston Thomas and Nathan Zhang 64

When Is a Name Sensitive? Eponyms in Clinical Text and Implications for De-Identification
Thomas Vakili, Tyr Hullmann, Aron Henriksson and Hercules Dalianis 76

Did the Names I Used within My Essay Affect My Score? Diagnosing Name Biases in Automated Essay Scoring
Ricardo Muñoz Sánchez, Simon Dobnik, Maria Irena Szawerna, Therese Lindström Tiedemann and Elena Volodina 81

Program

Thursday, March 21, 2024

09:00 - 09:10	*Opening Remarks by Elena Volodina*
09:10 - 10:00	*Invited talk 1. Anders Søgaard. Title: NLP is Dead - Now What?, chair: Elena Volodina*
10:00 - 10:30	*Session 1, chair: Maria Irena Szawerna*
	Handling Name Errors of a BERT-Based De-Identification System: Insights from Stratified Sampling and Markov-based Pseudonymization Dalton Simancek and VG Vinod Vydiswaran
	Automatic Detection and Labelling of Personal Data in Case Reports from the ECHR in Spanish: Evaluation of Two Different Annotation Approaches Maria Sierro, Begoña Altuna and Itziar Gonzalez-Dios
10:30 - 11:00	*COFFEE break*
11:00 - 12:00	*Session 2, chair: Hercules Dalianis*
	PSILENCE: A Pseudonymization Tool for International Law Luis Adrián Cabrera-Diego and Akshita Gheewala
	Extending Off-the-shelf NER Systems to Personal Information Detection in Dialogues with a Virtual Agent: Findings from a Real-Life Use Case Mario Mina, Carlos Rodríguez, Aitor Gonzalez-Agirre and Marta Villegas
	Data Anonymization for Privacy-Preserving Large Language Model Fine-Tuning on Call Transcripts Shayna Gardiner, Tania Habib, Kevin Humphreys, Masha Azizi, Frederic Mailhot, Anne Paling, Preston Thomas and Nathan Zhang
12:00 - 13:00	*LUNCH break*
13:00 - 13:50	*Invited talk 2. Ildikó Pilán. Title: Pseudonymisation and related techniques: a quest for determining what personal information to rewrite and how, chair: Elena Volodina*
13:50 - 14:00	*Short break*
14:00 - 14:45	*Session 3, chair: Ricardo Muñoz Sánchez*

Thursday, March 21, 2024 (continued)

	Assessing Authenticity and Anonymity of Synthetic User-generated Content in the Medical Domain Tomohiro Nishiyama, Lisa Raithel, Roland Roller, Pierre Zweigenbaum and Eiji Aramaki
	Deidentifying a Norwegian Clinical Corpus - an Effort to Create a Privacy-preserving Norwegian Large Clinical Language Model Phuong Ngo, Miguel Tejedor, Therese Olsen Svenning, Taridzo Chomutare, Andrius Budrionis and Hercules Dalianis
	When Is a Name Sensitive? Eponyms in Clinical Text and Implications for De-Identification Thomas Vakili, Tyr Hullmann, Aron Henriksson and Hercules Dalianis
14:45 - 14:50	*Short break*
14:50 - 15:30	*Session 4, chair: Ildikó Pilán*
	Detecting Personal Identifiable Information in Swedish Learner Essays Maria Irena Szawerna, Simon Dobnik, Ricardo Muñoz Sánchez, Therese Lindström Tiedemann and Elena Volodina
	Did the Names I Used within My Essay Affect My Score? Diagnosing Name Biases in Automated Essay Scoring Ricardo Muñoz Sánchez, Simon Dobnik, Maria Irena Szawerna, Therese Lindström Tiedemann and Elena Volodina
15:30 - 16:00	*COFFEE break*
16:00 - 17:00	*Panel discussion with Ildikó Pilán, Thomas Vakili, etc., moderator: Elena Volodina*

Handling Name Errors of a BERT-Based Text De-Identification System: Insights from Stratified Sampling and Markov-based Pseudonymization

Dalton Simancek
Department of Learning Health Sciences
University of Michigan
daltonsi@umich.edu

V.G.Vinod Vydiswaran
School of Information
University of Michigan
vgvinodv@umich.edu

Abstract

Missed recognition of named entities while de-identifying clinical narratives poses a critical challenge in protecting patient-sensitive health information. Mitigating name recognition errors is essential to minimize risk of patient re-identification. In this paper, we emphasize the need for stratified sampling and enhanced contextual considerations concerning Name tokens using a fine-tuned Longformer BERT model for clinical text de-identification. We introduce a Hidden in Plain Sight (HIPS) Markov-based replacement technique for names to mask name recognition misses, leading to a significant reduction in name leakage rates. Our experimental results underscore the impact on addressing name recognition challenges in BERT-based de-identification systems for heightened privacy protection in electronic health records.

1 Introduction

Clinical narratives and unstructured documentation within electronic health records (EHRs) are considered valuable assets in epidemiological research (Sheikhalishahi et al., 2019; Patra et al., 2021) and the creation of prognostic clinical prediction models (Seinen et al., 2022). The advancement of these applications is frequently impeded by the limited availability of de-identified clinical text corpora. Clinical notes must remove protected health information (PHI) to safeguard patient privacy and align with privacy regulations exemplified by the United States' HIPAA Safe Harbor privacy guidelines (OfC, 2022).

Bidirectional Encoder Representations from Transformers (BERT) models have shown promise in automatically identifying sensitive PHI in clinical texts (Johnson et al., 2020; Ahmed et al., 2020). Previous research has explored BERT variants with hyper-parameter tuning, comparing their efficacy in clinical text de-identification across PHI subcategories, including dates, phone numbers and names (Meaney et al., 2022). Less focus has been given to the shrinking but persistent margins of error that plague even the best-performing de-identification pipelines. For instance, our base de-identification model uses a Longformer BERT variant (Beltagy et al., 2020) fine-tuned using discharge summaries from a US-based tertiary healthcare institution. In preliminary work as a part of Alkiek et al. (2023), we discovered that the Longformer model performed exceptionally well during preliminary testing among the pretrained models we sampled. Our base model achieved an impressive but far-from-optimal overall F1 score of 0.90 for names (Table 1). Considering the inherent privacy risks of missed PHI, even small margins of error have the potential to result in substantial numbers of exposed patient records with identifiable health information when de-identification systems are deployed in the real world.

This study aims to contribute to characterizing Name errors in BERT-based transformer models on real-world discharge summaries. The goal is to provide insights into the development of comprehensive de-identification strategies capable of both correcting bias and tolerating mistakes related to names. We first compare the effect on recognizing names using a fine-tuned Longformer model with a stratified sample that uses demographic information against a model fine-tuned with a standard randomized sample. We suggest that enhancing the recognition of name tokens in our de-identification system is achieved by including sets of name tokens found in stratified training samples compared to those in random training samples. Next, we investigate a Hidden in Plain Sight (HIPS) Markov-based replacement technique for names. Using real-world discharge summaries from an academic healthcare institution, we compare the effectiveness of a Markov-based replacement strategy against a random replacement strategy in reducing name leakage.

Proceedings of the Workshop on Computational Approaches to Language Data Pseudonymization
CALD-pseudo 2024, pages 1–7
March 21, 2024 ©2024 Association for Computational Linguistics

PHI	Mean True Token Count	Precision	Recall	F1-Score
PROVIDER NAMES	503	.984 (.007)	.984 (.007)	.984 (.007)
NON-PROVIDER NAMES	1836	.904 (.019)	.850 (.027)	.876 (.010)
NAMES IN WHITE RECORDS	1756	.923 (.022)	.889 (.019)	.905 (.006)
NAMES IN URM RECORDS	583	.925 (.018)	.860 (.024)	.892 (.014)
ALL NAMES	2339	.923 (.016)	.880 (.019)	.900 (.007)
ALL PHI	13103	.953 (.005)	.952 (.005)	.952 (.004)

Table 1: Baseline fine-tuned Longformer performance, averaged over 5 runs, on identifying name tokens over a test set of discharge summaries (n=80). For performance metrics, the numbers in parentheses show standard deviation. Name tokens from full name entities that matched with doctor, nurse or specialist names in a given EHR provider list were labeled as provider names. Name tokens from unmatched full name entities in the EHR provider list were labeled as non-provider. Underrepresented minority (URM) records are notes associated with patients reporting any non-white racial identity or a Hispanic/Latino ethnicity.

2 Related Work

2.1 Name-related biases in BERT Models

Naming a person often involves a deliberate or subconscious choice conveying racial, ethnic, class-based, gender-normative, or religious affiliations (Seguin et al., 2021; Lindsay and Dempsey, 2017). These choices collectively contribute to naming trends or groups of names characterized by gender, race, or association with a specific locality or decade (Lockhart et al., 2023). Learned contextual embeddings in BERT models have been shown to capture such signals in socio-demographic phenomena, which may then contribute to discriminative biases in recruitment and other systems informed by trained contextual embeddings (Ramezanzadehmoghadam et al., 2021). Name tokens like "Smith" are expected to be prominent in United States based, English-language datasets, making them more easily identifiable by systems trained on those datasets. In contrast, names that are rare, unique, or correspond to underrepresented minority (URM) groups in the training data may carry a higher risk of being overlooked by the model. Our work is inspired by Xiao et al. (2023), who studied learned name biases in pretrained BERT models for de-identification using synthetic patient data to evaluate fairness across demographic patient groups. Others, such as Yue and Zhou (2020), have proposed solutions involving training data augmentation.

2.2 Hidden in Plain Sight (HIPS) strategies

Multiple strategies have been explored to enhance privacy through de-identification. Notable among these are the HIPS approaches, which involves substituting personally-identifiable information (PIIs) with authentic pseudonyms to mitigate false negatives (Carrell et al., 2013). For example, instead of replacing a real name token "John" with a placeholder tag "[NAME]", HIPS uses a realistic pseudonym like "Tony". As an extension of this methodology, Osborne et al. (2022) proposed Bratsynthetic, which utilizes a Markov-based substitution component to introduce randomness in the selection of pseudonyms. Building on this foundation, our study applies a similar approach to a real-world dataset of discharge summaries, extending the scope of its evaluation beyond simulated environments.

3 Methods

3.1 Stratification of Training Data

Our methodology challenges the conventional practice of randomly selecting clinical notes for training data annotation, that tends to predominantly include the majority patient population of white patients. Instead, we advocate for a stratified sampling approach to diversify the training data, that would select disproportionately more patients from underrepresented minority communities. This method aims to improve the generalizability of the Longformer-based de-identification model previously proposed by Alkiek et al. (2023), particularly in identifying patient names during inference. We propose that the name token sets found in a stratified training samples containing a higher proportion of documents from URM patients, would result in superior name de-identification performance than the performance achieved with the name token set found in random training samples.

Sampling	Demographic	# Names	Precision	Recall	F1 score
Random	All	654 (17)	0.918 (0.021)	0.843 (0.019)	0.878 (0.008)
	White	483 (24)	0.916 (0.014)	0.849 (0.022)	0.881 (0.009)
	URMs	171 (29)	0.901 (0.029)	0.837 (0.042)	0.867 (0.020)
Stratified	All	654 (17)	0.897 (0.032)	0.842 (0.018)	0.868 (0.014)
	White	483 (24)	0.900 (0.026)	0.857 (0.032)	0.877 (0.015)
	URMs	171 (29)	0.892 (0.030)	0.837 (0.025)	0.863 (0.020)

Table 2: Test set performance of patient name identification models fine-tuned on (a) random sample (URM patients: 21%, s.d. 0.01) and (b) stratified sample (URM patients: 34%, s.d. 0.01). Averaged over five runs. The numbers in parentheses are standard deviations.

Our annotated dataset consists of 400 discharge summary notes from a tertiary academic medical center, annotated by trained medical professionals to label eighteen PHI categories, including provider and patient names. The average discharge summary consists of 1643 tokens containing 43 PHI entity annotations, of which 12 are names. The average name entity has two tokens, typically a first name and a surname. For this study, full-name entities that did not match with doctor, nurse, or specialist names in a given EHR provider list were labeled as non-providers and assumed to patient or family names.

The discharge summary notes were randomly split 80:20 into train-test splits. To implement the stratified sampling approach and evaluate its effectiveness, we created two subsamples of 200 notes each from the train set. One subsample followed random selection, while the other used stratified sampling that leveraged structured EHR race and ethnicity fields to create a white stratum and an underrepresented minority (URM) stratum. A patient was categorized into the URM stratum if their record indicated any non-white racial identity or Hispanic/Latino ethnicity. In the stratified sample, we included the maximum number of available notes from URM (Underrepresented Minority) patients in the train split. The remaining notes were randomly sampled from white patients. This process was repeated five times, starting from a new 80:20 split.

On average, the number of instances from the underrepresented minority patients increased from 21% in the random sample to 34% in the stratified sample. Subsequently, two new Longformer models were trained and tested on the same held-out test set (n=80): one fine-tuned with the random subsample and the other with the stratified subsample.

3.2 Markov-based name pseudonymization

Inspired by the strategy used by Osborne et al. (2022), we designed the following Markov-based strategy to replace the names identified by the Longformer models with surrogates. For each note, when the Longformer identifies k name token predictions, our approach will select k surrogates. There's a $p = 0.5$ chance that the preceding surrogate name will be reused, and a $p = 0.5$ chance that a new surrogate name will be chosen. In addition, each surrogate name is constrained to be used at most $t = 4$ times, which follows the observation that the mode frequency of name tokens in the training documents is four. Once identified, the surrogate names are used to replace the original names at random. This strategy was contrasted with random pseudonymization strategy, where the k surrogate names are selected at random without replacement. All surrogate names were selected from a United States Census name list (Bureau, 2021) and the sampling strategies are document-independent, ensuring that names are not sampled repetitively for the same name tokens across multiple documents. The values for the probability and repetition threshold was set empirically based on the mode of the name frequency distribution.

3.3 Name leakage

We defined name leakage as instances where a name token appears more frequently than allowed by a perfect re-identification system and replacement strategy. For example, a name token appearing five times in a document would flag that document as leaking real name tokens with our Markov-based replacement strategy, as it contains a name token count exceeding the maximum threshold of $t = 4$ uses. The overall leakage rate was calculated across the entire test set by considering the proportion of notes where the mode of the name frequency distribution was indeed a true patient name. This follows a heuristic that in a clinical note, the patient's name is the one most likely to repeat. Wilcoxon signed-rank tests (Wilcoxon, 1945) were conducted to test statistical significance of differences in mode of name frequency distribution in the original data and each replacement strategy. McNemar's test (Sundjaja et al., 2023) was conducted to test if the leakage rate of Markov-based strategy is significantly lower than the random replacement strategy.

4 Results

4.1 Stratification of training data

Across the five iterations, the performance of the Longformer models fine-tuned with stratified samples exhibited comparable results to the models fine-tuned with random samples (Table 2). A slight reduction in precision and F1-score was observed across all test notes and within each demographic subgroup. Recall remained consistent for all test notes and URM notes, with a modest and statistically insignificant increase in recall for names in notes from white patients. Consequently, our demographic stratification rule, aimed at enhancing the representation of URMs in the training set of notes from 21% to 34%, did not yield an improvement in name recognition.

4.2 Markov-based name pseudonymization

Pseudonymization strategies significantly influenced the frequency of name tokens in documents, impacting the risk of name leakage. For each note, the random replacement strategy assigns a unique surrogate to each name token prediction, ensuring no repetition. This results in an expected mode of 1 among all name token frequencies in a given document. In contrast, Markov-based replacement may reuse a name token surrogate for up to four predictions, adjusting the expected mode to 4 among all name token frequencies. Our analysis showed that instances of a name being missed twice, even with random replacement, could signal potential name leakage.

Over the five iterations, random strategy displayed significant differences in mode values, whereas Markov distributions exhibited smaller differences, compared to the original name frequency distribution. In Iteration 5 (Figure 1), the Markov name distribution closely resembled the original distribution and was statistically similar per Wilcoxon's signed rank test.

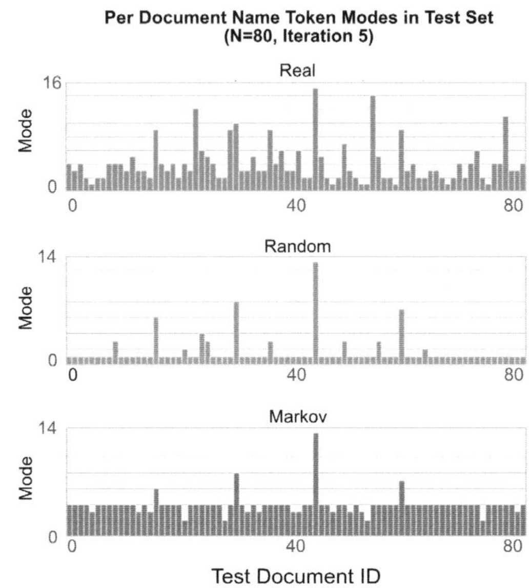

Figure 1: Distributions of unique name modes in the test set by replacement strategy on a sample iteration.

Further, the average leakage rate decreased from 13.1% with random replacement to 3.8% with Markov replacement across all iterations (Table 3). Markov replacement significantly reduced the name leakage rate compared to random replacement, as evidenced by McNemar's test.

5 Discussion

While previous research has emphasized the effectiveness of strategies such as data augmentation for improving name diversity and contextual patterns (Yue and Zhou, 2020), we focused on enhancing name performance through stratification. We aimed to increase the proportion of URM patients in the train dataset by using a stratified sampling approach. Surprisingly, this approach did not significantly improve the name performance of our de-identification system. This lack of improvement could be attributed to a relatively small sample size, where the change in URM representation was not substantial enough to impact name performance in a predominately White patient population. Additionally, higher URM representation in the training sample through stratification may not perfectly correlate with a more robust set of name tokens. URM patients may have names more commonly associated with white demographics and white patients may also have rare or unique names.

Iter.	Original data		Random replacement		Markov-based replacement	
	Avg. Mode	Leakage (%)	Avg. Mode	Leakage (%)	Avg. Mode	Leakage (%)
1	3.5	100	1.2	7.5	3.8	1.3*
2	3.8	100	1.5	17.7	4.1	3.8***
3	3.7	100	1.4	11.3	4.0	3.8*
4	3.9	100	1.6	14.1	4.0	5.1**
5	4.0	100	1.6	15.0	4.0	5.0**
AVG	3.8	100	1.5	13.1	4.0	3.8

Table 3: Average mode and rate of name leakage on the test set across five runs. Statistically significant drop relative to leakage in random approach using McNemar's test:* ($p<0.05$), ** ($p<0.01$), *** ($p<0.001$)

In our discharge summaries, there is a single patient with two notes. To prevent name token leakage, we deliberately included both notes from this patient exclusively in the training sets. This ensures that the names associated with this particular patient do not leak between the training and test sets through their notes.

However, this method does not address the potential leakage of provider names between training and test sets, as a provider's name may appear in notes from multiple patients. Additionally, our stratification rule for creating the white and URM strata does not consider the demographics of the providers. Consequently, not only may provider names leak between the training and test sets, but the set of provider name entities could also remain similar between the stratified and random training samples, posing a challenge to the effectiveness of our methodology." The higher performance for provider names in Table 1 is therefore unsurprising considering the possibility of name leakage for this subgroup. This observation reinforces the importance of name token distributions represented in the training data as a vector for improving de-identification performance on names.

Future work could expand on efforts to explore how shifts in training data effect embedding or attention mechanisms (Clark et al., 2019) to better understand causal mechanisms for targeting name distributions as a parameter to improving de-identification system performance on names.

Nevertheless, achieving complete elimination of name errors through incremental model improvements is unlikely, especially as the model is applied to different note types or health system contexts. In such scenarios, our Markov-based HIPS strategy holds theoretical efficacy in diminishing document-level leakage associated with false negatives related to name tokens. However, missed names that appear more than the allowable repeats in the Markov method remain at risk for PHI leakage. Our results propose that implementing such a strategy would be beneficial for BERT-based de-identification systems, effectively masking name errors and providing enhanced privacy protection for patients.

6 Conclusion

Our study aims to address errors in name recognition of a Longformer-based de-identification model fine-tuned on discharge summaries. Stratified sampling for fine-tuning did not significantly improve name recognition. However, the introduction of a HIPS Markov-based pseudonymization strategy showed promising results, significantly reducing name leakage rates compared to random replacement. This research contributes to the ongoing efforts to address the persistent challenges associated with de-identification of clinical texts, offering valuable guidance for the development of robust and privacy-conscious clinical text de-identification.

Limitations

While we recognize the importance of acknowledging and addressing disparities in healthcare, the term "Underrepresented Minorities (URM)" utilized in this study is acknowledged as not being an ideal or precise grouping, potentially oversimplifying the diverse range of minority patient populations in a tertiary, academic healthcare institution. The rationale behind the chosen stratification rule was to establish a straightforward method that could yield sufficient samples in each stratum to ensure a stable signal for analysis.

Moving forward, we advocate for future research endeavors in stratified sampling to prioritize annotation efforts aimed at including more substantial samples from demographic subgroups. It is important to acknowledge and accept this limitation as a conscious choice made to address the inherent dominance and potential bias arising from a larger representation of White patient records in this specific experiment. Our commitment remains steadfast in contributing to a nuanced understanding of healthcare disparities, and we encourage ongoing efforts to refine and expand upon our methodology in future investigations.

Additionally, using name lists from US Census data for pseudonymization may not be ideal for all contexts due to potential biases and limitations. Careful consideration of the specific context and potential biases is crucial when selecting and utilizing name lists for pseudonymization purposes.

Finally, we acknowledge that fine-tuning of our BERT-based de-identification system used discharge summaries written exclusively in American English clinical language and not other languages.

Ethics Statement

The experiments in this study use 400 discharge summaries sampled from patient populations in a tertiary, academic healthcare institution. The handling of sensitive medical data prioritized participant privacy, with robust data handling protocols in place. The research was conducted under the oversight of an Institutional Review Board, ensuring continual adherence to ethical guidelines.

Acknowledgements

We acknowledge the authors of Alkiek et al. (2023), who developed the DeiDoc de-identification model and shared code, annotated data, and model insights used in conceiving the experiments conducted in this paper. These contributions significantly enhanced the quality of this research.

References

Tanbir Ahmed, Md Momin Al Aziz, and Noman Mohammed. 2020. De-identification of electronic health record using neural network. *Scientific Reports*, 10(1):18600.

Kenan Alkiek, Dalton Simancek, Jiaye Tan, Noah Weissman, Jane Ferraro, and Vydiswaran V.G. Vinod. 2023. DeiDoc: Automatic De-identification of Notes Using Long-Document Transformers. In *Annual Symposium of the American Medical Informatics Association*.

Iz Beltagy, Matthew E. Peters, and Arman Cohan. 2020. Longformer: The Long-Document Transformer. ArXiv:2004.05150 [cs].

United States Census Bureau. 2021. Frequently Occurring Surnames from the 2010 Census.

David Carrell, Bradley Malin, John Aberdeen, Samuel Bayer, Cheryl Clark, Ben Wellner, and Lynette Hirschman. 2013. Hiding in plain sight: use of realistic surrogates to reduce exposure of protected health information in clinical text. *Journal of the American Medical Informatics Association*, 20(2):342–348.

Kevin Clark, Urvashi Khandelwal, Omer Levy, and Christopher D. Manning. 2019. What Does BERT Look At? An Analysis of BERT's Attention. ArXiv:1906.04341 [cs].

Alistair E. W. Johnson, Lucas Bulgarelli, and Tom J. Pollard. 2020. Deidentification of free-text medical records using pre-trained bidirectional transformers. In *Proceedings of the ACM Conference on Health, Inference, and Learning*, pages 214–221, Toronto Ontario Canada. ACM.

Jo Lindsay and Deborah Dempsey. 2017. First names and social distinction: Middle-class naming practices in Australia. *Journal of Sociology*, 53(3):577–591.

Jeffrey W Lockhart, Molly M King, and Christin Munsch. 2023. What's in a Name?: Name-Based Demographic Inference and the Unequal Distribution of Misrecognition. *Nat Hum Behav*, 7:1084–1095.

Christopher Meaney, Wali Hakimpour, Sumeet Kalia, and Rahim Moineddin. 2022. A Comparative Evaluation Of Transformer Models For De-Identification Of Clinical Text Data. ArXiv:2204.07056 [cs, stat].

Rights (OCR) OfC. 2022. Guidance Regarding Methods for De-identification of Protected Health Information in Accordance with the Health Insurance Portability and Accountability Act (HIPAA) Privacy Rule.

John D Osborne, Tobias O'Leary, and Richard E Kennedy. 2022. BRATsynthetic: Text De-identification using a Markov Chain Replacement Strategy for Surrogate Personal Identifying Information. ArXiv:2210.16125 [cs.CR].

Braja G Patra, Mohit M Sharma, Veer Vekaria, Prakash Adekkanattu, Olga V Patterson, Benjamin Glicksberg, Lauren A Lepow, Euijung Ryu, Joanna M Biernacka, Al'ona Furmanchuk, Thomas J George, William Hogan, Yonghui Wu, Xi Yang, Jiang Bian, Myrna Weissman, Priya Wickramaratne, J John Mann, Mark Olfson, Thomas R Campion, Mark Weiner, and Jyotishman Pathak. 2021. Extracting social determinants of health from electronic health records using natural language processing: a systematic review. *Journal of the American Medical Informatics Association*, 28(12):2716–2727.

Maryam Ramezanzadehmoghadam, Hongmei Chi, and Edward L Jones. 2021. Inherent Discriminability of BERT towards Racial Minority Associated Data. volume 12951. Springer, Cham.

Charles Seguin, Chris Julien, and Yongjun Zhang. 2021. The stability of androgynous names: Dynamics of gendered naming practices in the United States 1880–2016. *Poetics*, 85:101501.

Tom M Seinen, Egill A Fridgeirsson, Solomon Ioannou, Daniel Jeannetot, Luis H John, Jan A Kors, Aniek F Markus, Victor Pera, Alexandros Rekkas, Ross D Williams, Cynthia Yang, Erik M Van Mulligen, and Peter R Rijnbeek. 2022. Use of unstructured text in prognostic clinical prediction models: a systematic review. *Journal of the American Medical Informatics Association*, 29(7):1292–1302.

Seyedmostafa Sheikhalishahi, Riccardo Miotto, Joel T Dudley, Alberto Lavelli, Fabio Rinaldi, and Venet Osmani. 2019. Natural Language Processing of Clinical Notes on Chronic Diseases: Systematic Review. *JMIR Medical Informatics*, 7(2):e12239.

Joshua Henrina Sundjaja, Rijen Shrestha, and Kewal Krishan. 2023. McNemar And Mann-Whitney U Tests. *StatPearls Publishing*.

Frank Wilcoxon. 1945. Individual Comparisons by Ranking Methods. *Biometrics Bulletin*, 1(6):80–83.

Yuxin Xiao, Shulammite Lim, Tom Joseph Pollard, and Marzyeh Ghassemi. 2023. In the Name of Fairness: Assessing the Bias in Clinical Record De-identification. In *2023 ACM Conference on Fairness, Accountability, and Transparency*, pages 123–137, Chicago IL USA. ACM.

Xiang Yue and Shuang Zhou. 2020. PHICON: Improving Generalization of Clinical Text De-identification Models via Data Augmentation. ArXiv:2010.05143 [cs].

A Base De-identification Model Details

In our experiments, we employed a pre-trained Longformer model as the baseline for fine-tuning the de-identification approach over discharge summaries, based on work conducted by Alkiek et al. (2023). Each experiment consisted of five iterations of model training with different train-test splits, with each iteration consisting of 5 epochs. Training hyperparameters include a learning rate of 2e-5 and a batch size of 4. These parameters were chosen to balance the model's learning capacity and computational efficiency during the fine-tuning process. The utilization of a pre-trained Longformer model served as a foundation for our experiments, allowing us to leverage its inherent understanding of contextual information in medical text.

Assessing Authenticity and Anonymity of Synthetic User-generated Content in the Medical Domain

Tomohiro Nishiyama[1*] **Lisa Raithel**[2,3,4*] **Roland Roller**[2]
Pierre Zweigenbaum[4] **Eiji Aramaki**[1]
[1]Nara Institute of Science and Technology
[2]German Research Center for Artificial Intelligence (DFKI)
[3]TU Berlin, BIFOLD [4]Université Paris-Saclay, CNRS, LISN
[1]{nishiyama.tomohiro.ns5,aramaki}@is.naist.jp [3]raithel@tu-berlin.de
[2]roland.roller@dfki.de [4]pz@lisn.fr

Abstract

Since medical text cannot be shared easily due to privacy concerns, synthetic data bears much potential for natural language processing applications. In the context of social media and user-generated messages about drug intake and adverse drug effects, this work presents different methods to examine the authenticity of synthetic text. We conclude that the generated tweets are untraceable and show enough authenticity from the medical point of view to be used as a replacement for a real Twitter corpus. However, original data might still be the preferred choice as they contain much more diversity.

1 Introduction

Medical text is difficult to share, even for research purposes, as it contains information about patients that might reveal an individual's identity. This makes natural language processing in that domain difficult. Moreover, there have been concerns about sharing even publicly available data from social media in recent years. This is partially due to legal reasons (e.g., X (Twitter)) but also due to privacy concerns. While data sensitivity can be at least addressed by de-identification (removal of personal health identifiers) and anonymization (irreversible removal of all information that possibly links back to an individual) (Meystre et al., 2010), privacy aspects constitute an additional barrier (see (Vakili et al., 2022; Volodina et al., 2023; Ben Cheikh Larbi et al., 2023)).

Synthetic data generation bears much potential and a way out of this misery, particularly with the rise of generative models. Various attempts within and outside the medical domain generate synthetic clinical data and show that large datasets can be easily generated and models trained on them can compete with models trained on real data (Ive et al., 2020; Libbi et al., 2021; Giuffrè and Shung, 2023). Apart from that, the use of generative data has advantages such as structural similarity, information relevance, and subjective assessment (Guillaudeux et al., 2023). Furthermore, synthetic dataset have been shown to be useful in, e.g., epidemiology research, medical education and training, and algorithm testing (Gonzales et al., 2023).

> ***Ex1:*** I've heard a lot about people going blind after inoculation, but the ears too. If you have pneumonia, you can recover instantly with steroids, but the eyes and ears...

> ***Ex2:*** I've been taking azathioprine for 2 days now and I feel like it's working really well. But the side effect is a rash all over my body..

Figure 1: Example of a source (top) and a pseudo (bottom) tweet translated into English. The original Japanese text can be found in the appendix.

For example, Choi et al. (2017) employ Generative Adversarial Networks (GANs) (Goodfellow et al., 2014) to generate (English) electronic health records (EHRs) while Abedi et al. (2022) synthesize tabular medical data such as laboratory values. Amin-Nejad et al. (2020) use GPT-2 (Radford et al., 2019) amongst other models to create datasets of discharge summaries in English. These data are then used as either pure training/fine-tuning material (Choi et al., 2017) or to augment existing resources (Amin-Nejad et al., 2020; Abedi et al., 2022), resulting in a better performance of the trained models when compared to the low-resource setup in which they are usually fine-tuned. Hiebel et al. (2023) report that linguistic phenomena are reproduced while privacy is preserved in their generated datasets of French clinical case reports. The usefulness of the authors' synthetic corpus is extrinsically investigated by fine-tuning models for a clinical named entity recognition task. The perfor-

* Equal contribution

Proceedings of the Workshop on Computational Approaches to Language Data Pseudonymization
CALD-pseudo 2024, pages 8–17
March 21, 2024

mance of the models yields promising results.

Although the use of generated data in corpora is highly significant from the viewpoint that medical language resources are difficult to make public, few studies evaluate the anonymity or authenticity of the data, including medical aspects. Melamud and Shivade (2019) investigate the privacy-preserving characteristics and utility of synthetic EHRs by introducing a new measure based on Pointwise Differential Training Privacy (PDTP) (Long et al., 2017). Another work is provided by Mclachlan et al. (2018), who propose a framework to investigate the "realism" of synthetic EHRs. They compare the generated information with the rules, constraints, and concepts used in the original EHR data. Their approach, however, does not apply to unstructured user-generated texts.

In contrast to related work, this paper examines the authenticity of synthetic *user content* with respect to health-related topics in Japanese. More precisely, we examine whether artificially generated user tweets about potential adverse drug effects (ADE) are authentic and privacy-preserving and, therefore, might be a valuable alternative resource for future research.

2 Dataset

The baseline of this work is a synthetic corpus of Japanese tweets in the context of drug intake and symptoms (Wakamiya et al., 2023). The source data (original) was collected using 68 medication names as keywords from a Japanese drug-name dictionary[1] in the Twitter API. During preprocessing, URLs and user names were removed. Only tweets containing mentions of drugs and symptoms were kept in the data. T5 (Raffel et al., 2020), a transformer-based encoder-decoder model, was fine-tuned on these data and finally used to generate 10,000 tweets per medication name. The created texts were filtered and manually annotated with 22 different adverse drug reactions. More details about the synthetic data can be found in the appendix and in Wakamiya et al. (2023). In this paper, we are examining how authentic these synthetic data are. In the following, we distinguish between *source* tweets, i.e., the original data, and *pseudo*-tweets, i.e., the synthetics tweets.

[1]https://sociocom.naist.jp/hyakuyaku-dic/

3 Method

We analyze the data in different ways to measure the authenticity and validate the anonymity of the pseudo-tweets. First, we examine the source and the pseudo data on the word level and compare the vocabulary of both datasets. Next, we analyze if the distribution of our target events in the synthetic data is similar to that in the source data. Finally, we directly compare a subset of synthetic and source tweets manually as well as automatically with respect to *naturalness*, *comprehensibility*, *medical correctness* and *anonymity*.

3.1 Vocabulary

First, we compare the vocabulary of both corpora to analyze the diversity of the source and the pseudo data. Since there are considerably more source tweets (441,151) than pseudo-tweets (10,000), we sample 5 times 10,000 messages from the source tweets and compare each sample to the pseudo-tweets. To this end, we tokenize all tweets using spaCy[2] and report the number of tokens, types, and the mean lengths of source versus pseudo-tweets.

Additionally, we compare the similarity of original and pseudo tweets with the FAISS library[3]. All tweets (original and pseudo) are embedded using SentenceBERT (Reimers and Gurevych, 2019)[4] and compared using cosine similarity. Finally, we compute the type-token ratio (TTR) (Johnson, 1944) as a function of corpus size, and we check the frequency of part-of-speech tags.[5]

3.2 Analysis of ADEs

We compare the distribution of adverse drug effects in the pseudo data to their distribution/frequency in the real world. We compare the data to the Japanese Adverse Drug Event Report database (JADER) [6], which contains information about medications and ADEs. Since JADER reports every single ADE, the relative frequency of an ADE is calculated by dividing the number of reports for each adverse drug reaction pair by the total number of reports on the 22 ADEs for that drug. Using the frequency,

[2]https://spacy.io/api, version 3.7.2., model "ja_core_news_trf"

[3]https://github.com/facebookresearch/faiss

[4]https://huggingface.co/sonoisa/sentence-luke-japanese-base-lite

[5]More details on the corpus statistics can be found in Appendix B.

[6]https://www.pmda.go.jp/safety/info-services/drugs/adr-info/suspected-adr/0003.html (in Japanese)

we calculate Pearson's and Spearman's correlation coefficients for each drug individually and for all drugs globally. We also categorize ADEs into a more frequent (MFG) and a less frequent group (LFG) based on this frequency, for each drug individually and for all drugs globally, and compare MFG and LFG using a t-test. As the source data is not annotated, we draw only a comparison between pseudo data and world knowledge (JADER), but not to the source data. In addition, we examine whether we can find ADEs in the pseudo data that are unknown according to JADER.

3.3 Direct Comparison

Next, we directly compare the content of the source and pseudo-tweets. For this, we randomly select 100 source tweets and 100 pseudo-tweets. We conduct a manual and an automatic (GPT-4 (OpenAI, 2023)) analysis, giving the following questions to human annotators and GPT-4. Both of the human annotators are native Japanese speakers and medically trained.

Q1: "Do you think a human wrote this message?" (*naturalness*)

Q2: "Do you understand what the person wants to say with this message?" (*comprehensibility*)

Q3: "Is this message medically correct?" (*medical correctness*)

Q4: "Does the message contain any identifying information?" (*anonymity*)

Each question could only be answered with "yes" or "no". The human annotators were encouraged to answer quickly, i.e., without overthinking their response. Based on the responses, we calculated the inter-annotator agreement using Cohen's κ (Cohen, 1960).

4 Results

In the following section, we briefly present the results of our analyses. More details, particularly tables and figures, can be found in the appendix.

4.1 Vocabulary

For the pseudo-tweets, we count 441,022 tokens in total and on average 646,773 $\pm$ 1,568 tokens for the sampled source tweets. When comparing the number of types in the vocabulary, we find 6,499 different types in the pseudo data, whereas the source tweets exhibit 21,079 $\pm$ 121 types per random sample batch. Further, the mean length of pseudo-tweets is 44 (median is 44), while the source tweets have a mean length of 64 (median is 68). The results of the other statistics are summarized in Appendix B.

4.2 Analysis of ADEs

The comparison between the overall drug-ADE pairs is presented in Figure 2. The left figure indicates that according to the frequency in JADER, frequent ADE pairs in the pseudo data also occur more frequently than the less frequent ADE pairs. The right figure analyzes the single drug-ADE pairs in more detail. A deeper analysis, however, shows that we cannot find a correlation between the frequency of drug-ADE pairs in our pseudo data and their occurrence in the real world, as reported in JADER. The figure shows, for instance, that various drug-ADE pairs occur with a much higher frequency in the pseudo data than JADER. Conversely, we can observe some frequent drug-ADE pairs hardly occur in the pseudo data.

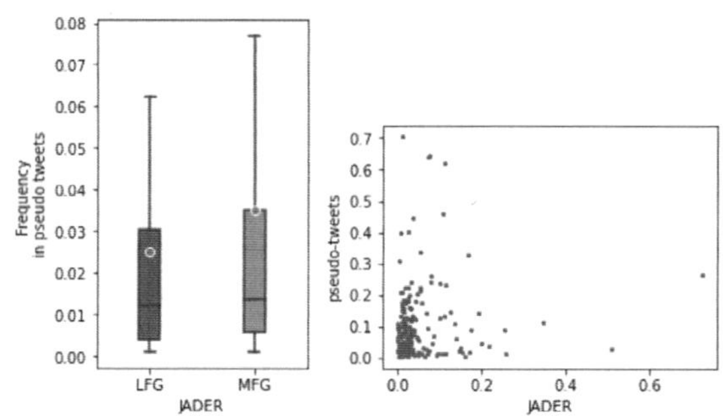

Figure 2: The frequency of ADEs from JADER and the pseudo data. (left): Comparison between MFG and LFG in the pseudo data. (right): Scatter plot between JADER and the pseudo data.

Figure 2 (right) does not show a strong association between JADER and the pseudo data, but the t-test result between MFG and LFG from all drug-ADE pairs indicated some association. When looking at the drugs individually, we found that only two of the drugs, *amiodarone* and *azathioprine*, were correlated with Pearson's and Spearman's correlation coefficient, respectively. Although the results of the t-tests in each drug showed no statistically significant differences, each of the means of MFG was greater than each of the means of LFG.

Next, we analyzed the drug-ADE pairs of the pseudo data. We found six pairs that were not listed in JADER, namely *azathioprine-constipation*, *amiodarone-insomnia*, *infliximab-insomnia*,

> *Ex3:* Colchicine has been used for a long time and I have either constipation or diarrhea... I was told that if I get any side effects I can reduce it... but so far I've only had side effects.

Figure 3: Original tweet mentioning colchicine and constipation. (Translated from Japanese into English)

colchicine-asthma, *colchicine-constipation*, and *colchicine-hemorrhagic cystitis*. Of those six pairs, however, three could be found in the drug leaflets of the corresponding medications. For the remaining three, we cannot judge if this is correct from a medical perspective. Further analysis revealed that the pair *colchicine-constipation* at least occurred in the source data as shown in Figure 3, while the combinations *azathioprine-constipation* and *colchicine-asthma* did not.

4.3 Direct Comparison - Human

The human analysis shows a considerable disagreement between the two annotators on what can be considered a message written by a human (Q1). Normally, a higher Cohen's kappa closer to one is desirable, but in this result the Cohen's kappa closer to zero is desirable. The closer to zero, the better, because it means that the two human annotators are choosing more randomly which tweets are written by humans and which are generated by the model. Moreover, the results show that both annotators consider a slightly higher number of pseudo-tweets human-like than those from the source data.

Regarding the tweets' comprehensibility (Q2), most can be understood by both annotators. Again, there seems to be no major difference between pseudo and source tweets. Interestingly, both annotators agreed not to understand only eight pseudo and 13 source tweets.

Although our two annotators are medical experts, the results show a considerable disagreement (Cohen's kappa of 0.290) regarding which messages can be considered medically correct (Q3). However, there is a slight tendency towards source tweets being considered by both as medically correct (37 original versus 29 pseudo-tweets). The same applies to the joint agreement for medically incorrect tweets (23 versus 25).

Finally, regarding the anonymity of the data (Q4), the agreement of both annotators is very strong. Only up to four tweets (overlap of one tweet) were considered to contain identifying information. Notably, none of those four tweets were

> *Ex4:* Hanako, good evening... I couldn't tell him about my mental health... instead he gave me some Calonal because of a pressure headache...

Figure 4: Example of a part of a source tweet that contained a person's name, manually replaced here with 'Hanako' for publication.

from the pseudo data. More details can be found in the appendix.

4.4 Direct Comparison - Model

In contrast to the human analysis, GPT-4 only responded to the above-described questions for 198 tweets. Of those tweets, the model considered all messages human-generated and nearly all understandable (196/198). Moreover, 144 tweets were regarded as medically correct, of which a slightly larger portion came from the pseudo-tweets. The number of tweets considered medically correct by GPT-4, but as incorrect by both annotators, was 30. On the other hand, the number of messages considered medically incorrect by GPT but correct by both annotators was six. Finally, no message was considered by GPT-4 to be not anonymous.

5 Discussion

5.1 Vocabulary

Vocabulary inspection reveals a lower diversity of the pseudo-tweets compared to the source text messages, i.e., the source data generally contains more types and longer messages. The similarity comparison shows that given the pseudo-tweets and 4,000 source tweets, 1% of the pseudo-tweets are very similar to the original tweets, but not equal[7]. The generation process added content or reformulated the messages, leading to pseudo-tweets covering the same topics as the original tweets. The distribution of POS tags is similar in both datasets. Therefore, with respect to vocabulary, the pseudo data seems to be diverse, but not as diverse and creative as the source data. This aligns with research on the diversity of generated content (Chung et al., 2023) and might lead to an easy-to-learn dataset from which a machine-learning model cannot be generalized to other data.

5.2 Analysis of ADEs

Based on the investigated distribution of drug-ADE pairs, we conclude that the data is medically au-

[7]Except for one tweet, see details in Appendix B.

thentic to a certain degree. Further investigation by medical experts would be needed to arrive at a final conclusion.

5.3 Direct Comparison – Human Annotators

Naturalness A large number of pseudo-tweets were considered to be written by humans, whereas many source tweets were considered to be not written by humans. Moreover, the inter-annotator agreement on this task was very low (Cohen's kappa of 0.089). Therefore, we conclude that it is difficult to detect tweets written by humans and that our pseudo-tweets are sufficiently human-alike.

Comprehensibility Many tweets, even those written by humans, were not understood, and in fact, a larger percentage of the source tweets written by humans did not make sense to the annotators. This suggests that our pseudo-tweets are at least as comprehensible as the source tweets.

Medical correctness The annotations show that both annotators considered more source tweets medically correct. On the other hand, the annotators also show a strong disagreement with many tweets. Therefore, it is difficult to conclude that source data might be medically more accurate than synthetic data. Conversely, we can see a similar distribution of messages labeled as medically incorrect by both annotators (source=23; pseudo=25). In other words, this means that one out of four messages is medically incorrect. Although our subset was randomly sampled, this shows a concerning tendency and raises concerns about health-related information from social media.

Anonymity Most tweets did not include identifying information, as critical information and messages were filtered out beforehand. Interestingly, the only messages considered problematic regarding anonymity were still from the source data, not the pseudo data, as shown in Figure 4. However, we cannot guarantee that pseudo-tweets per se do not include identifying information, but we believe that removing critical information before training a generative model helps.

5.4 Direct Comparison – Model

While the question about comprehension might be too abstract for GPT-4, it fails to identify messages with identifying information. Moreover, regarding medical correctness, the model identified multiple tweets as correct, which, on the other hand, were labeled by both humans as incorrect and vice versa. Finally, regarding the differentiation between human-generated and synthetic tweets, GPT-4 and humans come to a similar conclusion: they are difficult to differentiate. However, GPT-4 is too optimistic and assigns all messages to human-alike.

6 Conclusion

In this work, we analyzed synthetically-generated tweets in the context of drug intake and adverse drug reactions. The data was compared to (real) user-generated messages regarding authenticity, privacy preservation, and medical correctness. The results show that the synthetic data has characteristics similar to the source data. From a linguistic point of view, the data shows less variation, but it contains a similar number of data with questionable medical correctness (as the original), and has a similar authenticity. In addition to that, pseudo data could serve as a "safety net" as it might be less likely to provide identifiable information. Finally, we believe that the findings are generally valid for different languages; however, larger and more complex models than T5 might increase the authenticity and correctness level but might easily reproduce sensitive information it has seen during training.

Acknowledgements

We thank the anonymous reviewers for their constructive feedback on our paper. Our work was supported by the Cross-ministerial Strategic Innovation Promotion Program (SIP) on "Integrated Health Care System" Grant Number JPJ012425, and by JPMJCR20G9, ANR-20-IADJ-0005-01, and DFG-442445488 under the trilateral ANR-DFG-JST AI Research project KEEPHA. Furthermore, we gratefully acknowledge funding from the German Federal Ministry of Education and Research under the grant BIFOLD24B.

Limitations and Ethical Considerations

JADER has a reporting bias because some of the reports are voluntary, which may have affected the results. The study targets generated Japanese social media messages. However, most analyses should also apply to other languages, especially those in the original corpus (Wakamiya et al., 2023). We recognize that the above data analysis is domain-specific, but similar tests could also be conducted for other areas.

Regarding ethical considerations, the following three methods were implemented to avoid privacy issues in the original Twitter data: Deleting the usernames in training data for the model, deleting the exact duplicates in the generated text from the source, and, with manual work of annotators, checking all of the synthetic data and making sure no identifying information remains. Models using original data were trained locally.

We further acknowledge that questions used to judge tweets with GPT-4 and the corresponding responses are (1) not reproducible as soon as an updated version of GPT-4 is released, and (2) might result in different responses when the questions are slightly modified or set up differently.

Finally, to assess the authenticity and diversity of the data, many more linguistic measures could be applied. This paper only presents a few as a complement to the medically inspired investigations.

References

Masoud Abedi, Lars Hempel, Sina Sadeghi, and Toralf Kirsten. 2022. Gan-based approaches for generating structured data in the medical domain. *Applied Sciences*, 12(14).

Ali Amin-Nejad, Julia Ive, and Sumithra Velupillai. 2020. Exploring transformer text generation for medical dataset augmentation. In *Proceedings of the Twelfth Language Resources and Evaluation Conference*, pages 4699–4708, Marseille, France. European Language Resources Association.

Iyadh Ben Cheikh Larbi, Aljoscha Burchardt, and Roland Roller. 2023. Clinical Text Anonymization, its Influence on Downstream NLP Tasks and the Risk of Re-Identification. In *Proceedings of the 17th Conference of the European Chapter of the Association for Computational Linguistics: Student Research Workshop*, pages 105–111, Dubrovnik, Croatia. Association for Computational Linguistics.

Edward Choi, Siddharth Biswal, Bradley Malin, Jon Duke, Walter F. Stewart, and Jimeng Sun. 2017. Generating multi-label discrete patient records using generative adversarial networks. In *Proceedings of the 2nd Machine Learning for Healthcare Conference*, volume 68 of *Proceedings of Machine Learning Research*, pages 286–305. PMLR.

John Chung, Ece Kamar, and Saleema Amershi. 2023. Increasing diversity while maintaining accuracy: Text data generation with large language models and human interventions. In *Proceedings of the 61st Annual Meeting of the Association for Computational Linguistics (Volume 1: Long Papers)*, pages 575–593, Toronto, Canada. Association for Computational Linguistics.

Jacob Cohen. 1960. A Coefficient of Agreement for Nominal Scales. *Educational and Psychological Measurement*, 20(1):37–46.

Mauro Giuffrè and Dennis L. Shung. 2023. Harnessing the power of synthetic data in healthcare: innovation, application, and privacy. *npj Digital Medicine*, 6(1):186.

Aldren Gonzales, Guruprabha Guruswamy, and Scott R. Smith. 2023. Synthetic data in health care: A narrative review. *PLOS Digital Health*, 2(1):e0000082.

Ian Goodfellow, Jean Pouget-Abadie, Mehdi Mirza, Bing Xu, David Warde-Farley, Sherjil Ozair, Aaron Courville, and Yoshua Bengio. 2014. Generative adversarial nets. In *Advances in Neural Information Processing Systems*, volume 27. Curran Associates, Inc.

Morgan Guillaudeux, Olivia Rousseau, Julien Petot, Zineb Bennis, Charles-Axel Dein, Thomas Goronflot, Nicolas Vince, Sophie Limou, Matilde Karakachoff, Matthieu Wargny, and Pierre-Antoine Gourraud. 2023. Patient-centric synthetic data generation, no reason to risk re-identification in biomedical data analysis. *npj Digital Medicine*, 6(1):37.

Nicolas Hiebel, Olivier Ferret, Karen Fort, and Aurélie Névéol. 2023. Can synthetic text help clinical named entity recognition? a study of electronic health records in French. In *Proceedings of the 17th Conference of the European Chapter of the Association for Computational Linguistics*, pages 2320–2338, Dubrovnik, Croatia. Association for Computational Linguistics.

Julia Ive, Natalia Viani, Joyce Kam, Lucia Yin, Somain Verma, Stephen Puntis, Rudolf N. Cardinal, Angus Roberts, Robert Stewart, and Sumithra Velupillai. 2020. Generation and evaluation of artificial mental health records for Natural Language Processing. *npj Digital Medicine*, 3(1):69.

W. Johnson. 1944. *Studies in Language Behavior*. Psychological Monographs. American Psychological Association.

Claudia Alessandra Libbi, Jan Trienes, Dolf Trieschnigg, and Christin Seifert. 2021. Generating synthetic training data for supervised de-identification of electronic health records. *Future Internet*, 13(5).

Yunhui Long, Vincent Bindschaedler, and Carl A. Gunter. 2017. Towards measuring membership privacy. *CoRR*, abs/1712.09136.

S. Mclachlan, K. Dube, T. Gallagher, B. Daley, and J. Walonoski. 2018. The ATEN Framework for Creating the Realistic Synthetic Electronic Health Record. *Technologies (BIOSTEC 2018), 11th International Joint Conference on Biomedical Engineering Systems*.

Oren Melamud and Chaitanya Shivade. 2019. Towards automatic generation of shareable synthetic clinical notes using neural language models. In *Proceedings of the 2nd Clinical Natural Language Processing Workshop*, pages 35–45, Minneapolis, Minnesota, USA. Association for Computational Linguistics.

Stephane M Meystre, F Jeffrey Friedlin, Brett R South, Shuying Shen, and Matthew H Samore. 2010. Automatic de-identification of textual documents in the electronic health record: a review of recent research. *BMC medical research methodology*, 10(1):1–16.

OpenAI. 2023. GPT-4 Technical Report. Publisher: arXiv Version Number: 3.

Alec Radford, Jeff Wu, Rewon Child, David Luan, Dario Amodei, and Ilya Sutskever. 2019. Language models are unsupervised multitask learners.

Colin Raffel, Noam Shazeer, Adam Roberts, Katherine Lee, Sharan Narang, Michael Matena, Yanqi Zhou, Wei Li, and Peter J. Liu. 2020. Exploring the limits of transfer learning with a unified text-to-text transformer. *The Journal of Machine Learning Research*, 21(1):140:5485–140:5551.

Nils Reimers and Iryna Gurevych. 2019. Sentence-BERT: Sentence embeddings using Siamese BERT-networks. In *Proceedings of the 2019 Conference on Empirical Methods in Natural Language Processing and the 9th International Joint Conference on Natural Language Processing (EMNLP-IJCNLP)*, pages 3982–3992, Hong Kong, China. Association for Computational Linguistics.

Thomas Vakili, Anastasios Lamproudis, Aron Henriksson, and Hercules Dalianis. 2022. Downstream task performance of BERT models pre-trained using automatically de-identified clinical data. In *Proceedings of the Thirteenth Language Resources and Evaluation Conference*, pages 4245–4252, Marseille, France. European Language Resources Association.

Elena Volodina, Simon Dobnik, Therese Lindströ m Tiedemann, and Xuan-Son Vu. 2023. Grandma karl is 27 years old – research agenda for pseudonymization of research data. In *2023 IEEE Ninth International Conference on Big Data Computing Service and Applications (BigDataService)*, pages 229–233.

Shoko Wakamiya, Lis Kanashiro Pereira, Lisa Raithel, Hui-Syuan Yeh, Peitao Han, Seiji Shimizu, Tomohiro Nishiyama, Gabriel Herman Bernardim Andrade, Noriki Nishida, Hiroki Teranishi, Narumi Tokunaga, Philippe Thomas, Roland Roller, Pierre Zweigenbaum, Yuji Matsumoto, Akiko Aizawa, Sebastian Möller, Cyril Grouin, Thomas Lavergne, Aurélie Névéol, Patrick Paroubek, Shuntaro Yada, and Eiji Aramaki. 2023. NTCIR-17 MedNLP-SC Social Media Adverse Drug Event Detection: Subtask Overview. In *Proceedings of the 17th NTCIR Conference on Evaluation of Information Access Technologies, NTCIR-17. National Institute of Informatics (NII)*.

A Appendix

A.1 Corpus Generation

The synthetic data creation consists of two steps, data generation and pre-processing. First, Japanese tweets were collected from Twitter (X), using 68 drug queries extracted from a Japanese drug-name dictionary[8] and the public Twitter API[9]. The text generation model was built from the collected tweets to produce Japanese pseudo tweets. URLs and user names in the original tweets were replaced with masks. Using a Japanese medical named entity recognizer, MedNER-CR-JA[10], tweets without any symptom expression were filtered out. T5 was fine-tuned on the remaining tweets to generate synthetic tweets mentioning a subset of 17 drugs.

During post-processing, the following tweets were filtered out; (i) pseudo-messages that do not mention any drug or symptom, (ii) pseudo-messages that are identical to any of the original tweets, and (iii) duplicates.

Finally, all tweets mentioning any of the 17 drugs were annotated manually. After counting the number of annotations describing positive ADE mentions, the 24 most frequent ones were chosen. In two cases, two similar ADEs were merged into one. Then, 22 ADEs were obtained as labels. More details can be found in Wakamiya et al. (2023).

A.2 Tables and Figures about analysis of ADEs and human comparison

Tables 1 and 2 and Figure 6 present the detailed results of the direct comparison of source and pseudo data, analyzed by human annotators and GPT-4. Figure 5 presents the detailed distribution of the drugs and their ADE in the pseudo data compared to JADER. Table 3 and Figures 10 and 11 show a detailed overview of the data's drug-ADE correlation. Finally, Figure 8 presents all example tweets from above in the original language (Japanese).

B Details on Corpus Statistics

The following will give more details on the corpus statistics we used to compare the original and pseudo-tweets. This is not exhaustive; there are many more interesting analyses that can be applied to the data.

[8]https://sociocom.naist.jp/hyakuyaku-dic/

[9]https://developer.twitter.com/en/support/twitter-api

[10]https://huggingface.co/sociocom/MedNER-CR-JA

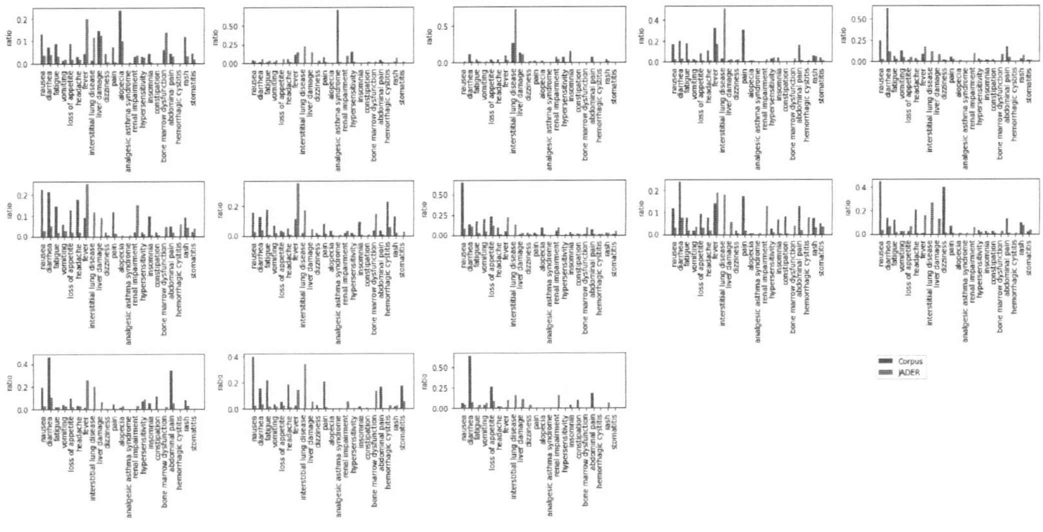

Figure 5: Distributions between JADER and the corpus

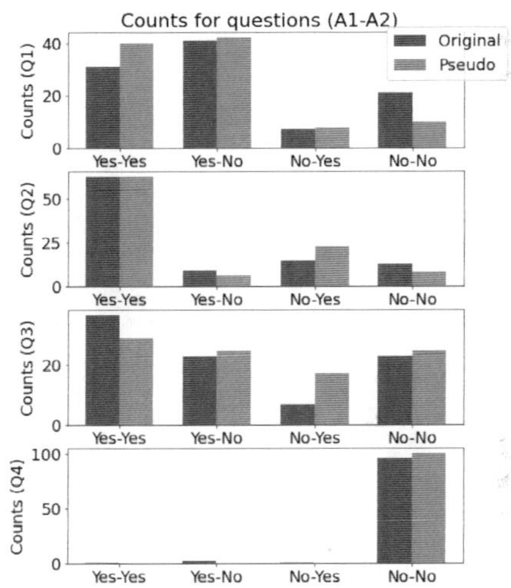

Figure 6: Results from human judgment by A1 and A2 (Barplots of Table 1) .

Q1		A1	
		yes	no
A2	yes	71 (31 / 40)	15 (7 / 8)
	no	83 (41 / 42)	31 (21 / 10)
Cohen's kappa		0.089	
Q2		A1	
		yes	no
A2	yes	126 (63 / 63)	38 (15 / 23)
	no	15 (9 / 6)	21 (13 / 8)
Cohen's kappa		0.281	
Q3		A1	
		yes	no
A2	yes	66 (37 / 29)	24 (7 / 17)
	no	48 (23 / 25)	48 (23 / 25)
Cohen's kappa		0.290	
Q4		A1	
		yes	no
A2	yes	1 (1 / 0)	1 (1 / 0)
	no	2 (2 / 0)	196 (96 / 100)
Cohen's kappa		0.393	

Table 1: Results from human judgment by annotator1 (A1) and annotator2 (A2).*The numbers are counts of original + pseudo (original / pseudo)

	GPT-4 Answer		Cohen's kappa	
	yes	no	A1	A2
Q1	198 (98 / 100)	0 (0 / 0)	0.000	0.000
Q2	196 (97 / 99)	2 (1 / 1)	0.088	0.014
Q3	144 (67 / 77)	54 (31 / 23)	0.237	0.298
Q4	0 (0 / 0)	198 (98 / 100)	0.000	0.000

Table 2: Results from model judgment by GPT-4

B.1 Statistics

Type-Token Ratio The type-token ratio (TTR) (Johnson, 1944) counts the number of types and divides the result by the number of tokens as a measure of diversity in a corpus. However, this ratio strongly depends on the corpus size, and therefore, it is often shown as a function of the corpus size.

Part-of-Speech Tags We further calculate the relative frequencies of the occurring POS tags in the data using spaCy for tagging.

Similarity We index the pseudo-tweets with the FAISS library and compare them using cosine similarity with a sample from the original data. This

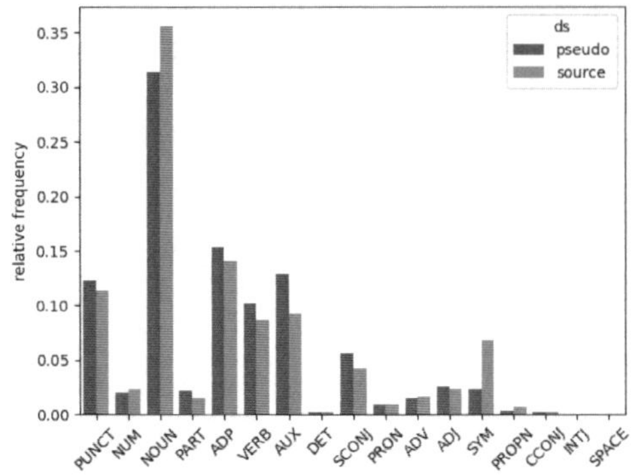

Figure 7: The relative frequency of the POS tags for the pseudo- and source tweets.

Ex1: 接種後失明は良く聞くけど耳もなんだ肺炎だとステロイドで即回復だけど目や耳って

Ex2: アザチオプリンを飲み始めて2日目だけどめっちゃ効いてる気がする。でも副作用で全身の発疹が凄い..

Ex3: コルヒチンは昔から使われてるし、便秘か下痢のどっちかかな…副作用出たら減らしてもいいから、次の病院まで飲み続けてって言われたんだけど、副作用しか今のとこないんだけど

Ex4: はなこちゃん，こんばんは... 精神的なことは伝えられずに終わりました～，そのかわり気圧頭痛が酷くてカロナール出して…

Figure 8: Japanese version of examples Ex1–Ex4. Ex1: source tweet. Ex2: pseudo tweet. Ex3: tweet mentioning colchicine and constipation. Ex4 where a person's name remained in the tweet (manually replaced here with 'はなこ' for publication).

sample contained only 4,000 original tweets since the computation was time-consuming.

B.2 Results and Discussion

Type-Token Ratio In Figure 9, we show the TTR for both datasets (the first 20,000 tokens), plotted against the corpus size. The source tweets clearly show a higher type-token ratio which decreases slower than the ratio of the pseudo-tweets.

Part-of-Speech Tags We show the relative frequencies of the occurring POS tags in Figure 7. The pseudo-tweets get tagged with 15 different POS tags, while the original data gets 16 POS tags. Nouns (NOUN), adpositions (ADP), auxiliaries (AUX) and punctuation markers (PUNCT)[11] are the most common POS tags for both corpora.

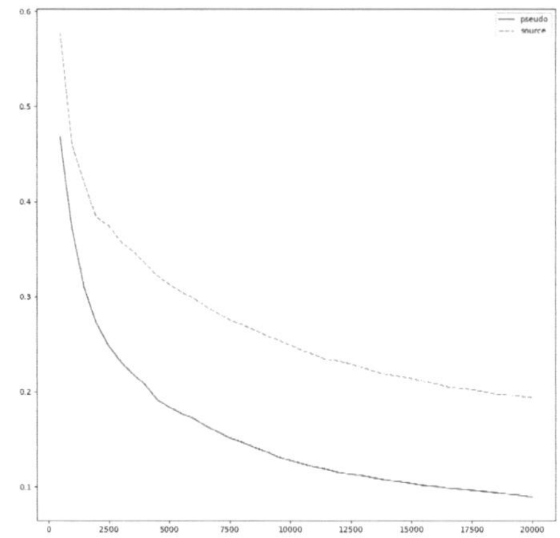

Figure 9: The type-token ratio as a function of corpus size for the source (orange) and pseudo data (blue) for an excerpt of the data.

	Pearson		Spearman		KS
drug	CC	p-value	CC	p-value	p-value
azathioprine	0.316	0.153	0.508	0.016	0.049
aspirin	-0.154	0.493	-0.014	0.951	0.007
amiodarone	0.762	0.000	0.391	0.072	0.020
infliximab	0.040	0.859	0.176	0.435	0.109
colchicine	0.314	0.154	0.205	0.359	0.632
cyclosporine	-0.096	0.670	-0.072	0.750	0.394
cyclophosphamide	0.110	0.627	0.205	0.361	0.109
cisplatin	0.184	0.411	0.269	0.226	0.872
tacrolimus	0.025	0.911	-0.137	0.542	0.394
minocycline	-0.212	0.343	-0.064	0.776	0.218
mesalazine	0.104	0.646	0.102	0.652	0.632
methotrexate	-0.215	0.336	-0.086	0.705	0.109
metformin	0.107	0.635	0.210	0.349	0.007
all drugs	0.088	0.140	0.126	0.034	-

Table 3: Pearson's and Spearman's correlation coefficient and p-values of the tests in each drug

Similarity From the 4,000 samples we compared to the pseudo-tweets, we retrieved 86 hits that showed a cosine similarity higher than 0.9 and one that was exactly the same. However, from the 86 hits, only 39 were unique, i.e., one pseudo-tweet can have several very similar, but not exact nearest neighbors. The single pseudo-tweet that was identical to the source tweet did not contain any identifiable information and was basically a sequence of hashtags. However, this shows that even though the generation process included a diversity penalty, synthetic data might still be repetitive or near-repetitive.

[11] https://universaldependencies.org/u/pos/

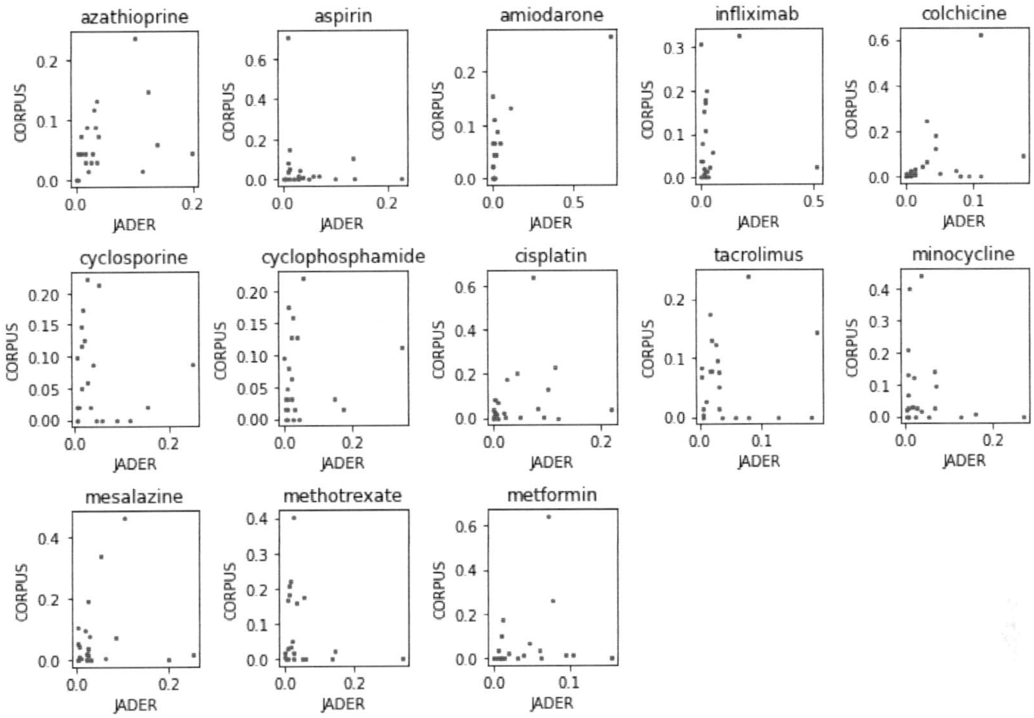

Figure 10: The frequency between JADER and the corpus in each drug

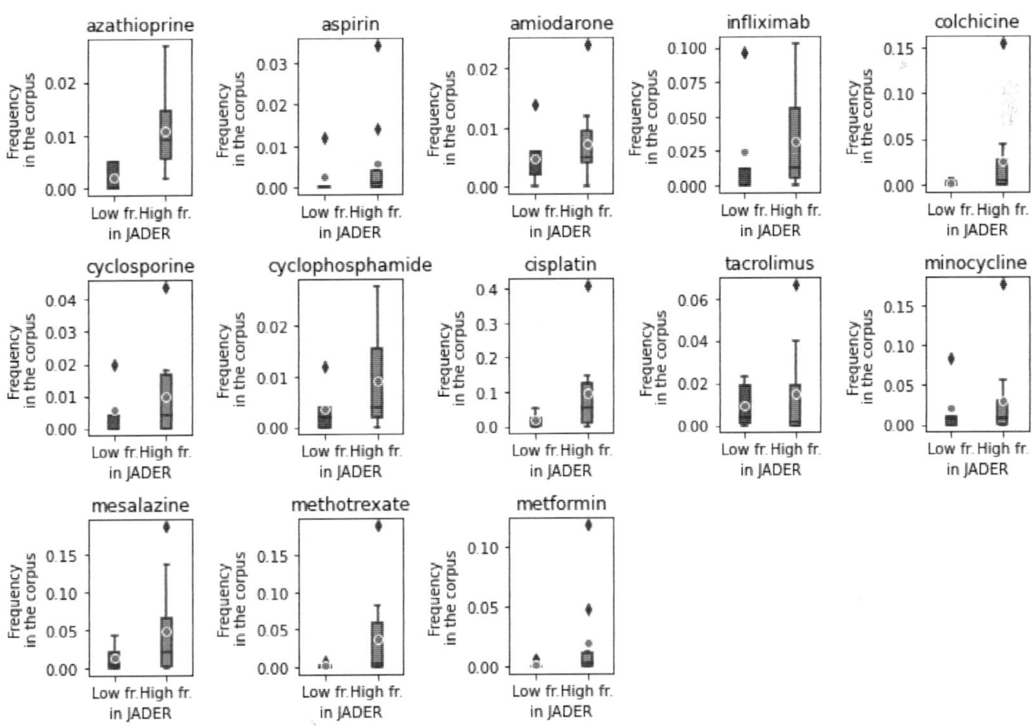

Figure 11: Comparison between MFG and LFG in each drug

Automatic Detection and Labelling of Personal Data in Case Reports from the ECHR in Spanish: Evaluation of Two Different Annotation Approaches

Maria Sierro
LASLAB
University of the Basque Country (UPV/EHU)
maria.sierro@ehu.eus

Begoña Altuna
HiTZ Center - Ixa
University of the Basque Country (UPV/EHU)
begona.altuna@ehu.eus

Itziar Gonzalez-Dios
HiTZ Center - Ixa
University of the Basque Country (UPV/EHU)
itziar.gonzalezd@ehu.eus

Abstract

In this paper we evaluate two annotation approaches for automatic detection and labelling of personal information in legal texts in relation to the ambiguity of the labels and the homogeneity of the annotations. For this purpose, we built a corpus of 44 case reports from the European Court of Human Rights in Spanish language and we annotated it following two different annotation approaches: automatic projection of the annotations of an existing English corpus, and manual annotation with our reinterpretation of their guidelines. Moreover, we employ Flair on a Named Entity Recognition task to compare its performance in the two annotation schemes.

1 Introduction

One of the reasons why research on the automatic detection and labelling of personal information in legal texts (such as case reports) is important is that many countries, including Spain, have the legal requirement of removing sensitive information from these texts before publishing them. However, Pilán et al. (2022) have argued that most research on sensitive entities detection and classification has focused on clinical data, and publicly available evaluation datasets outside this domain are scarce. Moreover, as indicated by Csányi et al. (2021), carrying out this process manually is extremely inefficient.

Regarding datasets for automatic detection and labelling of personal data in the legal domain in Spanish, few datasets have been published, and often they have been built from texts subjected to previous anonymization, thus making the evaluation performed on this data less realistic. This is the case of the work of Arranz et al. (2022), which introduces very detailed annotation guidelines (Arranz et al., 2020).

In contrast, the privacy-oriented annotated corpus in English built by Pilán et al. (2022) stands out due to the use of case reports from the European Court of Human Rights (ECHR), which are publicly available in the HUDOC database[1] in full-text with the consent of the applicants involved in the cases. Additionally, they annotated the corpus by taking into consideration not just direct identifiers, following the usual procedure, but also quasi or indirect identifiers. Nevertheless, their annotation approach presents some ambiguity, given that it leaves room for interpretation and some of their selected entities cover a broad variety of forms.

The ambiguity of annotation guidelines is an important factor to take into consideration when investigating automatic detection and labelling of personal information because it might cause annotations to be non-homogeneous. As argued by Benesty (2019a), non-homogeneous annotations may decrease the performance of Language Models (LMs) on Named Entity Recognition (NER) tasks (the tasks that precede the masking or replacement of sensitive information for anonymization or pseudonymization in legal texts).

Drawing from the work of Pilán et al. (2022), in this paper we intend to contribute to the field of automatic detection and labelling of personal information by (1) building one evaluation corpus of case reports from the ECHR in Spanish, and annotating it following two different annotation approaches; and (2) employing this corpus for assessing the performance of Flair (Akbik et al., 2018) on a NER task and comparing the results of the two annotation schemes. On the one hand, we annotate the corpus via automatic annotation projection, respecting the annotation approach of Pilán et al. (2022). Separately, we annotate the same corpus by following our own reinterpretation of their annotation approach, inspired by the guidelines of Arranz et al. (2020). Our goal is to observe the effects of the different level of ambiguity of the

[1] https://hudoc.echr.coe.int (accessed on July 2023)

Proceedings of the Workshop on Computational Approaches to Language Data Pseudonymization
CALD-pseudo 2024, pages 18–24
March 21, 2024

annotation approaches on the results of the NER task per entity type. We publish the code employed as well as the annotated datasets on GitHub[2] under a MIT license.

2 The TAB corpus

In order to build an evaluation corpus of case reports from the ECHR in Spanish, we departed from the test set of the English corpus built by Pilán et al. (2022). Their corpus is called the Text Anonymization Benchmark (TAB) corpus and it is available on GitHub[3] in json format under a MIT license. This json file contains both the annotations as well as the texts from the ECHR, taken from the HUDOC database. In regards to the reproduction of its website content, the EHCR (n.d.) claims that:

> The information and texts available on the Court's website may be reproduced provided the source is acknowledged (© ECHR-CEDH) and the reproduction is made for private use or for the purposes of information and education in connection with the Court's activities. This authorisation is subject to the condition that the source is indicated and that any such reproduction is free of charge.

As it is explained by Pilán et al. (2022), the texts included in their annotated corpus only contain judgments from the "Grand Chamber" and the "Chamber", and they are restricted to the document sections called "Introduction" and "Statement of Facts", given that they contain the largest quantity of personal identifiers. In addition to that, they selected the judgements by ensuring that their annotators would have knowledge of the national language of the country accused of human rights violations.

It is important to note that the TAB corpus was annotated by 12 annotators. In the work of Pilán et al. (2022), annotators were instructed to annotate all sensitive entities and their semantic types in a first step. In a second step, they were asked to use their interpretation to determine whether to mask each sensitive entity for protecting a person's identity while preserving data utility. Moreover, annotators were instructed to indicate whether the entities to be masked were direct or quasi-identifiers. In a third step, they added a second attribute to the entity mentions indicating whether they corresponded to confidential information (such as religious beliefs, ethnicity or health data). The TAB corpus maintains the masking decisions by all the annotators given that Pilán et al. (2022) consider that there are often multiple correct masking choices in the same text.

3 Dataset creation

In this section we explain our workflow for creating the Spanish corpus.

3.1 Data collection and translation

We extracted 44 random texts from the TAB test set and automatically translated them into Spanish with DeepL.[4] The use of Machine Translation (MT) for building our corpus implies that a number of translation errors are expected. In our corpus, the texts translated with DeepL were not post-edited, but they were inspected by native speakers during the review of the projected annotations. In general, the most common flaw in the Spanish automatic translations was the inconsistent translation of organization names (e.g. "Poole Magistrate's Court" sometimes translated as "*Tribunal de Magistrados de Poole*" and sometimes left untranslated in the same text).

3.2 Projection of annotations

Before projecting the annotations, we collapsed the annotations by all the annotators in the test set of the TAB corpus (they are all considered equally correct examples). When collapsing all the annotators' decisions, only the annotations of the spans to be masked (which are both direct and quasi-identifiers) were kept.

Furthermore, in order to project the annotations with the T-Projection method (García-Ferrero et al., 2023) we transformed the data to get a CoNLL file with IOB tags, with sentences separated by double-space, and only one layer of annotations. The downside of this process was that there was some loss of information. The entity types (shown in the first column of Table 1) of the spans to be masked were transferred. However, the additional labels (which include the distinction between direct and quasi-identifiers and the indication of confidential information) were lost. Consequently, our work

[2] https://github.com/mariasierrofer/sensitive-entity-detection-ECHR-Spanish

[3] https://github.com/NorskRegnesentral/text-anonymization-benchmark

[4] https://www.deepl.com/translator

is limited to the recognition of the different entity types.

After projecting the annotations of the selected texts into the Spanish translations, two persons (a Natural Language Processing (NLP) Master's student and a linguist) reviewed them with the INCEpTION tool.[5] We measured the Inter-Annotator Agreement (IAA) with the same tool at the entity level using the metric Cohen's Kappa, resulting in a value of 0.89.

3.3 Reinterpretation and reannotation

Our reinterpreted guidelines, which combine the annotation approach of Pilán et al. (2022) with the detailed guidelines of Arranz et al. (2020), are available in the appendix. Table 1 compares the entity types included by Pilán et al. (2022) with the entity types included in our reinterpretation of their guidelines. Our goal is to pave the path for reducing label ambiguity. The most relevant changes of our reinterpreted guidelines include:

- The replacement of the DEM entity by two new labels: NATIONALITY (referring to a person's demonym) and ETHNIC CATEGORY (covering the ethnic parameters of a person's identity, such as race, religion, language, and regional origin). A disadvantage of this replacement is that the new labels do not cover some information that was included by the DEM entity (such as health information, political and sexual orientation). Due to the small size of our corpus, adding detailed labels for all types of personal information would produce few occurrences of each one. For the same reason, the MISC label is not addressed in our reinterpreted guidelines.

- The split of the DATETIME entity into two new labels: DATE and TIME. In regards to these labels, our reinterpreted guidelines contain one specific adaptation for Spanish language: the annotation of dates and times covers their preceding articles (but not prepositions) in order to comply with the ISO-TimeML standard for temporal annotation (ISO, 2008) and to potentially ease its automatic detection with existing tools.

- A specification related to the ORG entity, which now only covers the spans which refer to distinct organizations and not to generic institutions (e.g. "High Court", "Supreme Court").

- The split of the PERSON entity into two new labels: PER and LEGAL PROFESSIONAL. These two labels make a distinction between the names of the people professionally involved in the cases and the names of the rest of the people mentioned in the texts. The reason for making this distinction is that in Spain (and other countries), the names of the people professionally involved in the cases do not have to be masked (van Opijnen et al., 2017).

- A difference regarding the QUANTITY entity, which now covers meaningful quantities (not directly deducible from the rest of the information of the text) without their units of measure. It also covers periods of time, which were previously included in the DATETIME label. Currency instead gets a separate treatment: these units of measure are annotated with the CURRENCY tag because they can reveal information about the locations involved in the cases.

Corpus with projected annotations		**Corpus with manual annotations**	
Entity	**nb. tags**	**Entity**	**nb. tags**
PERSON	355	PER LEGAL PROFESSIONAL	191 170
CODE	54	CODE	87
LOC	163	LOC	454
ORG	216	ORG	130
DEM	92	NATIONALITY ETHNIC CATEGORY	110 22
QUANTITY	55	QUANTITY CURRENCY	204 32
DATETIME	799	DATE TIME	786 5
MISC	50	-	-
total	1,784	total	2,191

Table 1: Comparison of the entity types and number of tags included in the corpora with projected and manual annotations.

It is also important to note that, as stated in Section 2, Pilán et al. (2022) included a second step of annotation where they instructed annotators to judge case by case which combination of sensitive entities to mask for protecting a person's identity while preserving data utility. We intend to simplify this process and avoid leaving any room for interpretation by annotating all the occurrences of the

[5]https://inception-project.github.io/

entity types included in our reinterpreted guidelines in a unique annotation step. With the intention of avoiding compromising the data utility of the texts, our strategy consisted in defining the entity types for targeting precise sensitive information.

Two persons (a NLP Master's student and a philologist) carried out the manual annotations with the INCEpTION tool by making modifications to the preceding projected annotations. In this case, we measured the IAA with the same tool at the entity level using the metric Cohen's Kappa, resulting in a value of 0.99. This higher agreement could indicate that the new annotation approach of the reinterpreted guidelines was indeed less ambiguous and the annotators had less room for interpretation.

4 Experimental setup

Once we built and annotated the corpus of legal texts in Spanish language, we used it for assessing Flair (Akbik et al., 2018), which has provided good results in the identification of sensitive information in legal texts in previous studies (Benesty, 2019a; Benesty, 2019b). We used Flair version 0.12.2. For all the experiments, the corpus was split into train, dev, and test set as shown in Table 2.

Set	nb. sents.	nb. tokens
train	1,245	34,924
dev	178	4,430
test	193	5,255

Table 2: Number of sentences and tokens of the train, dev, and test sets.

We trained a bi-LSTM-CRF sequence tagger[6] with default hyper parameters for 18 epochs in both our experiment on the corpus with projected annotations as well as our experiment with the manually annotated corpus. We used pre-trained embeddings (Akbik et al., 2019) from Flair "ner-multi" model.[7]

The metrics used in the assessment of Flair are precision, recall, and F1-score, computed at the mention level, but for brevity we will only focus on the F1-scores in Section 5 and Section 6.

5 Evaluation on corpus with projected annotations

On the corpus with projected annotations, Flair achieves a micro average F1 of 0.73.

Entity	F1-score
PERSON	0.73
CODE	0.92
LOC	0.67
ORG	0.39
DEM	0
QUANTITY	0.50
DATETIME	0.95
MISC	0
micro avg	0.73

Table 3: F1-scores per entity type and micro average F1 calculated on the test set of the corpus with projected annotations.

By looking at the results per entity type (shown in Table 3), it can be observed that there is a particularly stark contrast between Flair's performance on the DATETIME and CODE labels (F1-score over 0.9) vs. the DEM and MISC labels (0 F1-score). This difference could indicate that the DEM and MISC labels were more widely defined than the DATETIME and CODE labels and their annotations were less homogeneous. Pilán et al. (2022) noticed a similar difference in the performance of their selected LMs, and they stated that the reason could be related to the broad variety of forms that the DEM and MISC labels can take. Moreover, it could be argued that such an imbalanced performance might be due to a dissimilar number of tags for each label. However, while it is true that the DATETIME label presents the larger number of tags (799 tags in the corpus with projected annotations), the labels CODE, MISC, and DEM all have a similar number of tags (54, 50, and 92 tags respectively), and still the performance of Flair on the CODE label is much higher.

6 Evaluation on corpus annotated with our reinterpreted guidelines

On the corpus annotated with our reinterpreted guidelines, Flair outperforms the results of the previous experiment, achieving a micro average F1 of 0.80.

By looking at the results per entity type (shown in Table 4), it can be observed that the TIME and the ETHNIC CATEGORY labels obtained a 0 F1-score, likely due to the scarcity of tags of these types (5 and 22 tags respectively in the whole corpus).

On the other hand, the performance of Flair on the DATE label (0.98 F1-score) is slightly higher than it was on the DATETIME label (0.95 F1-score). With a similar number of tags of this type,

[6] https://github.com/flairNLP/flair/blob/master/flair/models/sequence_tagger_model.py

[7] https://huggingface.co/flair/ner-multi

Entity	F1-score
PER	0.67
LEGAL PROFESSIONAL	0.46
CODE	1
LOC	0.87
ORG	0.20
NATIONALITY	0.85
ETHNIC CATEGORY	0
QUANTITY	0.75
CURRENCY	0.60
DATE	0.98
TIME	0
micro avg	0.80

Table 4: F1-scores per entity type and micro average F1 calculated on the test set of the corpus annotated with our reinterpreted guidelines.

the increase in performance could indicate that it was beneficial to make a distinction between the annotation of dates, times, and durations. In particular, the annotation of durations was covered by the DATETIME label according to the guidelines created by Pilán et al. (2022). On the contrary, in our reinterpretation of their guidelines, durations were covered by the QUANTITY label, which also shows an increase in performance (0.75 F1-score vs. 0.50 F1-score in the previous experiment).

There is also a slight increase in Flair's performance on the CODE label (1 F1-score vs. 0.92 F1-score in the previous experiment). Regarding the labels PER and LEGAL PROFESSIONAL, the performance of Flair decreases when compared to the PERSON label.

In regards to the NATIONALITY label included in the manually annotated corpus, which replaces the previous DEM label, the performance of Flair is higher (0.85 F1-score). This is especially interesting considering that the DEM label included in the corpus with projected annotations got a 0 F1-score and the number of tags is similar in both corpora.

Furthermore, while the performance of Flair on the ORG label decreases, its performance on the LOC label is much higher (0.87 F1-score vs. 0.67 F1-score in the previous experiment). In this case, the main reason for the increase seems to be related to the larger number of LOC tags in the corpus annotated according to our reinterpreted guidelines (454 tags vs. 163 tags). The larger number of LOC tags is due to our indication of annotating all the occurrences of the entity types included in our reinterpreted guidelines.

Finally, the performance of Flair on the CURRENCY label is low (0.60 F1-score). Other than having few occurrences (32 tags in the whole corpus), this low performance could also indicate that this label is still ambiguous.

7 Conclusions and future work

Throughout this paper, we have evaluated two annotation approaches for the automatic detection and labelling of personal information in case reports from the ECHR in Spanish language. Our goal was to observe the differences in the performance of Flair (Akbik et al., 2018) in relation to the ambiguity of the selected entity types. We performed this evaluation by building one evaluation corpus of case reports from the ECHR in Spanish, and annotating it by following two different annotation approaches: automatic projection of the annotations of the English corpus built by Pilán et al. (2022), and manual annotation with our reinterpretation of their guidelines, also based on the work of Arranz et al. (2020). We used this newly-built corpus for assessing Flair on a NER task and comparing the results of the two annotation schemes. We make both the corpus and the code public under a MIT license to encourage research on automatic detection and labelling of personal data in legal texts in Spanish.

The results showed that our reinterpreted guidelines partly succeeded in getting less ambiguous labels and more homogeneous annotations. This idea is reinforced by the higher IAA obtained with our reinterpreted guidelines, which suggests that the more detailed approach of our guidelines might also help human annotators to be consistent in their annotations. As we mentioned, the manual annotation of entities may be very time-consuming. An automatic system that yields a good performance in the task will help decreasing the burden. Trying to make a more consistent annotation has proven to be a sensible approach to improve the performance of Flair. In the near future an anonymization analysis should be conducted to see whether our approach effectively reduces the risk of re-identification while not compromising the readability of the document.

In the future research, we will expand our corpora, adapt and apply our reinterpreted guidelines to other languages, and include new specific labels. We also plan to test other Language Models and other techniques such as zero-shot or few shot. Additionally, we intend to test privacy models such as C-sanitized (Sánchez and Batet, 2016) for a comprehensive risk analysis.

Limitations

We evaluated the performance of Flair (Akbik et al., 2018) on a NER task with one corpus of 44 case reports from the ECHR in Spanish. The texts of our corpus were translated from English into Spanish via MT (using DeepL) without post-editing. In future work, it would be interesting to either employ professional translations or post-edit the automatic translations. Additionally, our work could be extended to other languages. It would also be interesting to carry out similar experiments on larger corpora and add labels covering other types of information that we could not cover due to the size of our corpus, including a deeper treatment of quasi-identifiers. On the other hand, it should be noted that our work is restricted to the recognition of sensitive entities on legal texts and it does not reflect on the masking operations following this task. Moreover, since we do not annotate pronouns and possessive adjectives, our corpus is suited for anonymization rather than pseudonymization. Lastly, there is no comprehensive risk analysis which examines the connection between the detected sensitive entities and external knowledge bases, as recommended by Csányi et al. (2021).

Acknowledgments

Maria Sierro receives funding from the LASLAB group (IT-1426-22) funded by the Basque Government.

Begoña Altuna is supported by the Basque Government postdoctoral grant POS 2022 2 0024.

We also acknowledge the funding from the following projects: a) Ixa group A type research group (IT-1805-22) funded by the Basque Government. b) DeepKnowledge (PID2021-127777OB-C21) project funded by MCIN/AEI/10.13039/501100011033 and by ERDF A way of making Europe. c) AWARE: Commonsense for a new generation of natural language understanding applications (TED2021-131617B-I00): funded by MCIN/AEI /10.13039/501100011033 by the European Union NextGenerationEU/ PRTR. d) DeepR3 (TED2021-130295B-C31) funded by MCIN/AEI/10.13039/501100011033 and European Union NextGeneration EU/PRTR.

References

Alan Akbik, Tanja Bergmann, and Roland Vollgraf. 2019. Multilingual sequence labeling with one model.

Alan Akbik, Duncan Blythe, and Roland Vollgraf. 2018. Contextual string embeddings for sequence labeling. In *Proceedings of the 27th International Conference on Computational Linguistics*, pages 1638–1649, Santa Fe, New Mexico, USA. Association for Computational Linguistics.

Victoria Arranz, Chomicha Bendahman, Elena Edelman, Mickael Rigault, and Khalid Choukri (ELDA). 2020. Annotation Guidelines for Named Entities in MAPA.

Victoria Arranz, Khalid Choukri, Montse Cuadros, Aitor García Pablos, Lucie Gianola, Cyril Grouin, Manuel Herranz, Patrick Paroubek, and Pierre Zweigenbaum. 2022. MAPA project: Ready-to-go open-source datasets and deep learning technology to remove identifying information from text documents. In *Proceedings of the Workshop on Ethical and Legal Issues in Human Language Technologies and Multilingual De-Identification of Sensitive Data In Language Resources within the 13th Language Resources and Evaluation Conference*, pages 64–72, Marseille, France. European Language Resources Association.

Michael Benesty. 2019a. NER algo benchmark: spaCy, Flair, m-BERT and camemBERT on anonymizing French commercial legal cases. *Towards Data Science.*

Michael Benesty. 2019b. Why we switched from Spacy to Flair to anonymize French case law. *Towards Data Science.*

Gergely M. Csányi, Dániel Nagy, Renátó Vági, János P. Vadász, and Tamás Orosz. 2021. Challenges and Open Problems of Legal Document Anonymization. *Symmetry*, 13(8):1490.

EHCR. n.d. Copyright and Disclaimer.

Iker García-Ferrero, Rodrigo Agerri, and German Rigau. 2023. T-Projection: High Quality Annotation Projection for Sequence Labeling Tasks. In *Findings of the Association for Computational Linguistics: EMNLP 2023*, pages 15203–15217, Singapore. Association for Computational Linguistics.

ISO. 2008. *ISO DIS 24617-1: 2008 Language Resource Management - Semantic Annotation Framework - Part 1: Time and Events.* International Organization for Standardization, Geneva, Switzerland.

Ildikó Pilán, Pierre Lison, Lilja Øvrelid, Anthi Papadopoulou, David Sánchez, and Montserrat Batet. 2022. The text anonymization benchmark (TAB): A dedicated corpus and evaluation framework for text anonymization. *Computational Linguistics*, 48(4):1053–1101.

David Sánchez and Montserrat Batet. 2016. C-sanitized: A privacy model for document redaction and sanitization. *Journal of the Association for Information Science and Technology*, 67(1):148–163.

Marc van Opijnen, Ginevra Peruginelli, Eleni Kefali, and Monica Palmirani. 2017. On-Line Publication of Court Decisions in the EU: Report of the Policy Group of the Project 'Building on the European Case Law Identifier'.

A Reinterpreted guidelines

This appendix contains the annotation guidelines for the detection and labelling of personal information of case reports from the ECHR in Spanish language. The set of entity types to be annotated are:

- PER: this label comprises the names, initials, titles and honorifics (e.g. "*Mr.*", "*Dr.*") of people who are not legal professionals involved in the cases.
- LEGAL PROFESSIONAL: this label comprises the names, initials, titles and honorifics (e.g. "*Mr.*", "*Dr.*") of people who are legal professionals involved in the cases.
- CODE: the CODE label covers all types of identification numbers (e.g. passport numbers, phone numbers, report identifiers, etc.). Nevertheless, even if the CODE label includes case numbers (because they make reference to the cases being treated and can consequently be considered a direct identifier), this label does not comprise any other numbers making reference to legal texts involved in the cases (e.g. convention and law articles, protocols, rules, paragraphs, etc.).
- LOC: covers all types of geographical locations (e.g. countries, cities, addresses, etc.).
- ORG: covers the names of distinct organizations (with the exception of the "ECHR" and the "European Commission on Human Rights", which should not be annotated), and not generic institutions (e.g. "High Court", "Supreme Court", etc.). Still, if address information (e.g. city, country, etc.) is comprised within the expression of a generic institution (e.g. "Supreme Court of *Sweden*"), the address information (e.g. "*Sweden*") should be annotated using the LOC label.
- ETHNIC CATEGORY: covers the ethnic parameters of a person's identity, such as race, religion, language and regional origin.
- NATIONALITY: refers to a person's demonym (e.g. "*French*", "*Swedish*", "*Norwegian*").
- DATE: this label makes reference to dates (days, months, and years) including articles (but not prepositions) in order to comply with the ISO-TimeML standard for temporal annotation. As it happened with the CODE label, the DATE label does not apply to dates that serve to identify legal texts (with the exception of case reports) involved in the case (e.g. convention and law articles, protocols, rules, paragraphs, etc.).
- TIME: corresponds to hours (e.g. "at *4 p.m.*"; or in Spanish "a *las 4 horas*"), expressed in figures or in words (e.g. "*morning*", "*evening*", etc.). It does not include durations, since these are covered by the label QUANTITY.
- QUANTITY: covers quantities (e.g. surface areas, distances, percentages, etc.) without their units of measure. In this way, the QUANTITY label targets meaningful quantities (not directly deducible from the rest of the information of the text), including figures associated to periods of time (e.g. "it lasted for *9* years and *9* months"), which were previously covered by the DATETIME label, as well as ages (e.g. "she was *19* years old").
- CURRENCY: covers currency types (e.g. "*euro*", "*pound*", "*dollar*", etc.).

The general principles that should be kept in mind when annotating are:

- Annotate all the entities in all the selected texts that correspond to the selected entity types.
- Do not annotate pronouns and possessive adjectives revealing gender information, since they imply a low re-identification risk.
- Annotate all the mentions pertaining to the same entity.

PSILENCE: A Pseudonymization Tool for International Law

Luis Adrián Cabrera-Diego and **Akshita Gheewala**
Jus Mundi, 30 Rue de Lisbonne, Paris, 75008, France
a.cabrera@jusmundi.com

Abstract

Since the announcement of the GDPR, the pseudonymization of legal documents has become a high-priority task in many legal organizations. This means that for making public a document, it is necessary to redact the identity of certain entities, such as witnesses. In this work, we present the first results obtained by PSILENCE, a pseudonymization tool created for redacting semi-automatically international arbitration documents in English. PSILENCE has been built using a Named Entity Recognition (NER) system, along with a Coreference Resolution system. These systems allow us to find the people that we need to redact in a clustered way, but also to propose the same pseudonym throughout one document. This last aspect makes it easier to read and comprehend a redacted legal document. Different experiments were done on four different datasets, one of which was legal, and the results are promising, reaching a Macro F-score of up to 0.72 on the legal dataset.

1 Introduction

Although the redaction of sensitive information in different types of documents is a common practice in multiple domains, since the announcement of the GDPR and especially after its implementation, the need to find automatic or semi-automatic ways to redact documents has become a priority in many organizations. Historically, the redaction of documents has been done mostly by hand, following guidelines and, in some cases, pattern-matching tools. However, due to its nature, the redaction process is not only slow, but it is also expensive as in many cases an expert needs to be consulted.

In certain domains, like biomedicine, the automatic redaction of documents is well-known thanks to shared tasks, e.g. Stubbs and Uzuner (2015). However, in the legal domain, as in many others, the automatic redaction of documents is still a challenge. For instance, legal documents tend to be long and they have multiple types of entities, e.g. parties, witnesses, experts, judges, lawyers, and citations. Furthermore, some of these entities can be either individuals or organizations. Finally, as we get farther from the beginning of the document, entities become less clear to identify correctly.

Currently, in the legal domain, we can find two different redaction processes: anonymization and pseudonymization, and while both terms are similar, they differ in key aspects. Mourby et al. (2018) summarizes GDPR definition of pseudonymization as the task that "prevents direct identification through attribution, but not through any other mean". Certain organizations add to the definition of pseudonymization the use of a unique identifier for each individual across multiple data sources, that hides their actual identity (Graham, 2012; Elliot et al., 2020). Furthermore, it is a process, that if necessary, can be reversed (Elliot et al., 2020) as only the individuals are substituted, regardless of the occurrence of other elements which could reveal, for example, the gender or age of a person (Allard et al., 2021). In contrast, the goal of anonymization is to remove the complete link between individuals and data (Graham, 2012). Moreover, it is a process that should make the re-identification of people hard to achieve, sometimes by doing additional alterations to the source (Elliot et al., 2020).

We present in this work the first results of *PSILENCE (PSeudonymization of International Law casEs using* NER *and Coreference rEsolution)*, a tool created to pseudonymize international arbitration documents in English. These first results come from multiple experiments done over four different datasets, one of which has been created by a group of legal experts for this specific task.

The rest of the paper is organized as follows. We present the scope and objectives of this work in Section 2. In Section 3, we present the most relevant works found in the literature related to the automatic redaction of documents, i.e. methods

Proceedings of the Workshop on Computational Approaches to Language Data Pseudonymization
CALD-pseudo 2024, pages 25–36
March 21, 2024

and data, as well as some additional relevant tasks. Then, we present the methodology of our system in Section 4. The data collection explored in this work is described in Section 5 while the evaluation setup is detailed in Section 6. The experimental results and their discussion are presented in Section 7 and Section 8 respectively. Finally, we conclude and propose our future work in Section 9.

2 Scope and Objectives

PSILENCE has been developed to semi-automatize the pseudonymization process of English documents within Jus Mundi[1]. Currently, it focuses only on entities of type people, however, we are aware of the existence of other types of information that need to be hidden, such as emails and addresses. Furthermore, from all the entities of type people, only those of type witnesses are redacted. This means that we do not redact lawyers, judges, or parties.[2]

Therefore, PSILENCE has two main goals. First, to propose to a legal expert a list of people that should be redacted in the document to keep the sensitive information hidden. Secondly, to cluster the names of people to provide a unique identifier to each redacted person within a document. This means that different name variations of the same person are grouped together. For instance, *"Mariano Puerta"* and *"Mr. Puerta"* will compose one cluster, while *"Laura Puerta"* would be put into a different one. In this way, we can simplify the redaction process and improve the readability and comprehension of a redacted document.

3 Related Work

In the health and biomedical domains, we can find multiple tools developed for the anonymization, pseudonymization, and deidentification of information, as presented by Chevrier et al. (2019) and Leevy et al. (2020). However, in the legal domain, there is a reduced number of works. For instance, we can name ANOPPI (Oksanen et al., 2019; Arttu Oksanen et al., 2022), a pseudonymization tool for Finnish Court documents that makes use of multiple NER systems, based on rules and machine learning. It uses regular expressions and dictionaries to find elements such as registration plates or specific names. As Finnish inflects pronouns and nouns, they perform morphological analysis to correctly inflect pseudonyms. Individuals are not grouped, this means that each occurrence of them is assigned a different identifier. In Schamberger (2021), the authors present an anonymization tool for German court rulings. Specifically, the authors create a NER system by using BERT embeddings (Devlin et al., 2019) through a BiLSTM and CRF architecture. Pilán et al. (2022) compare different tools for anonymyzing legal documents: Presidio[3], a generic NER system based on RoBERTa (Liu et al., 2019) and a specialized NER based on Longformer (Beltagy et al., 2020).

Outside the legal domain, we can highlight the work of Biesner et al. (2022). In this paper, the authors present a full anonymization system for German financial documents. The system considers the anonymization task as a sequence tagging problem, thus, they make use of NER for detecting entities. They explored elements such as word embeddings, contextual embeddings, and different neural network architectures for creating the NER system. Similarly, Papadopoulou et al. (2022) use knowledge graphs and k-anonymity (Sweeney, 2002) to generate a weakly supervised dataset. Then, the generated dataset is used to fine-tune RoBERTa (Liu et al., 2019) and create an anonymization tool following a NER architecture.

Regarding pseudonymization and anonymization data there are not many publicly available datasets. The documents that need this kind of tool have to be pseudonymized or anonymized before becoming public, due to privacy reasons, and, annotating documents is an expensive and time-consuming task. Thus many of the legal datasets used in the literature are private, such as the works of Barriere and Fouret (2019) and Garat and Wonsever (2022). One exception is the TAB Corpus (Pilán et al., 2022), which is a collection of publicly available documents from the European Court of Human Rights that have been annotated for evaluating anonymization tasks.

Outside the legal domain, there are clinical datasets such as the *2014 i2b2/UTHealth* corpus (Stubbs and Uzuner, 2015) and the *2016 CEGS N-GRID Shared Task* (Stubbs et al., 2017). Papadopoulou et al. (2022) created an anonymization dataset using a collection of Wikipedia biographies.

As the pseudonymization and anonymization

[1] https://jusmundi.com/

[2] This was defined by Jus Mundi's legal team according to their needs. However, PSILENCE is capable of redacting all types of person entities if necessary.

[3] https://github.com/microsoft/presidio

tasks can be seen as a NER one (Pilán et al., 2022; Garat and Wonsever, 2022; Papadopoulou et al., 2022) it is not uncommon for researchers to use general NER datasets, such as CoNLL 2003 (Tjong Kim Sang and De Meulder, 2003), and then apply the (pre-) trained models through a zero-shot approach into the legal domain. This is the case of the works presented by Schamberger (2021) and Pilán et al. (2022). However, as Pilán et al. (2022) conclude, the zero-shot results are not the best as, in some cases, the entities to mask are different than those available in the original tagset.

Although the clustering of individuals for the pseudonymization and anonymization tasks has been considered relevant in some works (Pilán et al., 2022; Garat and Wonsever, 2022), the amount of available resources regarding this aspect is scarce. For instance, in TAB (Pilán et al., 2022) only 1.7k of 24k entities of type person belong to a cluster, the rest are singletons[4]. In the case of CoNLL 2012 coreference corpus (Pradhan et al., 2012) there are no singletons. The best exception is *LitBank* (Bamman et al., 2020), a collection of 100 fiction documents in English that are annotated with coreference resolution, and presents singletons and clusters.

Finally, we can find some additional tools in the literature related to the pseudonymization task. In Gupta et al. (2018), the authors present a tool for identifying parties of legal cases using NER and coreference resolution. Moreover, in Kalamkar et al. (2022), the authors present a NER system for annotating Indian legal documents on which they reconcile types of named entities using rules and coreference resolution. BookNLP[5] a Spacy-based tool created for processing long documents, especially fiction books. Among BookNLP's tools, we can name a character clustering and a coreference resolution module. Finally, PeTra (Toshniwal et al., 2020) is a model based on BERT (Devlin et al., 2019) which uses memory modules to keep track of people within short documents.

4 Methodology

In Figure 1, we present PSILENCE's architecture, which is composed of four modules. In the first module, we make use of a Python-based HTML parser and Spacy (Honnibal et al., 2020) to pre-

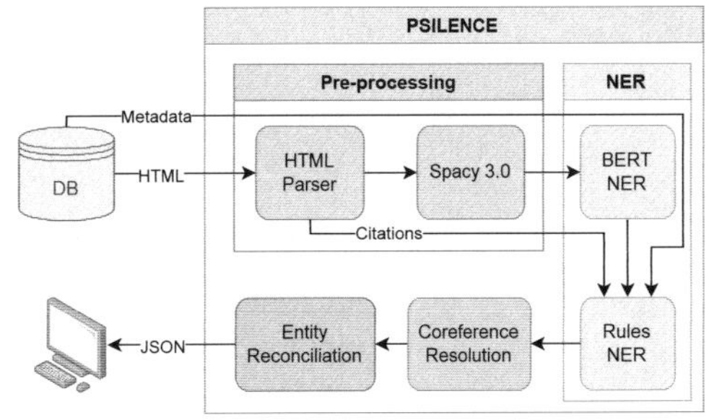

Figure 1: Global architecture of PSILENCE.

process the documents. During the pre-processing of documents, we convert HTML documents into plain text divided into paragraphs and we extract citations that were defined as HTML spans. The second module is a hybrid NER system, i.e. based on a machine learning model and rules; its goal is to detect different types of named entities within a document. The third module is a simplified coreference resolution model that only clusters names of entities and does not consider any kind of pronouns.[6] The fourth module is a reconciliation system, similar to the one used in Kalamkar et al. (2022), which tries to determine the exact type of entity in a document, even if the context in which it occurs, is not clear.

At the end of the pipeline, we create a pseudonymization dictionary, which is a JSON file, see Figure 2, indicating the different clusters found for each type of person entity. Each cluster contains all the variations found for the same person with their occurrences based on character positions. Based on the example presented in Figure 2, the occurrences of the names *"Bill Scott"*, *"William Scott"* and *"Scott"*, would be replaced with *"WITNESS_1"* while the name *"McConnell"* would be replaced with *"WITNESS_2"* in the pseudonymized document. Although in this work we focus on clusters of type Witness, we provide other types of clusters in the JSON output in case we make a mistake in the grouping or classification of entities.

The second, third, and fourth modules will be described in detail in the following subsections.

4.1 Named Entity Recognition (NER)

For extracting named entities, PSILENCE uses a hybrid NER system. It was done by coupling a

[4]A singleton is a type of cluster composed of only one person occurring only once in a document.

[5]https://github.com/booknlp/booknlp

[6]The reasons for not considering pronouns is that it makes the coreference resolution task harder to do and, as Pilán et al. (2022) indicate, pronouns do not tend to leak highly sensitive information even in anonymization tasks.

```json
{
 "clusters": {
  "WITNESS": [
   {
    "Bill␣Scott": [[2003,2013]],
    "William␣Scott": [[2317,2330]],
    "Scott": [[2443,2448], [3305,3310]]
   },
   {
    "McConnell": [[3300,3309]]
   }
  ],
  "LAWYER" : [
   {
    "Bermudez": [[1712,1720]]
   }
  ]
 }
}
```

Figure 2: Example of a PSILENCE's JSON output file. The file presents the different person entity types and the clusters found in the document. We indicate as well the character position in which the replacement needs to be done.

machine learning model, through a zero-shot approach, and a collection of rules.

The machine learning model is a transformer-based NER system trained on CoNLL 2003 (Tjong Kim Sang and De Meulder, 2003) using $\text{BERT}_{\text{LARGE}}$ (Devlin et al., 2019).[7] This model was used due to the lack training data[8] and it can predict four types of named entities, person, organization, miscellaneous, and location.

Regarding the collection of rules, we use regular expressions and string matching[9] to determine whether an entity found by the machine learning approach should be specialized. For instance, we do string matching between named entities of type person and metadata from the case database to find the names of judges, lawyers, and parties. In the case of authors, we use, for example, regular expressions to extract them from citations found in the pre-processing module.

In total, we can detect 12 types of entities: Party, Judge, Lawyer, Arbitrator, Tribunal member, Expert, Author, Law firm, Person, Organization, Miscellaneous, and Location. These are obtained using the following approaches. *Machine learning* - Person, Organization, Miscellaneous, and Location. *Metadata string matching* - Party, Judge, Lawyer, Arbitrator, Tribunal member, Expert, and Law firm. *Regular expressions* - Judge, Lawyers, Authors. As it can be seen, the category Witness is not present in the aforementioned list, this is because all the entities of type Person that could not become specialized, e.g. Judge and Author, are considered as witnesses at the end of PSILENCE's pipeline.

Although the approach described before can be counter-intuitive, i.e. to find specialized named entities rather than directly finding witnesses, it should be indicated that finding only witnesses is harder. In the first place, and especially as we get farther from the beginning of the document, the context in which the name of a person occurs might not be descriptive enough to determine whether it is a witness or not. At the beginning of a document, specialized people tend to be formally introduced either using titles or specific contexts. For instance, a lawyer can be introduced in a document as *"Doe QC"*, a judge as *"Honorable Doe"*, or an arbitrator as *"Arbitrator: Ms. Jane Doe"*. However, in the case of witnesses, these do not tend to be introduced directly as witnesses, such as in *"Mr. Doe was a personal trainer in the defendant's company and noticed that…"*. In the second place, this approach makes PSILENCE's output easier to correct by humans, for example, if a person is wrongly marked as an Expert, all their occurrences in a document can be easily converted into Witness, without having to find these by hand. Finally, it makes PSILENCE easier to use in different legal contexts, such as those where judges or lawyers need to be redacted as well.

4.2 Coreference resolution

For clustering named entities, we use a coreference resolution system based on the work of Clark and Manning (2016a,b). This means that it is composed of a mention-pair encoder, a cluster-pair encoder, a mention ranking model, and a cluster ranking model; moreover, the neural network has three fully connected hidden ReLU layers.

The input features of the neural network are presented as follows:

- Dense Embeddings: We use FastText with subword information (Bojanowski et al., 2017) to vectorize entities and entities contexts. Specifically, we use those trained on Common Crawl[10] and we reduced the size of

[7] This model was not trained by us, instead it was downloaded from https://huggingface.co/dbmdz/bert-large-cased-finetuned-conll03-english

[8] This research was done before the publication of Kalamkar et al. (2022), which proposes an English Indian Legal NER dataset. Moreover, it should be noted that we focus on international arbitration cases and not national legal cases as it happens in Kalamkar et al. (2022).

[9] This is done using RapidFuzz: https://github.com/maxbachmann/RapidFuzz.

[10] crawl-300d-2M-subword.zip

the embedding from a dimension of 300 to 100 using FastText API[11].

- Length of named entity: Using binary encoding, we set the number of characters in a named entity.
- Named entity location: It is the relative position of the named entity within a document.
- Matching root: Using Spacy's dependency parser, we compare whether the root of a named entity matches the root of other ones.
- Words intersection: Proportional number of words shared between couples of named entities.
- Exact match: We compare whether two named entities have an exact match.
- Relaxed match: We make use of RapidFuzz to determine the degree of string matching between a couple of named entities. In other words, we utilize fuzzy string matching metrics as digitized legal documents can contain misspelling mistakes, originated either by the OCR or by the data entry clerk.
- Cosine similarity: Using FastText embeddings, we calculate the cosine similarity between named entities.
- Named entity distance: We calculate the relative distance, in terms of words, between a couple of named entities.
- Dense representation of context: We calculate, using FastText embeddings, the dense representation of the named entities' contexts.

All the string comparisons are done using UTF-8 and ASCII encodings to prevent mistakes by the use of diacritics.

In Table 1, we present the hyperparameters used for training the coreference resolution model.

It should be indicated that during prediction time, we pre-cluster the named entities using RapidFuzz and a similarity score of 0.6. This allows us to decrease the processing time on long documents. This approach is similar to the one used by BookNLP[12] for the coreference resolution (Bamman et al., 2020).

4.3 Entities reconciliation

One common problem in NER tasks, especially in long documents, is the fact that certain entity names can be predicted with different types in multiple paragraphs or sentences (Kalamkar et al., 2022). The main reason is that the context in which an entity occurs might change. For instance, at the beginning of a document, it might be stated that *Mr. X* is a lawyer but, later on in the document it is just presented as *Mr. X*. In these cases, it might be impossible to determine the correct entity type, not only for humans (without reading the full document), but for machine learning models too. Therefore, it is necessary to reconcile entity types to have the best performance possible.

Table 1: Hyperparameters used for training the coreference resolution model.

Hyperparameter	**Value**
Maximum Epochs	200
Early Stop Patience	30
Learning Rate	0.001
Scheduler	Linear with warm-up
Warm-up Ratio	0.1
Optimizer	AdamW with bias correction
AdamW ϵ	1×10^{-8}
Random Seed	1111
Dropout rate	0.5
Weight decay	0.01
Embeddings size	100
h1 size	1000
h2 size	500
h3 size	500
Cost False New	0.8
Cost False Anaphoric	0.4
Cost Wrong Link	1.0

In this work, we use the output generated by the coreference resolution system along with some rules to reconcile entities. Specifically, for a given cluster of people, we start by counting the different types of entities. If only one type of entity exists, we consider the type of entity to be correct. However, if it is the opposite, i.e. more than one type, we use the following rules:

- If one of the entities is marked as a party, then all the entities become of type party and will be ignored for the pseudonymization process.
- If more than 30% of the entities are not of type person, i.e. Location, Miscellaneous, Law Firm, or Organization, the cluster will be ignored for the pseudonymization process.
- If the most frequent type of entity is a Judge, Author, Expert, Arbitrator, Tribunal Member, or Lawyer, then the cluster is ignored for the pseudonymization process.

The clusters considered to pseudonymize, i.e. Witness, are those of type Person that after the reconciliation process could not be specialized. These rules were developed and fine-tuned experimentally by

[11]https://fasttext.cc

[12]https://github.com/booknlp/booknlp

Table 2: Statistics of the legal corpus.

Per document	Median	Minimum	Maximum
Tokens	10 809	496	112 509
Witness entities	14	1	305
Clusters	4	1	38

assessing the performance of PSILENCE on the development part of a legal corpus (see Section 5).

5 Data

For training PSILENCE coreference resolution system, we use three different corpora. *LitBank* (Bamman et al., 2020) is the main training corpus because it contains singletons, documents are long and it is one of the biggest coreference resolution corpora. However, due to its literary nature, we decided as well to use two entity-linking-related corpora, *In Media Res* (Brasoveanu et al., 2020) and *AIDA-CoNLL-Yago* dataset (Hoffart et al., 2011); both of these corpora focus on news articles. Even though these two corpora are not annotated with coreference resolution groups, as we focus only on the clustering of people, we make use of their entity-linking annotations to determine clusters. In other words, named entities of type person can be grouped thanks to common knowledge-base links. For example, in AIDA-CoNLL-Yago, in a document talking about the signer *"Johnny Allen Hendrix"*, all his name variations, e.g. *"Hendrix"* and *"Jimi Hendrix"*, are linked to the same knowledge base Yago ID. To improve the quality of these two last corpora, we manually validated some of the clusters, and in the case of AIDA-CoNLL-Yago, we also included some heuristics to match some people that were not linked correctly.[13] For the three corpora, we use a training, development, and testing partition; therefore, we can fine-tune the models and evaluate their performance.

Besides, we have a collection of 140 international arbitration documents written in English covering different types of cases: sports (121), commercial (8), inter-state (5), Iran-US claims (2), and investor-state (4); see Table 2 for statistics. These 140 documents were manually annotated by a group of expert lawyers at Jus Mundi. Specifically, these experts created for each document a list of witness clusters; in other words, they found all the witnesses in a document and grouped their different occurrences into clusters.[14] It should be indicated that these documents are in HTML format and were previously enriched with citations using an in-house tool. Each document is associated with metadata which was manually verified by Jus Mundi's legal team. From the 140 documents, 33 were used for fine-tuning PSILENCE's pipeline, i.e. NER, and coreference resolution, and 107 were used for testing it.

6 Evaluation

In this paper, we use the evaluation framework proposed in CoNLL 2012 Coreference Shared Task (Pradhan et al., 2012). It asses in the first place whether all the named entities have been found within a document. And, in the second place, it evaluates how well these entities have been grouped into clusters. This evaluation framework is composed of three metrics, B^3 (Bagga and Baldwin, 1998), CEAF (Luo, 2005) and MUC (Vilain et al., 1995). However, instead of using MUC as defined by Vilain et al. (1995), we make use of a modified version that takes singletons into account. Specifically, for singletons, we define the minimum number of correct links as $|k(S)|$, instead of $|k(S)| - 1$, and the number of missing links as $|p(S)|$ instead of $|p(S)| - 1$; where $|k|(S)$ is the size of the key cluster for mention S, i.e. 1, and $p(S)$ is the intersection of the predicted cluster and the key cluster of mention S. In simple words, MUC for singletons becomes a binary metric. This change was necessary as the CoNLL 2012 Coreference Shared Task did not consider singletons but our four corpora do.

As indicated in Section 3, there are not many available tools for pseudonymizing legal documents. However, we compare PSILENCE coreference resolution tool with BookNLP[15]. Specifically, we assess the clustering performance of PSILENCE and BookNLP when they are provided with the gold standard entities, i.e., those that have to be pseudonymized. We use BookNLP because it was designed to process long documents and it is capable of performing coreference resolution (Bamman et al., 2020).[16] The comparison is done

[13] In AIDA-CoNLL-Yago, we used the original documents. However, for In Media Res, we create pseudo-documents by grouping sentences based on the co-occurrence of people.

[14] We did not include clusters of other types of entities in these lists, such as lawyers or judges, as they were out of the project scope. But also because their annotation would have become harder to achieve.

[15] https://github.com/booknlp/booknlp

[16] Although BookNLP has its own NER, we did not adapt its NER to predict and/or filter subtypes of people, like lawyers and judges, due to the complexity of the task.

on the legal documents, thus, we can assess how well the tools behave in the legal domain when all the correct entities are given.

7 Results

We present in Table 3 the results, in terms of Macro F-score, obtained by our coreference resolution system, when it was applied on the testing partitions of AIDA-CoNLL-Yago, In Media Res and LitBank. The results presented in Table 3 show us how well can we cluster the names of people in different types of documents and circumstances. It is clear that as the length of the documents increases, as it happens in LitBank, the performance decreases.

In Table 4 and Table 5, we show the F-scores obtained by our coreference tool and BookNLP, the baseline, regarding the clustering of gold standard entities, i.e. the names of people that had to be pseudonymized, over the legal development and testing corpora respectively. The macro outcomes presented in both Table 4 and Table 5 show that, despite applying the coreference resolution tools to an unseen domain, they manage to cluster people correctly in most documents. Nonetheless, the micro outcomes shown in Table 4 and Table 5, indicate that in documents where a great number of people co-occur, the performance decreases as it is harder to disambiguate people.

In Table 6, we introduce PSILENCE pipeline's results. We can observe in Table 6 that when we include the NER system into the pipeline, the performance of our coreference resolution tool is affected. This means that the detection of named entities is not perfect and the produced noise affects the clustering of people. Specifically, in the test corpus we pass from a macro CoNLL F-score of 0.95 (Table 5) to 0.82 (Table 6).

8 Discussion

Regarding the results presented in Table 3, we can observe that the macro F-scores achieved by the coreference system tend to be greater than 0.90, meaning that in general, most of the documents are clustered correctly. The performance decreases as the length of the document increases because the number of mentions increases, thus the number of pairs needed to be compared increases as well. Moreover, the documents from AIDA-CoNLL-Yago and In Media Res are relatively small and have fewer named entities and clusters than LitBank.

As we observed in Table 4 and Table 5, our coreference resolution system, performed in general, better than the one found in BookNLP. This can be due to several aspects. In the first place, PSILENCE coreference resolution system was trained on two more datasets. This means that PSILENCE was trained on more examples but also from different domains, literary and news. Secondly, to use BookNLP as a baseline, we had to introduce our gold standard named entities into BookNLP, meaning that we had to remove their NER system and modify certain pipelines. This could have affected the performance; also, BookNLP was designed to link personal pronouns to names too. Moreover, we do not see any change between BookNLP's small and big models (Table 4 and Table 5).

We performed a manual analysis of certain clusters found in our legal dataset to better understand Table 4 and Table 5. From this analysis, we determined that there are recurrent errors that occur in both PSILENCE and BookNLP. We found out that spelling name variations are one of the most common reasons for people not being correctly clustered. For instance, *"Mahmood"* can also be referred to as *"Mahmoud"*; *"Lief"* as *"Liefs"* and *"Kuan"* as *"Koan"*. Another frequent clustering error across both approaches occurs when the full name is used but then, only a part of it is used later in the text, like *"Michael S. Blatter"* as *"Blatter"* and *"Lalit Merchant"* as *"L Merchant"*. We noticed a drop in performance when the documents have people with long names, such as double last names, but also if they contain accentuated letters. Nonetheless, we also noticed that with PSILENCE, we can correctly cluster some entities among the above-mentioned instances. For instance, we manage to cluster *"Bill Essick"* and *"William Essick"* correctly whereas they remain as separate entities with BookNLP. It should be indicated that these types of errors are not uncommon, neither in PSILENCE or BookNLP. We believe it is related to the sentences' context, but a deeper analysis is needed.

Some of the previous errors might be able to be fixed by changing the embeddings type, from word to contextual ones like those provided by BERT (Devlin et al., 2019) or RoBERTa (Liu et al., 2019). However, this would mean that the architecture of the coreference resolution system would need to change completely, as contextual embeddings are not designed for single-word analysis, and have to be trained differently for calculating cosine similarity (Reimers and Gurevych, 2019). Moreover, mod-

Table 3: Results in terms of macro F-score for each testing partition of the corpora used for training the coreference resolution system.

Corpus	**MUC**	**BCUB**	**CEAFE**	**CoNLL**
AIDA-CoNLL-Yago	0.98	0.97	0.96	0.97
In Media Res	0.94	0.95	0.92	0.94
LitBank	0.96	0.93	0.80	0.90

Table 4: Results of the coreference resolution task in terms of F-score, micro and macro averaged, for legal development corpus.

System	**MUC**		**BCUB**		**CEAFE**		**CoNLL**	
	Micro	Macro	Micro	Macro	Micro	Macro	Micro	Macro
Ours	**0.90**	**0.95**	0.50	**0.95**	**0.64**	**0.90**	0.68	**0.93**
BookNLP Small	0.89	0.94	**0.61**	0.92	0.58	0.86	**0.69**	0.91
BookNLP Big	0.89	0.94	**0.61**	0.92	0.58	0.86	**0.69**	0.91

els such as Sentence BERT (Reimers and Gurevych, 2019) have been created to find similar sentences and not similar words, unlike FastText.

As we observed in Table 6, the coreference resolution F1-score decreases by 37% (micro) and 24% (macro) in comparison to the clustering-only task. This means that PSILENCE's NER has trouble in correctly detecting all the different types of named entities. For instance, the machine learning model sometimes cannot find all the entities in a sentence, or if they are found they can be tagged with the wrong type, or they are split into multiple smaller ones, or the boundaries are wrong, e.g. *"Romano F."* and *"Subiotto Q.C."* rather than *"Romano F. Subiotto"*. Regarding the collection of rules, sometimes it is hard to correctly apply them. For instance, in some documents, the parties were stated as *"Company (Country) Ltd."* or lawyers as *"John R. Doe"*, however in our metadata, these entities were *"Company Ltd."* and *"John Roe Doe"*.

To solve the aforementioned issues, we can propose certain solutions. First, we need to reduce our dependency on rules for the NER by training a specialized legal NER rather than using a generic one in a zero-shot way. Secondly, to reduce the number of entities with wrong boundaries, the new NER should be trained with a CRF layer, like in Ma and Hovy (2016), and use an IOBES encoding, as in Ratinov and Roth (2009). Also, we might need to use data augmentation methods, such as in Cabrera-Diego and Gheewala (2023), where a frustratingly easy domain adaption method is used to mix different legal NER corpora.

Moreover, some of the detected errors were caused by the reconciliation module. In other words, the rules used in this module were not robust enough to detect or solve issues generated by the NER model. For example, in one document a law firm was incorrectly tagged as a person rather than as an organization; in this case, the reconciliation module determined that the entity was of type person because it was the most frequent type, thus it was an entity that had to be pseudonymized.

Some other errors found during the analysis were caused by a wrong splitting of sentences. This was particularly noticeable when a paragraph contained citations that were not tagged in the HTML document, which in consequence made a paragraph be split into wrong sentences. In consequence, authors found in these undetected and wrongly split citations were considered many times as witnesses because specialization rules could not be applied. Other splitting errors in sentences come from the fact that Spacy, was not trained to analyze legal documents, thus it is not aware of specialized abbreviations such as *Hon'ble* and *Q.C.* Moreover, we found out that in general, Spacy is bad at processing long sentences, such as those that are found in legal documents. Therefore, when a paragraph is wrongly split into sentences, it has a consequence not only on the NER system but also on the coreference resolution one. To solve these errors, one option is to train our model for splitting sentences, although it can be complicated to achieve due to the number of data necessary to train this kind of model. Another option is to stop using sentences

Table 5: Results of the coreference resolution task in terms of F-score, micro and macro averaged, for the legal testing corpus.

System	**MUC**		**BCUB**		**CEAFE**		**CoNLL**	
	Micro	Macro	Micro	Macro	Micro	Macro	Micro	Macro
Ours	**0.94**	**0.97**	0.47	**0.96**	**0.45**	**0.92**	**0.62**	**0.95**
BookNLP Small	0.9	0.93	**0.51**	0.92	0.37	0.85	0.59	0.90
BookNLP Big	0.9	0.93	**0.51**	0.92	0.37	0.85	0.59	0.90

Table 6: Results of the pseudonymization pipeline, i.e., NER, coreference resolution, and entities reconciliation, in terms of F-score, micro and macro averaged, for the development and testing corpora.

Corpus	**MUC**		**BCUB**		**CEAFE**		**CoNLL**	
	Micro	Macro	Micro	Macro	Micro	Macro	Micro	Macro
Developement	0.70	0.87	0.24	0.86	0.32	0.80	0.42	0.82
Test	0.71	0.77	0.18	0.77	0.27	0.71	0.39	0.72

for delimiting the context in which a named entity occurs. However, this would mean that it could be harder to determine the actual context of a named entity in the coreference resolution system.

Despite the complexity of the pseudonymization task and the use of multiple deep learning models through a zero-shot approach, we consider the macro results shown in Table 6 good in general. Nonetheless, there is still work to be done, especially when we observe the micro results (Table 6). These results indicate that we need to continue working on the clustering of people in long documents because it becomes harder to keep track of people. We might need to explore more complex methods for clustering people using memory systems, such as PeTra (Toshniwal et al., 2020). However, we also need to consider that many of the works of coreference resolution are done on relatively short documents.

9 Conclusions

In this paper, we presented the first results of PSILENCE, a pseudonymization tool for the semi-automatic redaction of international arbitration documents in English, where people are clustered, to accelerate the human validation step and improve the readability of the document.

Experiments were done on different datasets, including one composed of legal documents. The obtained results were promising, especially for the clustering of people through coreference resolution. For instance, we got a macro F-score of 0.95, when clustering gold standard named entities, and a macro F-score of 0.72 when we use the NER.

An analysis of the results showed that some of the errors come from the fact that we use multiple rules at different levels. But also, because the current implementation of PSILENCE is based on multiple zero-shot approaches, meaning that the training data did not come from the legal domain. Therefore, to improve PSILENCE, it will be necessary to work on a specialized legal corpora.

In the future, we will work on the improvement of the PSILENCE system as discussed in Section 8. Moreover, we would like to cluster named entities through multiple documents to assign them the same pseudonym. This would be useful when a case has multiple documents and certain people occur in several of them, allowing us to increase the readability of complex cases.

Finally, we will train PSILENCE using multilingual language models on legal documents in other languages than English, especially those from the European Union where legal documents are subject to GDPR rules.

Acknowledgments

This work was possible thanks to the granted access of IDRIS (Institut du Développement et des Ressources en Informatique Scientifique) High-performance computing resources under the allocation 2022-AD011012667R1 and 2023-AD011012667R2 made by GENCI (Grand Équipement National de Calcul Intensif).

Limitations

PSILENCE has different limitations that need to be clarified. In the first place, while we indicate that PSILENCE can pseudonymize, if necessary, different types of person entities besides witnesses, it should be stated that we have not evaluated yet how well PSILENCE can detect these other person entities. The main reason is that we do not have those annotations and are very expensive to manually get. While we expect PSILENCE's coreference resolution system to perform similarly to the results presented in this work, we cannot ensure that the quality of the NER will be equal for all the types of named entities. Nevertheless, we expect that by deploying PSILENCE in Jus Mundi, we will be able to have more and better annotations that could be used to train specialized tools. In the second place, we have explored different types of international arbitration cases, however, there are many more. Thus, we cannot ensure that the current pipeline used in PSILENCE can be applied to all types of arbitration, at least without a fine-tuning process.

References

Tristan Allard, Louis Béziaud, and Sébastien Gambs. 2021. Publication of Court Records: Circumventing the Privacy-Transparency Trade-Off. In *AI Approaches to the Complexity of Legal Systems XI-XII*, pages 298–312, Cham. Springer International Publishing.

Arttu Oksanen, Minna Tamper, Jouni Tuominen, Aki Hietanen, and Eero Hyvönen. 2022. A Tool for Pseudonymization of Textual Documents for Digital Humanities Research and Publication. In *6th Digital Humanities in Nordic and Baltic Countries Conference (Book of Abtsracts)*, pages 107–108, Uppsala, Sweden.

Amit Bagga and Breck Baldwin. 1998. Algorithms for scoring coreference chains. In *The First International Conference on Language Resources and Evaluation: Workshop on Linguistics Coreference*, volume 1, pages 563–566, Granada, Spain. European Language Resources Association.

David Bamman, Olivia Lewke, and Anya Mansoor. 2020. An Annotated Dataset of Coreference in English Literature. In *Proceedings of the 12th Language Resources and Evaluation Conference*, pages 44–54, Marseille, France. European Language Resources Association.

Valentin Barriere and Amaury Fouret. 2019. May I Check Again? — A simple but efficient way to generate and use contextual dictionaries for Named Entity Recognition. Application to French Legal Texts. In *Proceedings of the 22nd Nordic Conference on Computational Linguistics*, pages 327–332, Turku, Finland. Linköping University Electronic Press.

Iz Beltagy, Matthew E. Peters, and Arman Cohan. 2020. Longformer: The Long-Document Transformer.

David Biesner, Rajkumar Ramamurthy, Robin Stenzel, Max Lübbering, Lars Hillebrand, Anna Ladi, Maren Pielka, Rüdiger Loitz, Christian Bauckhage, and Rafet Sifa. 2022. Anonymization of German financial documents using neural network-based language models with contextual word representations. *International Journal of Data Science and Analytics*, 13(2):151–161.

Piotr Bojanowski, Edouard Grave, Armand Joulin, and Tomas Mikolov. 2017. Enriching Word Vectors with Subword Information. *Transactions of the Association for Computational Linguistics*, 5:135–146.

Adrian M.P. Brasoveanu, Albert Weichselbraun, and Lyndon Nixon. 2020. In Media Res: A Corpus for Evaluating Named Entity Linking with Creative Works. In *Proceedings of the 24th Conference on Computational Natural Language Learning*, pages 355–364, Online. Association for Computational Linguistics.

Luis Adrián Cabrera-Diego and Akshita Gheewala. 2023. Jus mundi at SemEval-2023 task 6: Using a frustratingly easy domain adaption for a legal named entity recognition system. In *Proceedings of the 17th International Workshop on Semantic Evaluation (SemEval-2023)*, pages 1783–1790, Toronto, Canada. Association for Computational Linguistics.

Raphaël Chevrier, Vasiliki Foufi, Christophe Gaudet-Blavignac, Arnaud Robert, and Christian Lovis. 2019. Use and Understanding of Anonymization and De-Identification in the Biomedical Literature: Scoping Review. *Journal of Medical Internet Research*, 21(5):e13484.

Kevin Clark and Christopher D. Manning. 2016a. Deep Reinforcement Learning for Mention-Ranking Coreference Models. In *Proceedings of the 2016 Conference on Empirical Methods in Natural Language Processing*, pages 2256–2262, Austin, Texas. Association for Computational Linguistics.

Kevin Clark and Christopher D. Manning. 2016b. Improving Coreference Resolution by Learning Entity-Level Distributed Representations. In *Proceedings of the 54th Annual Meeting of the Association for Computational Linguistics (Volume 1: Long Papers)*, pages 643–653, Berlin, Germany. Association for Computational Linguistics.

Jacob Devlin, Ming-Wei Chang, Kenton Lee, and Kristina Toutanova. 2019. BERT: Pre-training of deep bidirectional transformers for language understanding. In *Proceedings of the 2019 Conference of the North American Chapter of the Association for Computational Linguistics: Human Language Technologies, Volume 1 (Long and Short Papers)*, pages

4171–4186, Minneapolis, Minnesota. Association for Computational Linguistics.

Mark Elliot, Elaine Mackey, and Kieron O'Hara. 2020. *The Anonymisation Decision-Making Framework: European Practitioners' Guide*, 2 edition. UKAN Publication, Manchester.

Diego Garat and Dina Wonsever. 2022. Automatic Curation of Court Documents: Anonymizing Personal Data. *Information*, 13(1).

Christopher Graham. 2012. Anonymisation: managing data protection risk code of practice. Technical report, Information Commissioner's Office, Wilmslow, UK.

Ajay Gupta, Devendra Verma, Sachin Pawar, Sangameshwar Patil, Swapnil Hingmire, Girish K. Palshikar, and Pushpak Bhattacharyya. 2018. Identifying Participant Mentions and Resolving Their Coreferences in Legal Court Judgements. In *Text, Speech, and Dialogue*, pages 153–162, Brno, Czech Republic. Springer International Publishing.

Johannes Hoffart, Mohamed Amir Yosef, Ilaria Bordino, Hagen Fürstenau, Manfred Pinkal, Marc Spaniol, Bilyana Taneva, Stefan Thater, and Gerhard Weikum. 2011. Robust Disambiguation of Named Entities in Text. In *Proceedings of the 2011 Conference on Empirical Methods in Natural Language Processing*, pages 782–792, Edinburgh, Scotland, UK. Association for Computational Linguistics.

Matthew Honnibal, Ines Montani, Sofie Van Landeghem, and Adriane Boyd. 2020. spaCy: Industrial-strength natural language processing in Python.

Prathamesh Kalamkar, Astha Agarwal, Aman Tiwari, Smita Gupta, Saurabh Karn, and Vivek Raghavan. 2022. Named Entity Recognition in Indian court judgments. In *Proceedings of the Natural Legal Language Processing Workshop 2022*, pages 184–193, Abu Dhabi, United Arab Emirates (Hybrid). Association for Computational Linguistics.

Joffrey L. Leevy, Taghi M. Khoshgoftaar, and Flavio Villanustre. 2020. Survey on RNN and CRF models for de-identification of medical free text. *Journal of Big Data*, 7(1):73.

Yinhan Liu, Myle Ott, Naman Goyal, Jingfei Du, Mandar Joshi, Danqi Chen, Omer Levy, Mike Lewis, Luke Zettlemoyer, and Veselin Stoyanov. 2019. RoBERTa: A Robustly Optimized BERT Pretraining Approach. arXiv.

Xiaoqiang Luo. 2005. On Coreference Resolution Performance Metrics. In *Proceedings of Human Language Technology Conference and Conference on Empirical Methods in Natural Language Processing*, pages 25–32, Vancouver, British Columbia, Canada. Association for Computational Linguistics.

Xuezhe Ma and Eduard Hovy. 2016. End-to-end Sequence Labeling via Bi-directional LSTM-CNNs-CRF. In *Proceedings of the 54th Annual Meeting of the Association for Computational Linguistics (Volume 1: Long Papers)*, pages 1064–1074, Berlin, Germany. Association for Computational Linguistics.

Miranda Mourby, Elaine Mackey, Mark Elliot, Heather Gowans, Susan E. Wallace, Jessica Bell, Hannah Smith, Stergios Aidinlis, and Jane Kaye. 2018. Are 'pseudonymised' data always personal data? Implications of the GDPR for administrative data research in the UK. *Computer Law & Security Review*, 34(2):222–233.

Arttu Oksanen, Minna Tamper, Jouni Tuominen, Aki Hietanen, and Eero Hyvönen. 2019. ANOPPI: A Pseudonymization Service for Finnish Court Documents. In *Legal Knowledge and Information Systems. JURIX 2019: The Thirty-second Annual Conference*, volume 322 of *Frontiers in Artificial Intelligence and Applications*, pages 251 – 254, Madrid, Spain. IOS PRESS.

Anthi Papadopoulou, Pierre Lison, Lilja Øvrelid, and Ildikó Pilán. 2022. Bootstrapping Text Anonymization Models with Distant Supervision. In *Proceedings of the Language Resources and Evaluation Conference*, pages 4477–4487, Marseille, France. European Language Resources Association.

Ildikó Pilán, Pierre Lison, Lilja Øvrelid, Anthi Papadopoulou, David Sánchez, and Montserrat Batet. 2022. The Text Anonymization Benchmark (TAB): A Dedicated Corpus and Evaluation Framework for Text Anonymization. *Computational Linguistics*, 48(4):1053–1101.

Sameer Pradhan, Alessandro Moschitti, Nianwen Xue, Olga Uryupina, and Yuchen Zhang. 2012. CoNLL-2012 Shared Task: Modeling Multilingual Unrestricted Coreference in OntoNotes. In *Joint Conference on EMNLP and CoNLL - Shared Task*, pages 1–40, Jeju Island, Korea. Association for Computational Linguistics.

Lev Ratinov and Dan Roth. 2009. Design Challenges and Misconceptions in Named Entity Recognition. In *Proceedings of the Thirteenth Conference on Computational Natural Language Learning (CoNLL-2009)*, pages 147–155, Boulder, Colorado. Association for Computational Linguistics.

Nils Reimers and Iryna Gurevych. 2019. Sentence-BERT: Sentence Embeddings using Siamese BERT-Networks. In *Proceedings of the 2019 Conference on Empirical Methods in Natural Language Processing and the 9th International Joint Conference on Natural Language Processing (EMNLP-IJCNLP)*, pages 3982–3992, Hong Kong, China. Association for Computational Linguistics.

Tom Schamberger. 2021. Customizable Anonymization of German Legal Court Rulings using Domain-specific Named Entity Recognition. Master's thesis, Technical University Munich, Munich, Germany.

Amber Stubbs, Michele Filannino, and Özlem Uzuner. 2017. De-identification of psychiatric intake records: Overview of 2016 CEGS N-GRID shared tasks Track 1. *Journal of Biomedical Informatics*, 75S:S4–S18.

Amber Stubbs and Özlem Uzuner. 2015. Annotating longitudinal clinical narratives for de-identification: The 2014 i2b2/UTHealth corpus. *Journal of biomedical informatics*, 58 Suppl(Suppl):S20–S29.

Latanya Sweeney. 2002. K-Anonymity: A Model for Protecting Privacy. *International Journal of Uncertainty, Fuzziness and Knowledge-Based Systems*, 10(5):557–570.

Erik F. Tjong Kim Sang and Fien De Meulder. 2003. Introduction to the CoNLL-2003 Shared Task: Language-Independent Named Entity Recognition. In *Proceedings of the Seventh Conference on Natural Language Learning at HLT-NAACL 2003*, pages 142–147, Edmonton, Canada.

Shubham Toshniwal, Allyson Ettinger, Kevin Gimpel, and Karen Livescu. 2020. PeTra: A Sparsely Supervised Memory Model for People Tracking. In *Proceedings of the 58th Annual Meeting of the Association for Computational Linguistics*, pages 5415–5428, Online. Association for Computational Linguistics.

Marc Vilain, John Burger, John Aberdeen, Dennis Connolly, and Lynette Hirschman. 1995. A Model-Theoretic Coreference Scoring Scheme. In *Sixth Message Understanding Conference (MUC-6)*, Columbia, Maryland.

Deidentifying a Norwegian clinical corpus - An effort to create a privacy-preserving Norwegian large clinical language model

Phuong Dinh Ngo[1,2], **Miguel Tejedor**[1,3], **Therese Olsen Svenning**[1]
Taridzo Chomutare[1,4], **Andrius Budrionis**[1,2], **Hercules Dalianis**[1,5]
[1]Norwegian Centre for E-health Research, Tromsø, Norway
[2]Department of Physics and Technology, UiT The Arctic University of Norway
[3]Department of Mathematics and Statistics, UiT The Arctic University of Norway
[4]Department of Computer Sciences, UiT The Arctic University of Norway
[5]Department of Computer and Systems Science, Stockholm University, Sweden
Corresponding author: `Phuong.Dinh.Ngo@ehealthresearch.no`

Abstract

This study discusses the methods and challenges of deidentifying and pseudonymizing Norwegian clinical text for research purposes. The results of the NorDeid tool for deidentification and pseudonymization on different types of protected health information were evaluated and discussed, as well as the extension of its functionality with regular expressions to identify specific types of sensitive information. This research used a clinical corpus of adult patients treated in a gastro-surgical department in Norway, which contains approximately nine million clinical notes. The study also highlights the challenges posed by the unique language and clinical terminology of Norway and emphasizes the importance of protecting privacy and the need for customized approaches to meet legal and research requirements.

1 Introduction

Today with the European General Data Protection Regulation (GDPR) law, and the Norwegian law for the processing of personal information *Lov om behandling av personopplysninger (personopplysningsloven)* it is notoriously difficult to get access to electronic patient record texts to perform research.

First of all, one needs to submit an application to the *Norwegian Regional Committees for Medical and Health Research Ethics (REK)* and after that approval, one needs to ask *Personvernsombud (PVO)* at the local hospital to access the data. One way to make it easier is to process the data before using it for research by sanitising the data, that is to deidentify and then pseudonymise it, very similar to what has been carried out in (Vakili et al., 2022).

2 Related research

The field of deidentifying and pseudonymizing clinical text for research purposes has been a subject of extensive research, with much of the previous work based on shared tasks related to datasets such as *i2b2* (now n2c2). In (Stubbs and Uzuner, 2015), and most studies model deidentification as a named entity recognition (NER) task, (Nadkarni et al., 2011). Making these datasets available to researchers has facilitated a lot of progress on this task over the years; starting with traditional NLP methods (Stubbs et al., 2015), then with deep learning using word embeddings, (Dernoncourt et al., 2017), then more recently to deep learning methods using contextual embeddings or large language models, (Vakili and Dalianis, 2022). These benchmark datasets partially solved the need for standardised evaluation metrics to facilitate the comparison and improvement of different deidentification methods. Regarding the generation of pseudonyms or surrogates there is a nice description carried out by Olstad et al. (2023) where the authors elaborate on the replacement at different generalisation levels.

More recent research have shown promising results in the field. Among others, López-García et al. (2023) conducted a study on the automatic deidentification of medical documents in Spanish. The study developed two different deep learning-based methodologies for the task and also developed a data augmentation procedure to increase the number of texts used to train the models. Vakili et al. (2022) carried out deidentification and pseudonymisation of 17.9 Gb of Swedish clinical text using a Swedish clinical BERT model called SweDeClin-BERT. The process of deidentification took over two weeks, while pseudonymisation, replacing the

Proceedings of the Workshop on Computational Approaches to Language Data Pseudonymization
CALD-pseudo 2024, pages 37–43
March 21, 2024 ©2024 Association for Computational Linguistics

found entities with pseudonyms or surrogates, was ready in a couple of days since it is a rule based approach. In total 83,914,340 sensitive entities were found in 49,715,558 sentences encompassing 2.8 billion words.

Zheng et al. (2021) reviewed the recent research for ensuring the correct usage of regular expressions, which is crucial for identifying specific types of sensitive information.

However, there is a growing focus on addressing the challenges posed by the diverse and nuanced nature of clinical narratives, including variations in language use, context, and medical jargon. For instance, different institutions have different standards on how they treat their electronic health record narratives. This highlights the importance of documenting deidentification processes in diverse contexts, such as Norway in this case.

3 Methods and Materials

3.1 Methods

The methods used are a combination of deep learning methods and rule-based methods in the form of regular expressions.

The NorDeid deidentification and pseudonymisation tool was used in this study. NorDeid utilises the ScandiBERT[1] language model based on all Scandinavian languages and fine-tuned on the Swedish Stockholm EPR PHI Pseudo Corpus augmented with Danish and Norwegian personal names, (Lamproudis et al., 2023). ScandiBERT is a Bidirectional Encoder Representations (BERT) that was specifically fine-tuned for understanding and processing the Scandinavian languages, including Danish, Norwegian, and Swedish. NorDeid's functionality was extended with a number of regular expressions to identify *email-addresses, Norwegian social security numbers, user name* and *family numbers*, and used to identify the Protected Health Information (PHI) described in Table 1. PHIs are entities in a text that can reveal the identity of a person.

The chosen strategy to sanitise the text is first the NER identification of the PHIs and secondly to pseudonymise the found PHI by replacing them with similar surrogates, (Dalianis, 2019). For example: A last name is replaced with another random last name, the same name is replaced with the same random name to keep the coherence within the discourse. Female names are replaced with another random female name. A gender-neutral first name is replaced with another random gender-neutral first name. A location is replaced with another location nearby.

The *HIPS, Hidden in Plain Sight* strategy proposed by Carrell et al. (2019) was used in this study which implies removing the tags around the identified and pseudonymised PHIs so the PHIs that have been missed to be identified will be hidden among the pseudonymised PHIs.

PHI classes	Found PHIs
First Name	26,250,587
Last Name	29,793,462
Phone Number	14,227,411
Full Date	20,063,639
Date Part	19,866,503
Health Care Unit	84,232,994
Location	11,407,571
Organisation	5,292,142
Family Number	15,215,076
Social Security Number	700,527
Email	125,572
User name	4,126,831
Summary	227,179,610

Table 1: The table presents the PHI-classes[2] to be deidentified.

3.2 Materials

A clinical corpus called ClinCode Gastro Corpus containing 31,378 adult patients treated between the years 2017 to 2022 at the Gastro-Surgical department at the University Hospital of North Norway, Tromsø was used[3]. The dataset includes approximately 8.8 million clinical notes (in total, 27.6 Gb).

4 Application of method

A server *Republic of Gamers* with the operating system Debian Linux installed and equipped with two GPUs (ASUS Geforce RTX 3090), 64 Gb of internal memory (RAM) (2 x 32GB 3200 MHz DDR4), 8 TB Gen4 x4 M.2 NVMes SSD hard disc etc and not connected to the Internet was used

[1] `https://huggingface.co/vesteinn/ScandiBERT`

[2] The PHI class *Age* was at some point excluded from the execution of NorDeid after some discussion within the research group, since it was not considered sensitive, but it can easily be included again.

[3] This research was approved by The Norwegian Regional Committees for Medical and Health Research Ethics (REK) North, decision number 260972

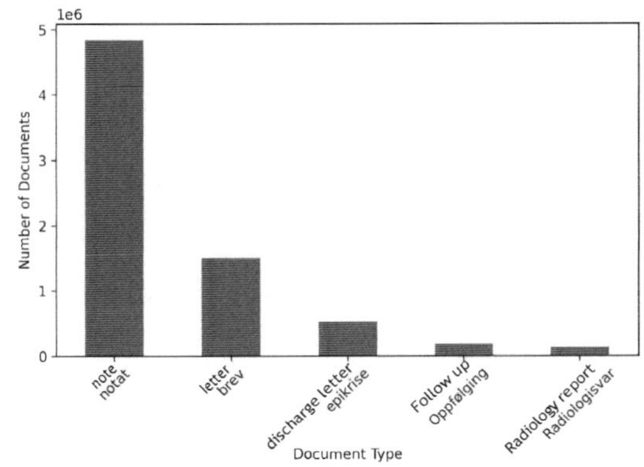

Figure 1: Top five types of clinical notes in the data. The letters are not clinical notes and will not be used in the research.

for the deidentification task. The server was also encrypted and situated in a server room only accessible to researchers who were specially authorised to work with the data and signed a confidentiality agreement. The server also remains offline during the project.

The process to deidentify and pseudonymise the corpus took approximately one week. The results can be seen in Table 2.

The evaluation of the current version of NorDeid is based on a comparison between human annotations and predictions made by the model. The evaluation dataset consists of 19 clinical notes that encompass about 13,000 tokens, annotated in the *CoNLL* format, a popular schema for text annotation used in natural language processing. The annotations target various entities of PHIs listed in Table 1.

The performance of the model is quantitatively measured using standard metrics: precision, recall, and F_1-score. Precision measures the proportion of correct positive identifications made by the model, recall assesses the model's ability to identify all relevant instances, and the F_1-score provides a harmonic mean of precision and recall, offering a balance between the two.

5 Analysis

The evaluation results are presented in a detailed format as shown in Table 2, covering various types of PHIs. The model shows varying levels of effectiveness across different PHI types. For example, it performs well in identifying entities like *First_Name, Full_Date*, and *Phone_Number*, but it struggles with *Family_Number, Organisation*, and *Social_Security_Number*.

The model achieves its highest F_1-scores with *Full_Date* (0.76), *Phone_Number* (0.73), and *First_Name* (0.68). These results indicate a strong ability to recognise and accurately tag full dates and names in clinical notes. Although the model shows no capability in correctly classifying *Family_Number, Organisation*, and *Social_Security_Number*, NorDeid was able to identify those entities as PHIs, according to the confusion matrix (Figure 2). By looking at the average scores (micro average, macro average and weighted average), the model demonstrates moderate effectiveness with a weighted average F_1-score of 0.53. While this indicates potential utility in a clinical setting, there is notable room for improvement.

Figure 2 shows the entity confusion matrix. Each row of the matrix represents the instances in an actual class, while each column represents the instances in a predicted class. For PHI types such as *Health_Care_Unit, Full_Date, First_Name*, and *Last_Name*, there is a higher number of true positives. This shows a strong alignment with human annotations. Certain types of PHIs, such as *Organisation* and *Social_Security_Number*, have higher false positives and false negatives. This suggests the challenge in classifying these PHIs correctly. There are also a high number of misclassifications between *Location* and *Health_Care_Unit*, as well as between *Date_Part* and *Full_Date*. This could be due to the similarity in format and context between these types of PHIs.

PHI class	**Precision**	**Recall**	**F_1-score**
Age	0.30	0.32	0.31
First_Name	0.61	0.76	0.68
Last_Name	0.66	0.70	0.68
Full_Date	0.65	0.93	0.76
Date_Part	0.28	0.44	0.34
Health_Care_Unit	0.29	0.40	0.34
Location	0.75	0.63	0.68
Organisation	0.00	0.00	0.00
Phone_Number	0.60	0.92	0.73
Social_Security_Number	0.00	0.00	0.00
Family_Number	0.00	0.00	0.00
Username	0.00	0.00	0.00
micro avg	0.47	0.59	0.52
macro avg	0.34	0.43	0.38
weighted avg	0.49	0.59	0.53

Table 2: Evaluation results of NorDeid on 19 random clinical notes, approximately 13,000 tokens

Precision, recall, and F_1-score do not consider

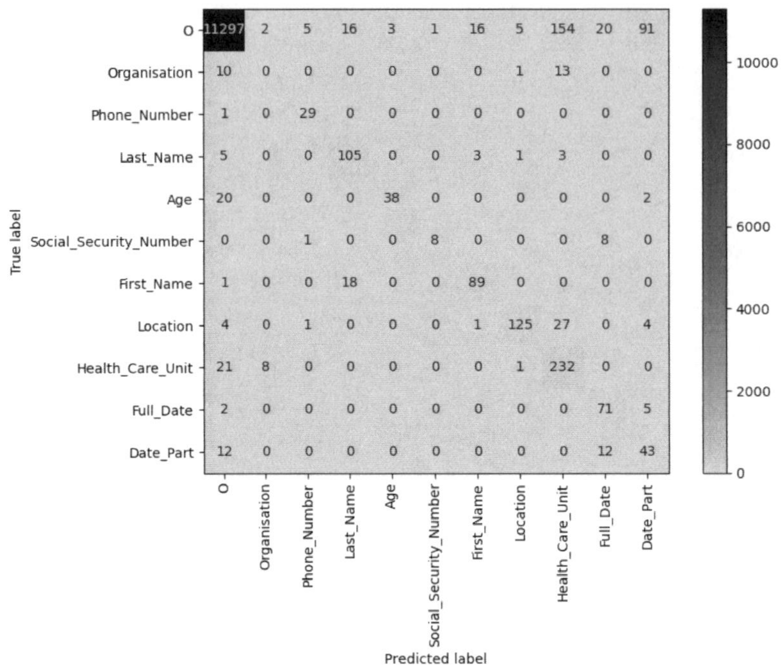

Figure 2: Entity level confusion matrix

the expected chance agreements that occur when humans annotate instances. We calculated the inter-annotator agreement to measure how well two different annotators made the same annotation decision. The two independent annotators annotated the same subset of clinical notes following the annotation guidelines developed in this work to qualitatively validate the labels. The inter-annotator agreement calculated using Cohen's Kappa was 0.86, indicating almost perfect agreement, (Landis and Koch, 1977).

6 Challenges

A major challenge was encountered in the beginning when trying to identify and classify sensitive data. This required a detailed understanding of the type and extent of sensitive information applicable to Norwegian texts, which included a wide variety of personal identifiers and confidential medical details. The difficulty was further increased by the subtle differences in language and clinical terminology that are unique to Norway. An example of illustrating this challenge is *personnummer*, which refers to a Norwegian social security number. This number is highly sensitive since it is unique to each person and contains information such as date of birth and gender. The model needed to distinguish between actual *personnummer* instances and other similar-looking numerical sequences. There are also different ways to represent this number depending on how healthcare professionals annotate notes. For example, a *personnummer* of *01010112345* can be rewritten as *010101-12345* or *010101 12345* or *01 jan 01 12345*.

The task of data management, such as cleaning and formatting, can be challenging. This included ensuring the data was in the correct text format, linking the data correctly, and dealing with issues when tokenizing Norwegian clinical texts. These processes were essential to ensure the data was accurate and reliable before using them with the model. Annotation of clinical texts requires a lot of resources. This process required both time and expertise, particularly in the medical domain. Therefore, providing enough resources for annotation is a major challenge in ensuring the overall efficiency and precision of the deidentification procedure.

Implementing the model to deidentify Norwegian clinical texts is also computationally intensive. It requires substantial computational resources, including processing power and memory, which was a limiting factor. Operating in an offline environment also introduced additional constraints, particularly in setting up the environment for model training and debugging code. This scenario limits the ability to take advantage of cloud computing resources and requires reliance on local computational capabilities.

Finally, there is a potential challenge in mitigating biases in the training and the output produced by NorDeid. Since the model relies on existing datasets for training, there is a risk of carrying the biases that exist within these datasets. Therefore, ensuring the unbiased and equitable functioning of the model in the deidentification of Norwegian clinical texts is essential and should not be overlooked.

7 Discussion

Each deidentification system needs to be customised on which PHIs to remove depending on the research task and type of data or what each country has for laws or rules. Lawyers and physicians do not always agree on which PHI is sensitive. For example, *Health Care Unit* can be valuable to keep sometimes, *Age* can also be important in certain research, most clinical researchers want to keep the class name while computer scientists consider it is much safer to replace identified PHIs with pseudonyms or surrogates, (Vakili and Dalianis, 2022). In the example with *Age* it can be replaced with an age close to the actual age, for example, random ± 2-3 years.

8 Conclusion

In conclusion, this paper has discussed the challenges and methods involved in deidentifying and pseudonymizing Norwegian clinical text for research purposes. The use of the NorDeid tool and regular expressions for identifying specific types of sensitive information proved effective in the deidentification process. The research highlighted the importance of privacy preservation and the need for tailored approaches to meet legal and research requirements. The significance of mitigating potential biases in the training and output of deidentification models were also emphasized.

9 Future work

The plan for the produced pseudonymised gastro corpus now called *ClinCode Gastro Pseudo Corpus* is to create a Norwegian Clinical BERT Model using the publicly available Norwegian language model NorBERT[4] based on general Norwegian Bokmål and Nynorsk, and perform continued pretraining from NorBERT on the pseudonymised gastro corpus. The aim of this is twofold first to improve the deidentification tool NorDeid and secondly to make a privacy preserved Norwegian large clinical language model available to researchers worldwide and improve the result of the current Norwegian clinical text mining. We will also extend the ClinCode Gastro Corpus with more manually annotated PHIs improve the performance of the NorDeid tool. The NordDeid tool is available for use by other researchers and research groups.

10 Limitations

The study may be limited by the availability of annotated Norwegian datasets for training and evaluating deidentification models. In addition to the limitation posed by the Norwegian language, it is important to note that there exist minor languages in Norway that were not considered in this study. The performance of the model has not been evaluated for these languages, which may introduce a bias in the results. This highlights a potential limitation of the study and underscores the importance of considering linguistic diversity in future research to ensure inclusivity and avoid bias.

The model's performance was not perfect and it had problems in classifying the PHIs in the correct PHIs class. In some cases, only parts of the health care unit or the social security number were identified, which led that only parts of it were pseudonymised, but NorDeid did its task in deidentifying and pseudonymising sensitive information. NorDeid also identified some false positives such as parts of ICD-10 codes or Drug names (as last names). In the Appendix some examples are shown. In the examples the SGML tags are left.

The clinical text used in the study was extracted only from a gastro-surgical department. Therefore, there may be a potential lack of generalizability of the findings to other healthcare domains or organizations. Finally, the potential impact of biases that exist in training data and how they affect deidentification and pseudonymization needs further investigation.

Acknowledgements

The research was funded by the Norwegian Research Council under the project *ClinCode - Computer-Assisted Clinical ICD-10 Coding for improving efficiency and quality in healthcare.*

[4]NorBERT, http://wiki.nlpl.eu/Vectors/norlm/norbert.

References

David S Carrell, David J Cronkite, Muqun Li, Steve Nyemba, Bradley A Malin, John S Aberdeen, and Lynette Hirschman. 2019. The machine giveth and the machine taketh away: a parrot attack on clinical text deidentified with hiding in plain sight. *Journal of the American Medical Informatics Association*, 26(12):1536–1544.

Hercules Dalianis. 2019. Pseudonymisation of Swedish electronic patient records using a rule-based approach. In *Proceedings of the Workshop on NLP and Pseudonymisation, In conjunction with Nodalida 2019*, pages 16–23, Turku, Finland. Linköping Electronic Press.

Franck Dernoncourt, Ji Young Lee, and Peter Szolovits. 2017. Neuroner: an easy-to-use program for named-entity recognition based on neural networks. *arXiv preprint arXiv:1705.05487*.

Anastasios Lamproudis, Sara Mora, Therese Olsen Svenning, Torbjørn Torsvik, Taridzo Chomutare, Phuong Dinh Ngo, and Hercules Dalianis. 2023. De-identifying Norwegian Clinical Text using Resources from Swedish and Danish. In *AMIA Annual Symposium Proceedings*, volume 2023. American Medical Informatics Association.

J. Richard Landis and Gary G. Koch. 1977. The Measurement of Observer Agreement for Categorical Data. *Biometrics*, 33(1):159–174.

Guillermo López-García, Francisco J. Moreno-Barea, Mesa Héctor, José M. Jerez, Nuria Ribelles, Emilio Alba, and Francisco J. Veredas. 2023. Named Entity Recognition for De-identifying Real-World Health Records in Spanish. In *Computational Science – ICCS*, pages 228–242.

Prakash M Nadkarni, Lucila Ohno-Machado, and Wendy W Chapman. 2011. Natural language processing: an introduction. *Journal of the American Medical Informatics Association*, 18(5):544–551.

Annika Willoch Olstad, Anthi Papadopoulou, and Pierre Lison. 2023. Generation of Replacement Options in Text Sanitization. In *Proceedings of the 24th Nordic Conference on Computational Linguistics (NoDaLiDa)*, pages 292–300.

Amber Stubbs, Christopher Kotfila, and Özlem Uzuner. 2015. Automated systems for the de-identification of longitudinal clinical narratives: Overview of 2014 i2b2/UTHealth shared task Track 1. *Journal of biomedical informatics*, 58:S11–S19.

Amber Stubbs and Özlem Uzuner. 2015. Annotating longitudinal clinical narratives for de-identification: The 2014 i2b2/UTHealth corpus. *Journal of biomedical informatics*, 58:S20–S29.

Thomas Vakili and Hercules Dalianis. 2022. Utility Preservation of Clinical Text After De-Identification. In *Proceedings of the 21st Workshop on Biomedical Language Processing*, pages 383–388.

Thomas Vakili, Anastasios Lamproudis, Aron Henriksson, and Hercules Dalianis. 2022. Downstream task performance of bert models pre-trained using automatically de-identified clinical data. In *Proceedings of the Thirteenth Language Resources and Evaluation Conference*, pages 4245–4252.

Li-Xiao Zheng, Shuai Ma, Zu-Xi Chen, and Xiang-Yu Luo. 2021. Ensuring the Correctness of Regular Expressions: A Review. *International Journal of Automation and Computing*, 18:521–535.

Appendix: De-identified clinical texts

Here follows examples with de-identified and pseudonymised Norwegian clinical text where the SGML tags has been kept (hence not HIPS), for pedagogical purposes.

1. Var henvist av egen lege til en kolonskopi som skulle vært tatt den <Date_Part>28.</Date_Part> < Date_Part>08,</Date_Part> men har utsatt denne grunnet operasjon.

2. Gjenomgikk så <Full_Date>17.02.19</Full_Date> fedmekirurgi (type Gastric sleeve) ved <Health_Care_Unit>en vårdenhet</Health_Care_Unit>, reoperert <Date_Part>20.02</Date_Part> pga blødning ved <Health_Care_Unit>en vårdenhet</Health_Care_Unit>.

3. Godkjent av/skrevet av lege i spesialisering 2 <First_Name>Signe</First_Name> <Last_Name>Rybakk</Last_Name> / <User_Name>/Sry001</User_Name> Da hun bor i <Location>Horten</Location> ble hun sendt hjem og kommer derfor i dag for kontroll.

4. <Full_Date>26.01</Full_Date> 17 Journalnotat SO, <Health_Care_Unit>en vårdenhet</Health_Care_Unit> <Health_Care_Unit>Bergen</Health_Care_Unit> v/Overlege endokrinologi <First_Name>Carrie</First_Name> <Last_Name>Rammus</Last_Name> /Cra2377aaa Pasienten er overflyttet hit fra <Location>Kongsberg</Location> pga akutt nekrotiserende pancreatitt med påfølgende langt behandlingsforløp og intensivt opphold.

5. J<Date_Part>UG05</Date_Part> Rektoskopi md biopsi

In Example 1. above, one can observe that the de-identifier splitted the *Date_Part* in two parts while *28.08* should be encompassed by one *Date_Part* tag.

In Example 4. the de-identifier missed to tag number *17* as in year *2017*, while *26.01* was tagged as *Full_Date* while it is actually a *Date_Part*. To be correct *26.01 17* should be tagged as *Full_Date*, moreover in the same example the User name */Msø2377* is not tagged.

In Example 5. a part of a procedure code is wrongly identified as a *Date_Part*.

Extending off-the-shelf NER Systems to Personal Information Detection in Dialogues with a Virtual Agent: Findings from a Real-Life Use Case

Mario Mina **Carlos Rodriguez-Penagos** **Aitor Gonzalez-Agirre** **Marta Villegas**
Barcelona Supercomputing Center
{mario.magued|carlos.rodriguez1|aitor.gonzalez|marta.villegas}
@bsc.es

Abstract

We present the findings and results of our pseudonymisation system, which has been developed for a real-life use-case involving users and an informative chatbot in the context of the COVID-19 pandemic. Message exchanges between the two involve the former group providing information about themselves and their residential area, which could easily allow for their re-identification. We create a modular pipeline to detect PIIs and perform basic deidentification such that the data can be stored while mitigating any privacy concerns. The use-case presents several challenging aspects, the most difficult of which is the logistic challenge of not being able to directly view or access the data due to the very privacy issues we aim to resolve. Nevertheless, our system achieves a high recall of 0.99, correctly identifying almost all instances of personal data. However, this comes at the expense of precision, which only reaches 0.64. We describe the sensitive information identification in detail, explaining the design principles behind our decisions. We additionally highlight the particular challenges we've encountered.

1 Introduction and Context

With current advances in NLP relying on data-hungry machine learning systems and even more data-hungry language models, user-generated data is becoming increasingly important: data from conversations with chatbots, crawls of internet forums, posts on social media, etc can and are often used to train deep learning systems. At the same time, respecting user privacy is critical.

The General Data Protection Regulation (GDPR) came into effect as of the 25th of May 2018, affecting any data identifying or allowing the identification of a natural person. For instance, in the previous examples of user-generated data, identifiable data could take the form of a username, a full name, or an address, among others (Francopoulo and Schaub, 2020). At its core, the aim of the GDPR is to bring EU data protection legislation in line with the new ways that personal data is now being used by giving users more control over the ways their data is bring processed.

One of the implications of the GDPR is for there to be no way to trace data back to a specific individual or a group thereof. As a result, anononimized data is exempt of GDPR requirements. In turn, much effort has gone into perfecting anonymization and pseudonymisation techniques to allow NLP practitioners to work directly with user-generated data.

However, each domain presents its own unique challenges. In this paper we tackle anonymization in user-generated messages with a virtual chatbot. Text originating from this domain presents the same characteristics as other instances noisy user-generated text; we encounter different types of text, with some of the messages being characterised with non-standard spelling, use of slang, etc, while others are written in a formal register (Barbieri et al., 2020; Baldwin et al., 2015a). Furthermore, information is exchanged between the user and the virtual agent in a dialog fashion, such that it is possible for no individual message to allow the identification of the user, but the conversation, taken as a whole, could.

In this paper we describe findings from our particular real-life scenario of automatically identifying PIIs in user-generated data from conversations involving a virtual agent serving as an informative tool while not being able to directly access the data. Users adhering to the contemplated use-case could use the virtual assistant to make inquiries regarding COVID restrictions in their area of residence. Such exchanges are a perfect example of personal information that can be used to identify an individual based on their location.

As stated, different domains present different challenges for anonymization. With this in mind,

Proceedings of the Workshop on Computational Approaches to Language Data Pseudonymization
CALD-pseudo 2024, pages 44–53
March 21, 2024

we design a flexible and modular pipeline[1] to anonymize GDPR protected text by allowing for different components that perform sensitive data identification and subsequent deidentification. We describe our experimental setup and methods used, and highlight particularly difficult aspects of working on real-life user-generated data in both Spanish and Catalan that we could not directly access.

2 Literature Review

The task of pseudonymisation is generally considered to be complex given that based on context, one can re-identify pseudonymised information and the. These difficulties can be in turn modulated by each domain's characteristics. Up until recently, most techniques were applied in either medical or legal domains, which were considered to be sensitive domains well before the GDPR (Sánchez-León, 2019; Langarizadeh et al., 2018; Yuwono et al., 2016). Methods typically vary between applications; generally speaking, pseudonymisation occurs in at least two steps: the first step is identifying personal information, where most of the our efforts in this paper are centered. Most methods that are applied to highly regular data rely on simple regular expressions, whereas less structured information requires more sophisticated Named Entity Recognition (NER) systems based on machine learning. Deidentification can vary more in terms of applicable methods, and is more dependent on the properties of the source text. That is to say, there are different methods that are more of less preferable depending on the use case (Belkadi et al.). Typically methods involve substituting sensitive information with a random sequence, a label, or a random entity of the same or similar type.

Nevertheless, Adams et al. (2019) posit that the need for robust anonymization is being extended to other domains, due to the GDPR affecting other sources of data, which has made the task of automatic text pseudonymisation more relevant than ever. To that end they develop a machine learning-based toolkit to perform automatic pseudonymisation in human-computer dialogue while taking into account information that could potentially identify persons (PIIs) but also corporations (CIIs).

[1] https://github.com/langtech-bsc/AnonymizationPipeline

2.1 Regular expression-based sensitive information identification

Hassan et al. (2019) create ReCRF, a named entity extraction system that extracts features based on orthography, lexis and regular expressions from a specific token and its surrounding context to classify a token as containing PII or not in medical text. The interesting aspect to their feature crafting method is the use of a data-driven method to automatically generate regex-based rules. These features are then used as input to Conditional Random Field models.

Still involving the medical domain, Sánchez-León (2019) develop a pseudonymisation system for Spanish clinical text. They enrich a simple grammar formalism with regular expressions to take into account spelling variations and then apply each rule in order of reliability, with generally favourable results.

Yuwono et al. (2016) apply regular expressions similarly to detect PIIs in clinical discharge papers. On top of the regular expressions they construct hand-crafted heuristics involving minimum edit distance to account for spelling and formatting inconsistencies between documents. Their simple heuristics-based approach does not require any sort of fine-tuning, model training, or manual annotation, but they do make use of their own database when detecting patient information.

2.2 Machine learning-based detection of sensitive data

A variety of machine learning methods can be utilised in several ways when detecting sensitive information. Juez-Hernandez et al. (2023) perform a comprehensive assessment of PII detection methods using current state-of-the-art methods and propose a few of their own, with a focus on several languages. They perform several experiments to derive optimal solutions for PII identification in different types of Spanish text (clinical texts and law-enforcement reports). They pose different research questions regarding the performance of NER models of PII detection. Specifically, they contemplate the effects of using off-the-shelf models on performance in comparison to training a model for each specific domain, as well as if an ad hoc trained model can be used in a cross-domain fashion. Their findings suggest that while off-the-shelf models can be used for PII detection, training domain-specific models yields superior results, given the variability across domains. Specifically, they note that a model trained on one domain can be used in another with acceptable performance, but performance will degrade when used on out-of-domain data.

In terms of methods, they test different NER architectures ranging from off-the-shelf Stanza (Qi et al., 2020) and Flair (Akbik et al., 2019) NER models to recurrent neural architectures with different combinations of embeddings, to pretrained transformers available on HuggingFace that were then fine-tuned on their task-specific data.

2.3 Challenges

Examining the requirements of the GDPR, and what constitutes genuinely anonymized data, a question that is continually asked is how do we manage the trade-off between privacy and utility? Francopoulo and Schaub (2020) determine that for an anonymization framework to be successful, it needs to: (1) avoid identifying the individuals in the text, (2) allow posterior analysis of the anonymized text, (3) allow for off-the-shelf NLP tools to be applied to the anonymized text, (4) produce a provable anonymization, (5) be usable in different European languages. They highlight that some of these are contradictory or at least that some requirements directly interfere with the effectiveness of the others, even if we assume a perfect detection of PIIs. The problem lies in that if resulting data from an anonymization or deidentification process is indistinguishable from a non-anonymized text, there would be no way to prove that it has actually been anonymized. For instance, anonymization by redaction (i.e. the elimination of PIIs by substituting them with a fixed character such as an *X*) leaves proof of the anonymization, but severely limits any posterior usability of the text. On the other hand, if a more sophisticated substitution is applied to the text, the result maximises posterior usefulness, but by definition should not leave a trace of the anonymization. As a solution they propose a relaxation of requirements based on the specific circumstance. They argue that requirement (3) is vital when using off-the-shelf tools within a secure environment, where requirement (4) can be relaxed, while requirement (4) is more important outside of a secure environment, where requirement (3) can be relaxed.

These concerns are echoed in Mozes and Kleinberg (2021). They argue that current methods do not correctly quantify anonymization performance, given that if a text contains several instances of PIIs, it is enough for one of them to go undetected to identify the person in question. Many metrics would still assign a high performance to the anonymization system, as evaluation is typically applied on a sentence or instance level, despite the anonymization essentially failing.

They propose specific evaluation criteria to measure the effectiveness of the anonymization. The criteria presented in TILD take into account an anonymization system's **t**echnical performance, the **i**nformation **l**oss resulting from the anonymization, and the human ability to **d**eanonymize the redacted documents. They highlight the importance of information loss and robustness against de-anonymization; to guarantee posterior utility, the authors argue that the anonymization process must introduce as minimal changes as possible to the original document such that utility loss (difference in performance when using anonymized data in comparison to the original data) and construct loss (difference according to a higher order construct) are minimised. However, while ensuring minimal differences between anonymized and original texts, the anonymization process must be irreversible, such that a human intruder with the ability to use external resources would not be able to identify the original PIIs.

We can draw parallelisms between Francopoulo and Schaub (2020) and Mozes and Kleinberg (2021). Both papers highlight the importance of the actual detection component (requirement (1) of Francopoulo and Schaub (2020) and criterion T of TILD), and both are concerned with the posterior utility of the data in terms of the analyses that can still be carried out (requirements (2) and (3) in Francopoulo and Schaub (2020) and criterion IL of TILD). However, we observe that Francopoulo and Schaub (2020) suggest modulating the importance of that requirement based on intended use and level of exposure of the anonymized data, while Mozes and Kleinberg (2021) make no such statement. After that point, both criteria diverge. Francopoulo and Schaub (2020) highlight the importance of having a provable anonymization, while Mozes and Kleinberg (2021) place more emphasis on the anonymization being non-reversible while maintaining the properties of the original data.

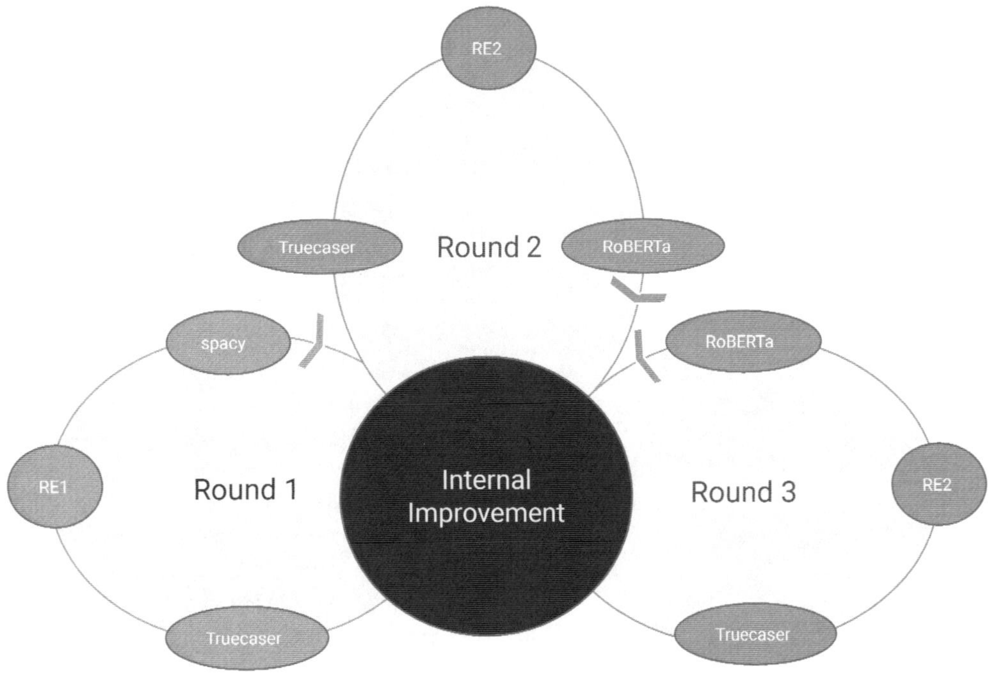

Figure 1: Diagram of our experimental design. round 1 was performed on the randomly sampled dataset (left, in pink), while rounds 2 and 3 were performed on the entire conversation dataset (top and right, in green).

3 Methods

3.1 Anonymization Data

As stated in section 1, our evaluation data originates from conversations between users and a virtual agent. For context, the conversations took place during the COVID-19 pandemic. We examine two subsets of the data. Initially, we randomly sample 23.000 messages for simplicity. However, after our initial assessment, discussion with annotators, and following Mozes and Kleinberg (2021), we decide to include full conversations, given that in some occasions, referents can be identified using contextual cues that do not individually constitute PIIs.

We decide to include messages from full conversations such that the individual messages sum to 23.000; annotators were instructed to compile a second dataset such that all messages sent by the users from a conversation were included. This resulted in the generation of a second evaluation dataset consisting of 23.000 messages from 953 unique conversations. We highlight that due to privacy restrictions, we only use the data for evaluating our system, as the data cannot be used to train or fine-tune a base model.

Regarding the annotation process, the data was selected and processed by two annotators, and then revised by a third such that the third annotator could essentially act as a tie-breaker. Cases where no consensus was reached were excluded from the experiments (this was the case for fewer than 15 messages in total, taking into account both datasets)

In terms of structure, only messages from the users are included. Messages are assigned two identifiers: a unique identifier and an identifier specifying to which conversation it belongs. Within each conversation, messages are ordered chronologically. Furthermore, the messages are unlabeled. We do not explicitly work with a gold standard. Instead, we rely on the annotators to examine the data on our behalf. They additionally analyse the performance of our system by checking what information is correctly pseudonymised and which information is incorrectly pseudonymised.

Our setup is as shown in Figure 1. The data is kept by the third party such that we cannot directly access or manipulate it. Given this data access constraint, the annotators were hired to perform three evaluation rounds. In each round, we submit a version of the pipeline which is run on the third party's systems. They in turn evaluate the PII identification component performance.

3.2 The Anonymization Pipeline

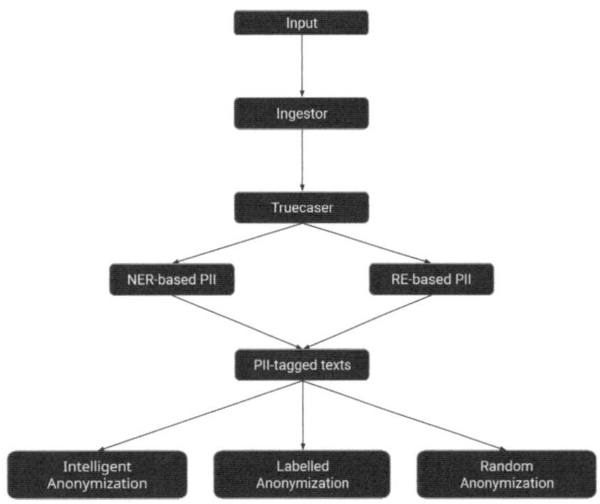

Figure 2: Diagram of the presented pipeline.

Despite the complexity of the task of pseudonymisation, the pipeline we present in this paper is relatively straightforward. In this subsection we proceed to describe our pipeline as shown in Figure 2.

Input data is provided textually. Currently, the pipeline supports different forms of textual input through different ingestors that, when fed a specific format, would output the data in a normalized format that the rest of pipeline can manipulate. The pipeline currently has ingestors for .csv, .json and .txt formats.

As explained in section 2, user-generated data is known to be noisy; while we do not explicitly add a preprocessing module, we have empirically determined during initial testing that in our specific case, performance is hindered by poor textual formatting. To mitigate this issue, we apply an implementation of the NLTK truecaser module[2] (Bird et al., 2009). This resolves simple cases where names of people, locations, organizations, etc are incorrectly cased.

Following ingesting the data, normalizing the input representation, and applying mild preprocessing, we proceed to the sensitive information identification task by combining regular expressions and machine learning models as described in subsection 3.3. While we take into account the labels provided by our regular expressions and one NER module, we highlight that the pipeline supports the use of multiple NER modules. In the case of a mismatch between any of the components, we establish a ranking such that the labelling of one can be determined to be more "trustworthy" and therefore take scope over the other in case of a discrepancy.

Once the sensitive information has been identified within the text, the pipeline can perform simple deidentification. Three methods are included: *random*, *labelled*, and *intelligent*. The *random* method substitutes the sensitive span with a series of random characters of varying length, the *labelled* method substitutes the span with the category of sensitive data detected (e.g. PERS, ID, LOC, etc). The *intelligent* method performs a limited substitution that attempts to substitute the marked span with a different entity of the same category. Currently, it is entirely possible for the *intelligent* anonymization system to substitute a street name with a city for instance, as we do not have a more fine-grained method of PII detection available. We conduct all of our experiments with the *labelled* setting to ease the annotation task.

3.3 PII identification

Given that pseudonymisation is a complex task and PIIs can occur in varying contexts, our pipeline is designed with flexibility and modularity in mind, such that components can be substituted based on the requirements and difficulty of the task. We differentiate between structured and non-structured PIIs and detect them using different methods; instances of structured data include phone numbers, zip codes, emails, etc. On the other hand, non-structured PIIs could include person and location names.

We take into account the domain properties of our domain of intended use. User-generated text is notorious for being noisy (Baldwin et al., 2015b; Jose and Raj, 2014). This can harm the robustness of PII detection module of our pipeline, increasing the number of false positives and negatives. We mitigate these problems in our pipeline differently for structured and unstructured data.

According to the intended use-case of the virtual agent, users are expected to provide information regarding their location, identity and contact in the form of structured PIIs of zip codes, ID number, email, phone number, and even land registry

[2] `https://huggingface.co/HURIDOCS/spanish-truecasing`

identifiers. To detect this sort of information we hand-craft regular expressions to match such information, allowing for some variation by users (e.g. a missing digit in a phone number, lower-case letters rather than upper-case letters in a license plate number).

For non-structured data such as location names and full names whose formats can vary, we use machine learning and deep learning methods for detection. We experiment with a large spacy model[3] and a RoBERTa NER[4] model that have been fine-tuned on Catalan and Spanish NER data. We additionally experiment with a truecasing module to ease the detection of named entities.

During each of the three evaluation rounds, we ask the annotators to classify each message using criteria that we provide. We establish the following typology to categorise PII detection performance:

A) Information that should not be anonymized (false positives)

B) PIIs that should have been detected but were not (false negatives)

C) PIIs that have been detected but assigned an incorrect type (true positives)

D) Correctly identified PIIs (true positives)

E) Potential PII but not in this context (true positives)

F) Not PIIs (true negative)

Many PIIs are contextually modulated, in the sense that the same span of text may allow the identification of the individual depending on the information in the surrounding context. For instance, a first name on its own might not identify an individual, but a full name probably would, and both would be detected by most off-the-shelf NER models. Similarly with locations, a user stating their city of residence may not be providing sensitive information. However, the likelihood of being able to identify the user increases the fewer the inhabitants that live in the area denoted by the message. Given our limited access to the data, we cannot use any of the messages to fine-tune a model and tailor it to our specific domain, and must rely on models trained on other datasets. This limits our system's ability to take this contextual modulation into account.

That being said, we still instruct the annotators to take into the account all messages sent by the user during the exchange in line with the points raised in Mozes and Kleinberg (2021) and the TILD evaluation framework; in one of our evaluation paradigms, if our system fails to detect critical PIIs that allow the identification of the individual, the entire exchange is labelled as B). We additionally instruct the annotators to highlight instances where users specify entities that would typically be detected by NER systems, but do not constitute PIIs, thereby creating category E). As stated, the models we use in this case are not specialised in anonymization, and therefore they are unable to pick up on explicit contextual cues that allow distinguishing PIIs from named entities (NEs). In light of this and that that sensitivity of specific entities is contextually modulated, for our evaluation we still consider them to be true positives. Similarly, we also consider correctly detected PIIs that are not correctly categorised (e.g. a location that is classified as a name) to be true positives, given that our main focus is PII identification.

3.4 Evaluation Rounds

Cleaning and aggregation On one hand, we believe that whatever PII detection system that is applied or deployed in a given environment should show robust performance despite noisy input. But on the other, in our specific case, without being able to adapt a model to this type of task and domain, the noise in the input negatively skews our results, both in terms of performance and evaluation. With the aid of the annotators, we identify two main issues:

1. Much of the input is noisy. Many users will misspell several words (e.g. *weno chao* instead of *bueno ciao* to end a conversation) in their messages or simply send nonsense (e.g. button mashing or sending the same random characters multiple times) to the virtual agent, which is detected by the model

2. Some users send several instances of the same message. If PII detection of that specific message is incorrect, it is then overrepresented in the data

Essentially, the first problem causes the model to detect several false positives through errors of

[3]https://huggingface.co/PlanTL-GOB-ES/es_anonimization_core_lg

[4]https://huggingface.co/BSC-LT/roberta_model_for_anonimization

type A). By sending several copies of some messages, the first problem is essentially exacerbated, such that false positives are overrepresented in our evaluation.

To mitigate this problem, we first detect poorly formatted or spelled messages similarly to Kudugunta et al. (2023); we apply the fasttext language identifier (Joulin et al., 2016) to each message. The language identifier outputs a probability distribution over languages. Poorly formed messages will have a lower probability associated with the expected languages. We discard any message with a probability lower than 0.8 of being either in Spanish or Catalan. Furthermore, in addition to evaluating performance by considering each message individually, we also examine performance by considering entire conversations. That is to say, rather than assign labels to individual messages, we assign them to the entire conversation. We do this by establishing a hierarchy of error types, such that graver errors take higher scope. The hierarchy is as follows: B > A > C > D > E > F. For instance, if in a conversation, one message is correctly anonymized (i.e. type D), but a critical PII is missed in another message belonging to the same conversation(i.e. type B, or a false negative), then that whole conversation is marked as B.

As stated in subsection 3.1, we do not have direct access to the data and instead provide the task to a third party. We iteratively make improvements to our pipeline based on their feedback. In Figure 1 we illustrate how we proceed through each evaluation round. We perform three sequential rounds of evaluation. During each round, we update the pipeline and make the new version available to the third party. The pipeline is then downloaded and run on their systems where the data is kept. For readability, model performance is based on the label-based pseudonymisation. Model performance is manually examined by comparing the original data with the anonymized data to examine if PIIs were correctly detected and replaced with the correct labels. The results of the examination are then forwarded back to us in terms of the error typology presented in the beginning of subsection 3.1. This feedback is then taken into account for the following round of evaluation.

Round 1 For the first round of evaluation, we experiment with lightweight approaches. We use a large spacy NER pipeline (which includes POS tagger, dependency parser, attribute matcher, and lemmatizer) (Honnibal et al., 2020). Initial experiments in-house additionally showed a benefit in performance by adding a truecaser as a preprocessing step. We use our initial set of regular expressions (RE1).

Round 2 For the second evaluation, we take into account the results and feedback from the second round and include a larger and more robust RoBERTa NER model to increase the quality of the PII detection. We additionally perform in-house experiments to determine if the truecaser adds any benefit and decide to still include it.

Round 3 After the second round, we observe that our system manages to detect the majority of the PII instances in the evaluation set. However, discussion with the annotators revealed that some instances were not detected due to user error (e.g. a phone number missing a digit, a misspelled email). We refine the regular expressions such that they are more flexible to account for user error (RE2). We additionally observe that the truecaser introduced whitespaces in specific contexts which interfered with the RoBERTa model tokenization, negatively impacting precision. We resolved this issue for the third and final round with the aim of reducing the number of false positives.

We show the results for each round in Table 1, presenting precision, recall and F_β ($\beta = 2$)for each round. We additionally present results for the datasets after filtering our the noisy text and assigning a label to each conversation, rather than each individual message.

4 Results

We present our results in Table 1. Within each round, we evaluate the effects of data cleaning and applying our evaluation metrics in different ways; we explore the effects of aggregating the data differently (as shown in the *Aggregation* column), and the effects of removing poorly formatted messages from consideration (expressed by the *-c* (for clean) suffix). Each round is separated by a horizontal line in the table. Cleaned and non-cleaned versions of the data are separated by a dashed line within each evaluation round.

In spite of not being able to directly access the data, Table 1 shows the clear benefits of our iterative evaluation paradigm. We can observe nontrivial improvement from one round to the next; the first round, using the Spacy model, yields moderate

Round	NER component	RE set	Aggregation	Precision	Recall	F_β
R1	Spacy	RE_1	Total	0.43	0.74	0.65
	-	-	-	-	-	-
R2	RoBERTa	RE_1	Total	0.06	0.95	0.23
			CONV	0.27	0.93	0.62
R2-c	RoBERTa	RE_1	Total	0.1	0.95	0.35
			CONV	0.29	0.93	0.64
R3	RoBERTa	RE_2	Total	0.40	0.99	0.77
			CONV	0.63	0.99	0.89
R3-c	RoBERTa	RE_2	Total	0.54	**0.99**	0.85
			CONV	**0.64**	0.99	**0.90**

Table 1: Results as classified by annotators for each evaluation round. Best performance in bold. $\beta = 2$. RE_n indicates the set of regular expressions used, whereas the *-c* suffix indicates that noisy messages have been removed from the dataset.

precision but relatively low recall. For the second round, we incorporate a more robust RoBERTa model into the pipeline, which drastically raises recall at the cost of precision. For the third and final round, we modify the system tokenization scheme and augment the set of regular expressions, further improving both recall and precision, ultimately yielding the highest F_β-score of 0.90.

Furthermore, we can see the clear impact of the data quality on pipeline performance. For each evaluated dataset, we create a *clean* counterpart after filtering out messages we believe have significant orthography or formatting issues. We observe superior model performance on cleaner datasets, especially in terms of precision. We observe this effect in evaluation rounds 2 and 3.

However, we observe a much stronger difference in precision based on the way we choose to aggregate the data; by aggregating the data by conversation we observe major improvements, which are more representative of actual PII detection performance. That is to say, by assigning a single label to each conversation based on whether a correct detection of PIIs was carried out, we attain much better precision. We observe these effects in both rounds where we collected several messages from the same conversation (rounds 2 and 3).

5 Discussion

PII detection performance The results shown in Table 1 in section 4 show clear improvement between consecutive iterations. In terms of trade-off between precision and recall, we note that performance is most balanced using the Spacy model. However, it does also present the lowest recall, which we consider to be the to be the most relevant metric given the sensitive nature of the data. In light of this, we find recall to be prohibitively low using the Spacy model. Comparing performance between the Spacy and RoBERTa models in similar conditions (i.e. considering individual messages and unclean data), it is clear that the RoBERTa models show lower precision. That said, their higher recall makes them more desirable in this context.

Our findings are in line with those of Juez-Hernandez et al. (2023). While we are able to achieve high recall with models trained on out-of-domain data, we do observe that performance is not optimal, given the relatively low precision of the RoBERTa models. That said, we have been able to determine that the low performance is largely due to the overrepresentation of noisy input in the data, which essentially interacts with the imperfect robustness of our model in this context, contributing to the deflation of the aforementioned metric. We have more or less mitigated this issue so that the results more accurately reflect model performance, but we also highlight that if the NER models were more robust to the noise in the input, the number of false positives would be drastically lower.

Francopoulo and Schaub (2020) and TILD Given the high recall of our system, we consider that we fulfill the first item of the criteria presented in TILD (Technical performance) and Francopoulo and Schaub (2020), which is to ensure that the data does not contain PIIs. However, we do note the low precision of our system may negatively impact Information loss, as obscuring more data than necessary may render the data less useful. On the other hand, tagging more entities than necessary as PIIs and their subsequent anonymization (via redaction or substitution) is more likely to make deanonymization much more difficult. In light of this, we argue that depending on use, the system we present in this paper could be more than adequate.

6 Conclusion and Future Work

In conclusion, we present the results and findings from a real life use-case where we have had to develop a PII detection system to pseudonymise exchanges between users and a virtual agent. We demonstrate the effectiveness of our system and the issues that can arise when extending a NER system beyond its original domain. We highlight the specific problems we have encountered with user-generated data. We additionally note that given the differences between the domains of training and deployment, our system performs well, achieving very high recall. We argue that the inter-domain differences may be detrimental to performance in general, PII detection can be achieved with robust off-the-shelf NER models, given that our system managed to detect almost all instances of PII.

While the performance of our system is more than adequate given the circumstances, anonymisation and pseudonymisation are tasks that are gaining more and more urgency and importance. In light of this we consider it of critical importance to develop more resources for domain-specific and domain-general pseudonymisation.

The focus of this paper has been examining the effectiveness of adapting off-the-shelf NER systems to the task of PII detection. Our future work should aim to address explore robust ways of deidentifying the data in accordance with the established literature (Francopoulo and Schaub, 2020; Mozes and Kleinberg, 2021).

7 Limitations

Given the relatively novel nature of this task, one of the major limitations of the work presented is only taking into account the benefits of examining entire conversations over individual messages from the second round of evaluation onwards. This negatively impacts the comparability of our results; we cannot compare the performance of the Spacy model with the RoBERTa model when considering entire conversations.

Additionally, we mention in section 3 that our system contains a rudimentary deidentification component that can substitute detected PIIs with either a sequence of random characters, a label, or a similar entity which was randomly sampled. For the purposes of our experiments, we have only considered the label-based deidentification (which is similar to redaction in the literature), as it made the anonymized text much more readable, and subsequently simplified the annotation task. We leave evaluating this component for future work.

8 Ethical Statement

The development of anonymisation or pseudonymisation systems is central to people's right to privacy. We view the work presented in this paper as a positive contribution, given that we provide the tools (pipeline, models, etc) to detect and deidentify sensitive data in Spanish and Catalan. Furthermore, we highlight the weaknesses we have observed both in our system and in early iterations of our improvement cycle with the aim of helping researches avoid similar pitfalls. However, while we do not foresee the methods described here to be used for unethical purposes, discussing any potential system weaknesses may facilitate system attacks down the line.

9 Acknowledgements

This work has been promoted and financed by the Generalitat de Catalunya through the Aina project. We would like to extend our thanks to the anonymous reviewers for their kind and insightful comments that have helped improve this paper. We additionally want to thank Belén Alemán and 1millionbot for their invaluable help in analysing user generated data used in this study.

References

Allison Adams, Eric Aili, Daniel Aioanei, Rebecca Jonsson, Lina Mickelsson, Dagmar Mikmekova, Fred Roberts, Javier Fernandez Valencia, and Roger Wechsler. 2019. AnonyMate: A toolkit for anonymizing unstructured chat data. In *Proceedings of the Workshop on NLP and Pseudonymisation*, pages 1–7, Turku, Finland. Linköping Electronic Press.

Alan Akbik, Tanja Bergmann, Duncan Blythe, Kashif Rasul, Stefan Schweter, and Roland Vollgraf. 2019. FLAIR: An easy-to-use framework for state-of-the-art NLP. In *NAACL 2019, 2019 Annual Conference of the North American Chapter of the Association for Computational Linguistics (Demonstrations)*, pages 54–59.

Timothy Baldwin, Marie-Catherine De Marneffe, Bo Han, Young-Bum Kim, Alan Ritter, and Wei Xu. 2015a. Shared tasks of the 2015 workshop on noisy user-generated text: Twitter lexical normalization and named entity recognition. In *Proceedings of the Workshop on Noisy User-generated Text*, page 126–135, Beijing, China. Association for Computational Linguistics.

Timothy Baldwin, Marie-Catherine De Marneffe, Bo Han, Young-Bum Kim, Alan Ritter, and Wei Xu. 2015b. Shared tasks of the 2015 workshop on noisy user-generated text: Twitter lexical normalization and named entity recognition. In *Proceedings of the workshop on noisy user-generated text*, pages 126–135.

Francesco Barbieri, Jose Camacho-Collados, Luis Espinosa Anke, and Leonardo Neves. 2020. TweetEval: Unified benchmark and comparative evaluation for tweet classification. In *Findings of the Association for Computational Linguistics: EMNLP 2020*, pages 1644–1650, Online. Association for Computational Linguistics.

Lydia Belkadi, Martine De Cock, Natasha Fernandes, Katherine Lee, Christina Lohr, Andreas Nautsch, Laurens Sion, Natalia Tomashenko, Marc Tommasi, Peggy Valcke, et al. 4.2 metrics for anonymization of unstructured datasets. *Privacy in Speech and Language Technology*, page 73.

Steven Bird, Ewan Klein, and Edward Loper. 2009. *Natural language processing with Python: analyzing text with the natural language toolkit.* " O'Reilly Media, Inc.".

Gil Francopoulo and Léon-Paul Schaub. 2020. Anonymization for the gdpr in the context of citizen and customer relationship management and nlp. In *workshop on Legal and Ethical Issues (Legal2020)*, pages 9–14. ELRA.

Fadi Hassan, Mohammed Jabreel, Najlaa Maaroof, David Sanchez, Josep Domingo-Ferrer, and Antonio Moreno. 2019. Recrf: Spanish medical document anonymization using automatically-crafted rules and crf. In *IberLEF@SEPLN*.

Matthew Honnibal, Ines Montani, Sofie Van Landeghem, and Adriane Boyd. 2020. spaCy: Industrial-strength Natural Language Processing in Python.

Greety Jose and Nisha S Raj. 2014. Noisy sms text normalization model. In *International Conference for Convergence for Technology-2014*, pages 1–6. IEEE.

Armand Joulin, Edouard Grave, Piotr Bojanowski, and Tomas Mikolov. 2016. Bag of tricks for efficient text classification. *arXiv preprint arXiv:1607.01759*.

Rodrigo Juez-Hernandez, Lara Quijano-Sánchez, Federico Liberatore, and Jesús Gómez. 2023. Agora: An intelligent system for the anonymization, information extraction and automatic mapping of sensitive documents. *Applied Soft Computing*, 145:110540.

Sneha Kudugunta, Isaac Caswell, Biao Zhang, Xavier Garcia, Christopher A Choquette-Choo, Katherine Lee, Derrick Xin, Aditya Kusupati, Romi Stella, Ankur Bapna, et al. 2023. Madlad-400: A multilingual and document-level large audited dataset. *arXiv preprint arXiv:2309.04662*.

Mostafa Langarizadeh, Azam Orooji, Abbas Sheikhtaheri, and D Hayn. 2018. Effectiveness of anonymization methods in preserving patients' privacy: A systematic literature review. *eHealth*, 248:80–87.

Maximilian Mozes and Bennett Kleinberg. 2021. No intruder, no validity: Evaluation criteria for privacy-preserving text anonymization. *arXiv preprint arXiv:2103.09263*.

Peng Qi, Yuhao Zhang, Yuhui Zhang, Jason Bolton, and Christopher D Manning. 2020. Stanza: A python natural language processing toolkit for many human languages. *arXiv preprint arXiv:2003.07082*.

Fernando Sánchez-León. 2019. Resource-based anonymization for spanish clinical cases. *IberLef@ SEPLN*, pages 704–711.

Steven Kester Yuwono, Hwee Tou Ng, and Kee Yuan Ngiam. 2016. Automated anonymization as spelling variant detection. In *Proceedings of the Clinical Natural Language Processing Workshop (ClinicalNLP)*, pages 99–103, Osaka, Japan. The COLING 2016 Organizing Committee.

Detecting Personal Identifiable Information in Swedish Learner Essays

Maria Irena Szawerna[†] **Simon Dobnik**[‡] **Ricardo Muñoz Sánchez**[†]
Therese Lindström Tiedemann[§] **Elena Volodina**[†]
[†]Språkbanken Text, SFS, University of Gothenburg, Sweden
[‡]CLASP, FLoV, University of Gothenburg, Sweden
[§]Department of Finnish, Finnougrian and Scandinavian Studies, University of Helsinki, Finland
mormor.karl@svenska.gu.se
[†]{maria.szawerna,ricardo.munoz.sanchez,elena.volodina}@gu.se
[‡]simon.dobnik@gu.se
[§]therese.lindstromtiedemann@helsinki.fi

Abstract

Linguistic data can — and often does — contain PII (Personal Identifiable Information). Both from a legal and ethical standpoint, the sharing of such data is not permissible. According to the GDPR, pseudonymization, i.e. the replacement of sensitive information with surrogates, is an acceptable strategy for privacy preservation. While research has been conducted on the detection and replacement of sensitive data in Swedish medical data using Large Language Models (LLMs), it is unclear whether these models handle PII in less structured and more thematically varied texts equally well. In this paper, we present and discuss the performance of an LLM-based PII-detection system for Swedish learner essays.

1 Introduction

While there is a constant need for linguistic data — fuelled recently by the advent of Large Language Models (LLMs) which require copious amounts of training data — legal and ethical sharing and use thereof is problematic. The EU Commission (2016) severely limits the use and sharing of data containing Personal Identifiable Information (PII). However, the regulation also presents a possible solution: pseudonymizing the data, defined as: "[...] the processing of personal data in such a manner that the personal data can no longer be attributed to a specific data subject without the use of additional information, provided that such additional information is kept separately and is subject to technical and organisational measures to ensure that the personal data are not attributed to an identified or identifiable natural person" (Art. 4 of EU Commission, 2016). Within the field of Natural Language Processing (NLP), this definition becomes more narrow — and while various researchers formulate it slightly differently, we understand pseudonymization as "the process of replacing an individual's personal data with a pseudonym, which is not related to the original data," with the same end goal as outlined in the GDPR (Volodina et al., 2023).

Naturally, conducting such a de-identification procedure manually is extremely time-consuming and costly, especially when the data in question is copious and very sensitive (Berg and Dalianis, 2020). It would therefore be beneficial to be able to automatize the process in a reliable and robust way. While there is existing research on automated de-identification systems, many of them are restricted to specific domains (especially healthcare), and not as much work has been conducted on less structured types of input, which we expect to be more problematic due to more varied types of personal information as well as a higher likelihood of various kinds of errors or non-standard forms (e.g. in terms of spelling, syntax, or semantics). We choose to work with L2 (second language) learner essays, as this kind of texts not only fulfills the requirement of larger structural and thematic variety but, as Volodina et al. (2020) show, the essays are also likely to contain PIIs. Since L2 corpora are relevant for various research applications, developing models that can handle PII detection and replacement in this kind of texts would be useful.

What exactly constitutes sensitive information can differ across domains, documents, or even paragraphs, and is heavily context-dependent. We believe that algorithms could learn something akin to human intuition about what is personal and/or sensitive in the data. With this in mind, we experiment with an approach where none of the PII and sensitive categories are labeled for their classes (e.g. name, city, etc.), but are binary (personal/sensitive or not). This distinction is formalized as inside-outside-beginning (IOB) classes, where non-sensitive tokens are labeled O (outside), while sensitive tokens or token spans are labeled with B (beginning) and, in the case of multi-token sensitive elements, I (inside) for every token after

Proceedings of the Workshop on Computational Approaches to Language Data Pseudonymization
CALD-pseudo 2024, pages 54–63

the first one. We replace manually assigned categories in our dataset of learner essays in Swedish (SweLL-pilot, Volodina et al. (2016)) with B(I) and O, and fine-tune two Large Language Models (LLMs, `KB/bert-base-swedish-cased` and `bert-base-multilingual-cased`) to distinguish between the two types of tokens (Malmsten et al., 2020; Devlin et al., 2018). While we are aware that pseudonym generation is likely to rely on a predicted PII class, we decide to focus on the detection step, which can precede classification – presuming that such a step is necessary in a pseudonymization pipeline. Our hypothesis is that the model will learn to distinguish between sensitive and non-sensitive information in a given context, and potentially even capture more types of personal information than we at the moment envisage, helping us identify new classes that can be added to the taxonomy or refine the existing ones. Simultaneously, we hope to assess the usefulness of fine-tuned LLMs for PII detection, especially in more free-flowing and error-prone genres such as learner essays.

2 Prior Research

As previously mentioned, pseudonymization, as we understand it, entails the replacement of sensitive tokens or groups of tokens with new and somewhat unrelated — but still contextually appropriate — surrogates. The replacement of PII with a pseudonym presupposes a step at which the sensitive data is detected and possibly classified; recently Eder et al. (2022) conceptualized the pseudonymization pipeline as consisting of the two aforementioned steps.

While Lison et al. (2021) consider the pseudonym generation step to be more of an open question than the detection of PIIs themselves, many previously presented detection systems do not account for, for example, misspellings or otherwise non-normative writing, which is essential when working with data like learner essays (Eder et al., 2019). Although Accorsi et al. (2012) highlights the issues stemming from spelling variation, these issues seem to mostly pertain to specific genres, which so far have been underrepresented in PII detection research, as the bulk of the existing research is focused on medical data.

As shown by Yogarajan et al. (2020), many of the well-performing systems for PII detection in medical data rely on neural or hybrid approaches. Recently, Pilán et al. (2022) have released a text anonymization benchmark corpus consisting of texts from the legal domain, and presented the results obtained by several models. While their custom metrics rely at least partly on there being more than one possible way to annotate a text, they do provide overall recall and precision as well, with the best model — a LongFormer model with a large window size — reaching 91.9% recall and 83.6% precision; however, an F1 score is not reported. Grancharova and Dalianis (2021), in turn, fine-tuned a Swedish BERT model for Named Entity Recognition and Classification (NERC) in Swedish medical texts. The NER categories in the corpus utilized in their experiment are actually PHI categories, which could be considered a type of PII, rendering this task sufficiently similar to warrant a comparison.

They report precision and recall scores for various models, with the best of them (KB-BERT trained and tested on data from the same source) reaching a weighted precision score of 92.26% and a weighted recall score of 92.20% (with the weighted F1 of 92.23%). They also reach relatively good scores on M-BERT (multilingual BERT) with the same data setup - 88.99% recall and 90.51% precision (and F1 of 89.74%). While Berg and Dalianis (2020) argue that high recall is more desirable in PII detection systems than high precision, the latter is also important, as it means that the model is not over-detecting the sensitive data and flagging innocent passages. We believe that the alterations to the text should be kept to a necessary minimum as any changes made to the linguistic data may affect its future usability in various types of research (e.g. linguistics or machine learning). While our experiment is meant to test an approach similar to that of Grancharova and Dalianis (2021), it is worth keeping in mind that the data we use is less structured and may contain a bigger variety of personal information, as described in Volodina et al. (2020), which may lead to a worse performance by the system.

3 Materials and Methods

In this experiment, we utilize 445 learner essays from the SweLL-pilot corpus, representing a wide variety of learner levels, topics, and types of writing (e.g. descriptive or argumentative essays) (Volodina et al., 2016). Some of the essays contain PIIs, and some do not, predominantly due to the variation in types of writing and the prompts (e.g. a descriptive essay with the topic"about me" is much more likely to contain PIIs than an argumentative essay with the topic "stress in the modern society"). We use the unpseudonymized[1] versions of the texts. The essays have also been tokenized and reannotated with tags for PII categories using the SVALA tool according to the SweLL pseudonymization guidelines developed for the SweLL-gold corpus and the corresponding tagset (Wirén et al., 2019; Megyesi et al., 2021; Volodina, 2024). This annotation includes not only typically NER-like categories such as place names or surnames, but also e.g. names of professions or references to one's faith, with only the tokens deemed sensitive in a given context being annotated as such. In our experiments, we ignore the categories of sensitive information and only differentiate between sensitive and non-sensitive information. We transform the existing category annotation into an inside-outside-beginning (IOB) annotation to represent the difference between PIIs and non-PII tokens. Due to BERT-imposed input sequence limitations, we subdivide the essays into sections that are at most 100 tokens long,[2] resulting in a total of 651 such sections, out of which 165 contain at least one token of sensitive information.

The data is then balanced so that the data splits (training, testing, development) contain equally many passages with PIIs as passages without PIIs, meaning that these splits are composed of 165 fragments with PIIs and 165 randomly chosen fragments without PIIs out of 486 such fragments. Importantly, this does not mean that half of the tokens include sensitive information, and the actual distribution of sensitive and non-sensitive tokens can be seen in Table 1. We also calculate weights that represent class importance for later use with a weighted loss function using Scikit-learn's `compute_class_weight` function (Pedregosa et al., 2011). The class distribution and the calculated weights for the data used in the experiment are presented in Table 1.

[1]This version is used only within the context of the project that this experiment is conducted in and is unavailable for anyone except the project team. The released version of SweLL-pilot is anonymized and the access form is linked in Appendix A.

[2]While BERT's maximum input sequence length is 512, this applies to the sequence length after tokenization using the BERT tokenizer, which often divides words into sub-word units; since the sectioning of the essays occurred at a much earlier step than BERT tokenization due to the framework used, an arbitrary length was chosen to mitigate the impact of the BERT tokenizer and maximum sequence length.

	Instances (%)	Count	Weight
B	2.64%	1142	12.64419148
I	0.20%	86	167.90310078
O	97.16%	42091	0.34305829

Table 1: The proportions of token instances of classes in the data used in the experiment and the corresponding calculated class weights.

The PII-detection system used in this paper is based on modified code for token classification included in the `transformers` library (see Appendix A) (Wolf et al., 2020). This code allows for the fine-tuning of a model of choice hosted by HuggingFace for a token classification task like NER (Named Entity Recognition) or part-of-speech (POS) tagging; in our case, we have chosen to work with the BERT model for Swedish (`KB/bert-base-swedish-cased`, KB-BERT)[3] developed by the National Library of Sweden (Kungliga Biblioteket, KB) as well as a multilingual BERT model (`bert-base-multilingual-cased`, M-BERT)[4] (Malmsten et al., 2020; Devlin et al., 2018). This was done to mirror the setup utilized by Grancharova and Dalianis (2021) for an easier comparison of results; simultaneously, our hope is that using a multilingual model may help mitigate the effect the foreign tokens found in learner essays may have on the performance of the system, since those tokens may then be parsed as something other than an unknown word. Additionally, having an insight into whether multilingual models can be used for this type of task could be useful when working with languages that are only featured in multilingual models.

We have fine-tuned the models on 80% of our data (after balancing the set) twice, once with a standard `CrossEntropyLoss` loss function, and once with a weighted version thereof, with the intent of accounting for the class imbalance in a task of this type[5]. We have also reduced the batch size to 8 since due to the length of the samples we did not have the computational resources to process that much data in one batch. Aside from that, we have proceeded with the default settings for the script (notably, 3 epochs and AdamW optimizer

[3]`https://huggingface.co/KB/bert-base-swedish-cased`

[4]`https://huggingface.co/bert-base-multilingual-cased`

[5]Similarly to regular NER tasks, sensitive and not sensitive tokens are not equally prominent in the data, with the majority of the tokens being not sensitive.

with a learning rate of 5e-05). The fine-tuning process also makes use of another 10% of our data for evaluation between the epochs (development set).

The fine-tuned model has been tested on the held-out test set (another 10% of the data). The Transformers evaluation code calculates average evaluation metrics but here we also additionally calculate per-class metrics. Additionally, tokens misclassified by the models relative to the manually annotated gold standard have been extracted with their contexts and analyzed manually to see if any patterns of what the model struggled with could be identified.

4 Results and Discussion

4.1 Evaluation Metrics

The standard KB-BERT model (using an unweighted cross-entropy loss function) performs better in terms of accuracy, with the standard M-BERT and weighted KB-BERT only slightly behind. Surprisingly, the M-BERT model with a weighted loss function performs drastically worse, as shown in Table 2. However, it is important to remember that accuracy is not a weighted metric and that the O class outnumbers the other two.

Accuracy			
Standard model		Weighted model	
KB	M	KB	M
99.11%	97.78%	97.73%	29.16%

Table 2: The models' accuracy.

Due to the aforementioned class imbalance, we find it important to inspect measures like per-class recall and precision instead of just accuracy in order to gain a better understanding of the performance of the models. We additionally follow the example of Grancharova and Dalianis (2021) and provide combined scores for the "sensitive" classes (B and I).

	Recall			
	Standard model		Weighted model	
	KB	Multi	KB	Multi
B	82.57%	38.53%	92.66%	74.31%
I	14.29%	0.00%	57.14%	0.00%
O	99.67%	99.46%	97.93%	28.05%
B+I[6]	77.79%	35.83%	90.17%	69.11%

Table 3: The models' per-class recall.

	Precision			
	Standard model		Weighted model	
	KB	Multi	KB	Multi
B	86.54%	64.62%	58.38%	2.58%
I	100.00%	0.00%	18.18%	0.00%
O	99.41%	98.28%	99.78%	97.46%
B+I[8]	87.48%	60.09%	55.57%	2.40%

Table 4: The models' per-class precision.

The scores presented in Table 3 show that using a weighted loss function in KB-BERT models has improved the detection of the two classes that are used to denote the sensitive information (B and I), at the cost of a small drop in the recall for O.

Simultaneously, while it helps with the detection of the B class in M-BERT models, it has no effect on the detection of I and causes a drastic drop in the detection of O. It is rather clear that the models are struggling with the detection of I-tags, likely due to them being extremely infrequent in the data, with most of the sensitive data being restricted to single tokens. Comparing this with the results obtained by Grancharova and Dalianis (2021) for their sensitive data detection models for the medical domain, we achieve 90.17% recall on the sensitive data in our best model compared to their 92.20%, leading us to the conclusion that in terms of recall, our weighted KB-BERT model is performing rather well, especially taking into account the fact that the types of PII present in learner essays are more diverse and potentially harder to detect than those found in medical data (a more narrow domain). However, the same cannot be said about any of the M-BERT models which fail much more noticeably when trained with the current hyperparameters: our 69.11% for the weighted M-BERT model is much lower than 88.99% reported in the aforementioned research. This is further illustrated in Figure 1, Figure 2, Figure 3, and Figure 4, which depict normalized confusion matrices for the models' predictions, where the numbers on the main diagonal correspond to per-class recall.[7]

[6]Weighted average of scores for the two sensitive classes.

[7]Please note that any value differences stem from different rounding in the table than in the confusion matrices.

[8]Weighted average of scores for the two sensitive classes.

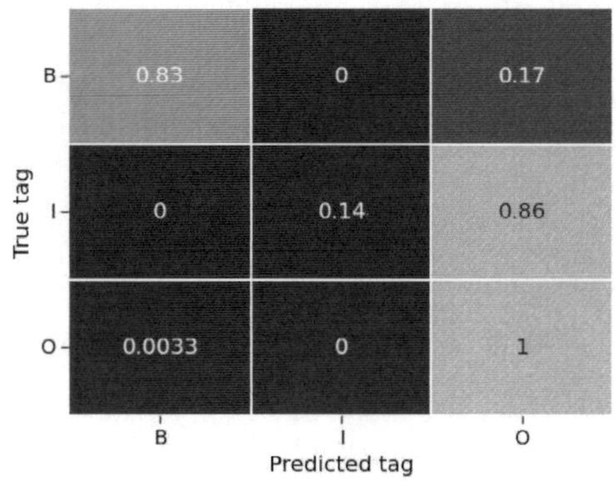

Figure 1: Normalized confusion matrix for PII detection with KB-BERT with the standard CrossEntropyLoss.

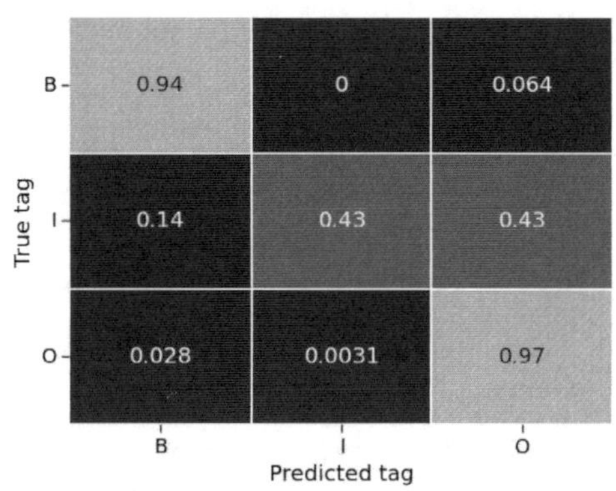

Figure 2: Normalized confusion matrix for PII detection with KB-BERT with the weighted CrossEntropyLoss.

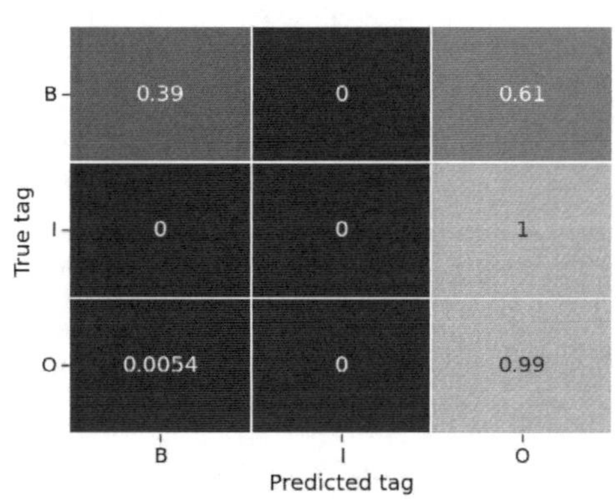

Figure 3: Normalized confusion matrix for PII detection with M-BERT with the standard CrossEntropyLoss.

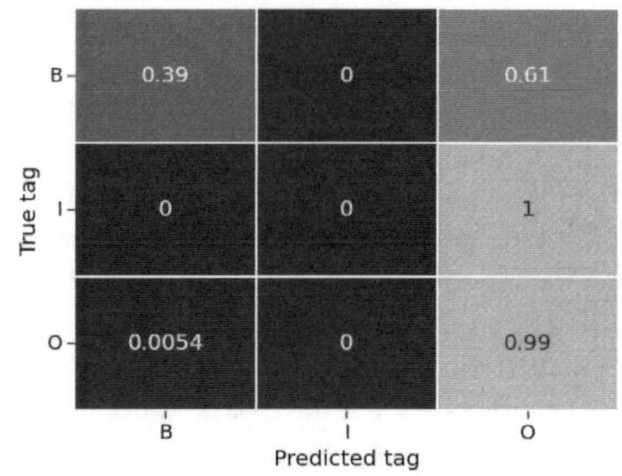

Figure 4: Normalized confusion matrix for PII detection with M-BERT with the weighted CrossEntropyLoss.

Contrary to the results for recall, precision for the sensitive classes is much better for the models without the weighted loss function, as shown in Table 4. Once again, the M-BERT models are overall performing worse, with the weighted version thereof achieving the worst result. This indicates that the weighted models are noticeably over-detecting tokens as sensitive — so although they now correctly identify more of the originally sensitive passages, they are also marking completely non-sensitive tokens as sensitive. While it is more important to correctly detect as many PIIs as possible, we are of the opinion that for the data to be useful for downstream tasks, such as semantic meaning extraction or information retrieval, it should be altered only as much as necessary, meaning that high precision would also be desirable.

One way to reconcile the need for considering both recall and precision in model evaluation is to look at the F1 score. One drawback of this score is that it assigns equal importance to its constituent parts, which is less ideal in the current scenario, where recall is considered to be more important. However, it is a widely used metric and it still allows us to compare the models to each other and to results from other research. Table 5 contains the per-class f1 scores alongside a weighted average of that score for the two sensitive classes.

In terms of the F1 score, the KB-BERT model with the standard cross-entropy loss function performs best on two out of three classes and as far as the combined B and I score is concerned. The KB-BERT with a weighted loss function slightly outperforms it on the I class. Both of the M-BERT models display significantly worse performance.

The standard KB-BERT model achieves the best

	F1			
	Standard model		Weighted model	
	KB	Multi	KB	Multi
B	84.51%	48.28%	71.63%	4.99%
I	25.00%	0.00%	27.59%	0.00%
O	99.54%	98.86%	98.85%	43.56%
B+I[9]	80.34%	44.89%	68.55%	4.64%

Table 5: The models' per-class F1 score.

result here - 87.48% weighted precision for the sensitive classes, which is still somewhat below 92.26% reported by Grancharova and Dalianis (2021); it is also not fair to compare only the highest results, as they are not achieved by the same model; the one with the best recall score only achieved 55.57% precision. When it comes to the F1 score, our best model (KB-BERT with a standard loss function) with a score of 80.34% on the sensitive classes is about 12 percentage points behind the best model for medical data, which is reported to have achieved 92.23% F1. This disparity stems from our model's decidedly lower precision.

Judging by all of the discussed metrics, KB-BERT models perform better than the multilingual BERT models. With the current hyper-parameters, the standard models suffer from relatively low recall, especially for the rarest class; weighted models, in turn, are over-detecting sensitive data, leading to lower precision. Nevertheless, the results seem to indicate that all the models except M-BERT with a weighted loss function are capable of distinguishing between sensitive and non-sensitive passages with a reasonable level of correctness. Importantly, the underdetection of the I class by all of the models suggests that they struggle with detecting multi-token spans of sensitive data.

It is also important to mention that we consider the task of learning to simply distinguish between sensitive and non-sensitive tokens or sequences of tokens to be more difficult than distinguishing specific classes of PIIs or PHIs, which is also reflected in the notably low precision of most of the models that we have trained. However, the results promisingly suggest that LLMs are indeed capable of learning, to some extent at least, what makes data sensitive in a given context.

[9]Weighted average of scores for the two sensitive classes.

4.2 Qualitative Prediction Analysis

A qualitative analysis of the predictions made by the models allows us to investigate what types of data marked as sensitive during manual annotation are particularly problematic for the models — and what kinds of generalizations lead to over-detection of PIIs they make. Importantly, due to the sensitive nature of the data used in this experiment sharing specific examples raises ethical concerns. We have decided to address this issue twofold: we manually pseudonymize the sensitive tokens in the examples and we provide the examples only in English (while simultaneously trying to mirror any kinds of learner errors).

The weighted M-BERT has failed to learn to differentiate between sensitive and non-sensitive data, as it does not mark some words with regular spelling (common Swedish given names, names of languages), and instead classifies words such as pronouns, determiners, some verbs as sensitive, in contexts where they with a great degree of certainty are not sensitive, as Examples 1 and 2 in Table 6 show. Simultaneously, some clearly sensitive tokens do not get recognized as such (Example 4). There are also instances of misspelled tokens being assigned the wrong category, but sometimes it is unclear whether the cause for the misclassification was the spelling or the model's disagreement as to what private data is, as in Example 3, where one could argue that *reltivs* "relatives" is a word denoting family members which could potentially be sensitive. This could be due to a language-specific model like KB-BERT being better at capturing specific semantic knowledge and being better able to generalize over e.g. street or place names; alternatively, it could be that while we have expected a multilingual model to improve the results since it would have representations for foreign language tokens, it actually struggled more with misspellings. While we did not explicitly notice that in our results, it is also possible that a multilingual model may have issues with tokens that have two separate meanings in two different languages.

The M-BERT model with the standard loss function, which has achieved low recall but somewhat higher precision appears to make more interpretable decisions: there are instances where this classification could be up for debate, and perhaps the token should have been marked as such by the annotator. This can be seen in Example 5, where *Stockholm* is not where the author lives, but

№	Token	Token in context	Prediction	Ground truth
		M-BERT WITH A WEIGHTED LOSS FUNCTION		
1	was	Historically, stress **was** a [...]	B	O
2	me	**me** and johnny at school sit	B	O
3	reltivs	Other **reltivs** have come	B	O
4	Alice	[...] they are called Sally, **Alice** and Sam.	O	B
		M-BERT WITHOUT A WEIGHTED LOSS FUNCTION		
5	Stockholm	We came to **Stockholm** city from Cairo directly	B	O
6	Germany	[...] one stress muc more in **Germany**.	B	O
7	Malmö	$$$$$[10] $$$ $$ $$$$s in **Malmö**. Later w$	O	B
8	Nobel street[11]	I live on **Nobel street**.	O	B
		KB-BERT WITH A WEIGHTED LOSS FUNCTION		
9	sweden	tim lives in the family in **sweden**	B	O
10	novmber	wynter is four months from **novmber** to February	B	O
11	small	because I have a **small** family here.	O	B
12	family	because I have a small **family** here.	B	I
		KB-BERT WITHOUT A WEIGHTED LOSS FUNCTION		
13	dad	and my **dad** was dizzy always	B	O
14	Cairo	**Cairo** has a verybig airport	B	O
15	Pierogi	they eat **Pierogi** which are traditional fud	O	B
16	%olis%	I am **$olis$**. We $$$$$$ $$$ $$	O	B
17	don't work[12]	I **don't work**.	O	B, I

Table 6: Examples of errors made by the M-BERT model with a weighted loss function.

constitutes an intermediate point in their travel, or in Example 6, where one can guess that someone writing about the reality of living in a given country in an argumentative essay has likely been born and raised there, or at least lived there for a longer period of time. We believe it is likely that in this case, the model has learned to classify all cities and countries that it has recognized as sensitive; this effect could at least partly be attributed to a possible imbalance between instances where such entities are not sensitive versus when they are sensitive.

When it comes to KB-BERT, the model with the weighted loss function provides even more examples of the model overgeneralizing certain entity types to always be sensitive — in the SweLL annotation, *Sweden* was not considered to be sensitive (as it was certain that all of the essays came from people living in Sweden), and yet in Example 9 the model predicts it to be sensitive. Similarly, *november* in Example 10 does not refer to a specific event in the author's life, but rather to a description of the climate, rendering it rather non-sensitive. Another interesting example here comes from two subsequent words in a sentence – since we differentiate between the start and the continuation of a sensitive passage, misclassifying the first token as non-sensitive, but classifying the second one as sensitive still leads to two errors, as in the case of the second error the class should be I, not B. Nevertheless, this suggests that a small fraction of the errors made by the model could be attributed to such cases, meaning that the model's performance is slightly better than the evaluation metrics may show.

The highest-scoring model in terms of evaluation metrics, KB-BERT without a weighted loss function, still has examples of the issue of overgeneralization (Example 14). However, it also illustrates that in some cases the annotators may have missed data that should be considered sensitive — like in Example 13, where the word for a specific family relation was not annotated as sensitive when it should have been according to the guidelines. Understandably, the model struggles with half-unintelligible tokens, such as in Example 16,

[10]$ is used to designate unintelligible handwriting.

[11]Names of streets are often just one token in Swedish.

[12]In Swedish the negation comes after the verb in the main clause, so in the original the I tag would refer to the negation, and the B tag to the verb. We have decided to display the two tokens together in the table for the sake of simplicity.

where a human annotator is perhaps better able to guess that the token refers to a nationality, while the model has very little to go off of, not just in the token, but also in the context. Finally, Example 15 shows that not all foreign-looking named entities get classified as sensitive, and that at least in the case of this sentence the model is not able to guess that a token would be sensitive just from the surrounding presence of the word "traditional" which describes it.

Both for M-BERT and KB-BERT, the models seem to run into difficulties when it comes to determining the sensitivity of data in cases where the tokens are misspelled, foreign, or surrounded by misspelled or unintelligible tokens, as in Examples 3, 7, or 10. While the model with a weighted loss function tends to flag more passages as sensitive (such as the ones in Examples 1–3, 9, and 10), the standard one errs on the side of caution in that regard (as in Examples 7 and 8, as well as 15).

One more notable feature shared by some of the under-detected PIIs is span. Most of the annotation in the data marks distinct tokens (e.g. a given name is separated from the surname, only the number of a bus or tram is marked as sensitive, etc.), and the multi-token instances are often somewhat longer passages that could be considered sensitive but do not fit into any of the categories in the annotation guidelines, e.g. talking about a political event or work status (e.g. being unemployed), as in Example 17. This shows how difficult detecting PII and determining what that concept means is, especially in the case where contextual information is essential for resolving whether a token is sensitive.

5 Conclusions

Within this paper we have presented the results of an investigation into the performance of LLMs on PII detection in learner essays, framing it as a task similar to Named Entity Recognition. We have shown that a finetuned `KB/bert-base-swedish-cased` model is capable of learning how to distinguish between sensitive and non-sensitive information in this kind of data, reaching up to 90.17% recall, suggesting that LLMs are able to approximate a human intuition when it comes to discerning what is sensitive in a given context, although they may struggle with overdetecting such data. We are also of the opinion that some of the model's disagreements with the original PII annotation could be informative when it comes to refining manual PII annotation, though perhaps not to the extent we would have wished for (the models did not discover any new kinds of PII).

While the current performance of the models is behind the ones presented by Grancharova and Dalianis (2021) (although they are relatively close in terms of recall) and the one discussed by Pilán et al. (2022) (comparing our top two models, one is slightly ahead in precision, but much worse in recall, while the other one has a similar recall with much worse precision), they are promising for PII detection in unstructured and non-standard texts in Swedish, and — with some improvements — a fine-tuned system like this could constitute a part of a pseudonymization pipeline. The current challenge is optimizing the model's hyperparameters so as to maximize the recall at the least possible cost to precision. In its current form, a weighted loss function does not seem to perform its function, but some method of accounting for class imbalance is necessary given the models' low performance on the I class.

Simultaneously, when discussing the performance of our models in relation to the ones reported by Grancharova and Dalianis (2021) we consider it relevant to mention that the latter were trained and tested on various medical datasets. We consider the medical domain to be much more regular in terms of the kinds of PII it may include (corresponding, in large part, to what the authors of that paper described as named entities), as well as less likely to include errors of various kinds. Therefore, PII detection in learner essays seems to us to be a more difficult task than PII detection in medical data.

6 Future Work

Aside from trying to optimize the model for this particular kind of data, we would like to see how well a model trained on our data would perform on other PII datasets for Swedish like the Stockholm EPR PHI Corpus, which consists of medical records or data from social media, which would also allow us to see what kinds of PII are present across domains, and what kinds are more domain-specific (Velupillai et al., 2009; Dalianis and Velupillai, 2010). Unfortunately, the TAB corpus mentioned earlier in the paper is in English, and therefore not suitable for such a comparison (Pilán et al., 2022).

Another step could be investigating to what extent the data from various domains like this can be combined in the fine-tuning process, possibly in a semi-supervised fashion, in order to produce a more universal PII detection model. The insights from the analysis of model predictions could help determine how to annotate data for sensitivity. In terms of the differences between KB-BERT and M-BERT it would be interesting to see whether the poor performance of the latter was indeed due to it being worse at handling misspelled tokens. It would also be really interesting to be able to utilize a Swedish version of the LongFormer architecture in order to see if more contextual information helps with PII detection — but, unfortunately, no such model exists as of now (Beltagy et al., 2020).

Finally, we aim to follow up this experiment with a pseudonym generation task where we intend to have LLMs simply generate suitable replacements for the passages flagged as sensitive, without the intermediate PII classification step, with only the surrounding context to inform the prediction.

Limitations

This paper presents only a short study, where we are not really striving to create the best possible model but we are instead more focused on exploring what personal information is and how it can be detected, with the only change from the default settings of the fine-tuning script being the use of a weighted loss function and smaller batch size (a technical constraint). Therefore, hyperparameter tuning may lead to a much better performance than the presented results.

While this approach may work well, it is not a universal solution, especially cross-linguistically, as it relies on a large language model like BERT, which need not be available for all the languages in the world.

Ethics Statement

Various kinds of linguistic data are likely to contain personal information, which has implications on how the data can be used in terms of ethics and even legality. This paper aims to investigate the use of pre-existing language models and small amounts of annotated data in a pseudonymization pipeline, possibly leading to an alleviation of this challenge.

Written consent was obtained for all the collected essays; the data was processed in accordance with the GDPR requirements and is made available individually on signing an agreement for use. At the moment of corpus release, no requirement for ethical review was relevant. The original, non-pseudonymized data is used strictly within the project, with real names never being disclosed, which is why we can share neither the data used in this paper nor the fine-tuned models.

Acknowledgements

This work has been possible thanks to the funding of two grants from the Swedish Research Council.

The project *Grandma Karl is 27 years old: Automatic pseudonymization of research data* has funding number 2022-02311 for the years 2023-2029.

The Swedish national research infrastructure Nationella Språkbanken is funded jointly by contract number 2017-00626 for the years 2018-2024, as well 10 participating partner institutions.

References

Pierre Accorsi, Namrata Patel, Lopez Cédric, Rachel Panckhurst, and Mathieu Roche. 2012. Seek&hide: Anonymising a french sms corpus using natural language processing techniques. *Linguisticae Investigationes*, 35:163–180.

Iz Beltagy, Matthew E. Peters, and Arman Cohan. 2020. Longformer: The long-document transformer.

Hanna Berg and Hercules Dalianis. 2020. A semi-supervised approach for de-identification of Swedish clinical text. In *Proceedings of the Twelfth Language Resources and Evaluation Conference*, pages 4444–4450, Marseille, France. European Language Resources Association.

Hercules Dalianis and Sumithra Velupillai. 2010. De-identifying swedish clinical text - refinement of a gold standard and experiments with conditional random fields. *Journal of biomedical semantics*, 1:6.

Jacob Devlin, Ming-Wei Chang, Kenton Lee, and Kristina Toutanova. 2018. Bert: Pre-training of deep bidirectional transformers for language understanding. *arXiv preprint arXiv:1810.04805*.

Elisabeth Eder, Ulrike Krieg-Holz, and Udo Hahn. 2019. De-identification of emails: Pseudonymizing privacy-sensitive data in a German email corpus. In *Proceedings of the International Conference on Recent Advances in Natural Language Processing (RANLP 2019)*, pages 259–269, Varna, Bulgaria. INCOMA Ltd.

Elisabeth Eder, Michael Wiegand, Ulrike Krieg-Holz, and Udo Hahn. 2022. "beste grüße, maria meyer" — pseudonymization of privacy-sensitive information in emails. In *Proceedings of the Thirteenth Language Resources and Evaluation Conference*, pages 741–752, Marseille, France. European Language Resources Association.

EU EU Commission. 2016. *General data protection regulation.* Official Journal of the European Union, 59, 1-88.

Mila Grancharova and Hercules Dalianis. 2021. Applying and sharing pre-trained BERT-models for named entity recognition and classification in Swedish electronic patient records. In *Proceedings of the 23rd Nordic Conference on Computational Linguistics (NoDaLiDa)*, pages 231–239, Reykjavik, Iceland (Online). Linköping University Electronic Press, Sweden.

Pierre Lison, Ildikó Pilán, David Sanchez, Montserrat Batet, and Lilja Øvrelid. 2021. Anonymisation models for text data: State of the art, challenges and future directions. In *Proceedings of the 59th Annual Meeting of the Association for Computational Linguistics and the 11th International Joint Conference on Natural Language Processing (Volume 1: Long Papers)*, pages 4188–4203, Online. Association for Computational Linguistics.

Martin Malmsten, Love Börjeson, and Chris Haffenden. 2020. Playing with Words at the National Library of Sweden – Making a Swedish BERT.

Beáta Megyesi, Lisa Rudebeck, and Elena Volodina. 2021. SweLL pseudonymization guidelines.

F. Pedregosa, G. Varoquaux, A. Gramfort, V. Michel, B. Thirion, O. Grisel, M. Blondel, P. Prettenhofer, R. Weiss, V. Dubourg, J. Vanderplas, A. Passos, D. Cournapeau, M. Brucher, M. Perrot, and E. Duchesnay. 2011. Scikit-learn: Machine learning in Python. *Journal of Machine Learning Research*, 12:2825–2830.

Ildikó Pilán, Pierre Lison, Lilja Øvrelid, Anthi Papadopoulou, David Sánchez, and Montserrat Batet. 2022. The Text Anonymization Benchmark (TAB): A Dedicated Corpus and Evaluation Framework for Text Anonymization.

Sumithra Velupillai, Hercules Dalianis, Martin Duneld, and Gunnar Nilsson. 2009. Developing a standard for de-identifying electronic patient records written in swedish: Precision, recall and f-measure in a manual and computerized annotation trial. *International journal of medical informatics*, 78:e19–26.

Elena Volodina. 2024. On two SweLL learner corpora – SweLL-pilot and SweLL-gold. In *Proceedings of the Huminfra Conference (HiC 2024)*, HiC 2024. Linköping University Electronic Press.

Elena Volodina, Yousuf Ali Mohammed, Sandra Derbring, Arild Matsson, and Beata Megyesi. 2020. Towards privacy by design in learner corpora research: A case of on-the-fly pseudonymization of Swedish learner essays. In *Proceedings of the 28th International Conference on Computational Linguistics*, pages 357–369, Barcelona, Spain (Online). International Committee on Computational Linguistics.

Elena Volodina, Simon Dobnik, Therese Lindström Tiedemann, and Xuan-Son Vu. 2023. Grandma Karl is 27 years old – research agenda for pseudonymization of research data.

Elena Volodina, Ildikó Pilán, Ingegerd Enström, Lorena Llozhi, Peter Lundkvist, Gunlög Sundberg, and Monica Sandell. 2016. SweLL on the rise: Swedish learner language corpus for European reference level studies. *Proceedings of the Tenth International Conference on Language Resources and Evaluation (LREC 2016), May 23-28, 2016, Portorož, Slovenia.*

Mats Wirén, Arild Matsson, Dan Rosén, and Elena Volodina. 2019. SVALA: Annotation of Second-Language Learner Text Based on Mostly Automatic Alignment of Parallel Corpora. In *Selected papers from the CLARIN Annual Conference 2018*, Selected papers from the CLARIN Annual Conference 2018. Linköping University Electronic Press.

Thomas Wolf, Lysandre Debut, Victor Sanh, Julien Chaumond, Clement Delangue, Anthony Moi, Pierric Cistac, Tim Rault, Rémi Louf, Morgan Funtowicz, Joe Davison, Sam Shleifer, Patrick von Platen, Clara Ma, Yacine Jernite, Julien Plu, Canwen Xu, Teven Le Scao, Sylvain Gugger, Mariama Drame, Quentin Lhoest, and Alexander M. Rush. 2020. HuggingFace's Transformers: State-of-the-art Natural Language Processing.

Vithya Yogarajan, Bernhard Pfahringer, and Michael Mayo. 2020. A review of automatic end-to-end de-identification: Is high accuracy the only metric? *Applied Artificial Intelligence*, 34(3):251–269.

A Appendix

- GitHub repository
- `transformers` code for token classification
- Application for access to the sanitized SweLL data

Data Anonymization for Privacy-Preserving Large Language Model Fine-Tuning on Call Transcripts

Nathan Zhang, Anne Paling, †Preston Thomas, Tania Habib,
Mahsa Azizi, Shayna Gardiner, Kevin Humphreys, †Frederic Mailhot*
Dialpad Canada Inc., †Dialpad Inc.
{nzhang, anne, preston, tania.habib, mahsa.azizi, sgardiner, kevin.humphreys, fred.mailhot}@dialpad.com

Abstract

Large language models in public-facing industrial applications must accurately process data for the domain in which they are deployed, but they must not leak sensitive or confidential information when used. We present a process for anonymizing training data, a framework for quantitatively and qualitatively assessing the effectiveness of this process, and an assessment of the effectiveness of models fine-tuned on anonymized data in comparison with commercially available LLM APIs.

1 Data Privacy in the era of LLMs

Recent progress in the capabilities of large language models (LLMs) (Devlin et al., 2019; Brown et al., 2020; Zhao et al., 2023), has led to their widespread adoption as the foundation for a variety of tasks in industrial and academic NLP (Bommasani et al., 2021). With parameter counts in the tens and hundreds of billions, these models require vast amounts of data to train and fine-tune (Hoffmann et al., 2022). At the same time, this overparameterization enables the memorization and potential leakage or extraction of large portions of LLMs' training data (Biderman et al., 2023; Carlini et al., 2023; Hartmann et al., 2023). Taken together, the required volume of training data and memorization capabilities of LLMs raise substantial issues concerning data privacy (Li et al., 2023). This risk is compounded because LLMs, like all supervised learners, perform best on test sets that have similar distributions to their training data. Thus, organizations seeking to deploy practically effective LLMs must train them with data that reflect the distribution of their deployment, with specific, sensitive data such as medical records or call transcripts leading to improved performance, but correspondingly greater risk of exposing that data to breaches or adversarial attacks (Nasr et al., 2023).

Furthermore, the lack of predictability and difficulty in constraining the outputs of LLMs means that including personal information (PI) in a training or fine-tuning data split runs the risk of this data being exposed in output generated by the model — even in the absence of adversarial attacks and when the task does not call for such data. Maximal mitigation of this risk requires removing all instances of PI from the training data, for example by excising any sentences that contain PI, or redacting any PI tokens. This kind of full exclusion leads to the challenge discussed above: depending on its use-case or deployment environment, a model may need to process and respond to PI at inference time. Suppressing all instances of PI, effectively removing the entire entity, is an approach seen when undertaking anonymization of structured data, however with unstructured text as in this context, this is not a realistic option due to resulting in training data that will be distributionally and semantically (Hassan et al., 2023) different from the input. Additionally, these types of data perturbations have been shown to negatively impact model performance (Malle et al., 2016, 2017). A more targeted approach to PI token redaction, tagging a set of candidate PI tokens with tags from a pre-defined taxonomy, is offered by some companies as a publicly-available anonymization service.

In this paper we leverage and modify such an anonymization service, proposing a nuanced approach to token redaction and risk assessment, showing that these measures can address the standard trade-off between privacy protection and performance. Our specific contributions are:

- Modifications to the taxonomy of PI categories defined by Google's Cloud Data Loss Prevention service[1] that serve to increase the

*Corresponding author. We would like to thank our anonymous reviewers for detailed and helpful feedback, and our colleagues Mel Andersen and Tere Roldán for their assistance with data annotation.

[1] https://cloud.google.com/security/products/

Proceedings of the Workshop on Computational Approaches to Language Data Pseudonymization CALD-pseudo 2024, pages 64–75

accuracy of anonymization of call transcripts generated by a proprietary *automatic speech recognition* (ASR) system.

- A framework for evaluating our modified anonymization pipeline with respect to *residual risk*: a measure encompassing both the likelihood of identifying an individual from residual PI that persists after anonymization, and the relative magnitude of harm based on the sensitivity of the remaining data. When properly calibrated, residual risk scoring for arbitrary combinations of PI or partial PI should closely align with the potential real-world impact of their exposure.

- A demonstration that a model fine-tuned with data that has been anonymized in accordance with our approach shows comparable F_1 and ROUGE scores to other popular LLMs on four in-domain tasks, with acceptable levels of residual risk.

1.1 Related Work

Data anonymization Elliot et al. (2020) present a framework for data anonymization, including a taxonomy of identifiers with different risk/exposure profiles. The framework's purpose is to furnish practical understanding of anonymization for use in business or organizational contexts. It is designed to control the risk of unintended re-identification and disclosure.

The problem of automated data anonymization specifically in the context of textual data is investigated by Lison et al. (2021). They draw links between work done in this area in the fields of NLP and privacy-preserving data publishing, and highlight some general challenges, including the trade-off between data utility and residual risk, and how to assess the quality of anonymization.

Privacy-preserving LLM/ML training Xu et al. (2021) provide a systematic review of existing privacy-preserving machine learning (PPML) approaches. They propose a Phase, Guarantee, and Utility based model to understand and guide the evaluation of various PPML solutions by decomposing their privacy-preserving functionalities.

Plant et al. (2022) empirically investigate the extent to which personal information is encoded in the representations of a variety of widely-available pre-trained LLMs. They demonstrate a positive correlation between the complexity of a model, the data volume used in pre-training, and data leakage. In addition, they present an evaluation and comparison of some popular privacy-preserving algorithms on a large multi-lingual sentiment analysis data set annotated with demographic information (location, age and gender). Their results show that larger and more complex models are more prone to leaking private information, and hence that the use of privacy-preserving methods is necessary. In addition to the preceding domain-general investigations, Yin and Habernal (2022) and Guerra-Manzanares et al. (2023) investigate some of the challenges of privacy-preserving training for machine learning and language modeling in the legal and healthcare domains, including increased resource needs to address the high computational complexity of some methods (e.g. homomorphic encryption), and privacy/accuracy trade-offs for methods with strong guarantees (e.g. differential privacy).

2 Data

The data set to be anonymized consists of transcripts generated by an internal proprietary ASR system. Raw transcripts are passed through an inverse text normalization module to generate final formatted transcripts. The transcripts in the data set include phone and video conference conversations between at least one and usually two or more speakers in business contexts, such as voicemails (single speaker), call center conversations (typically two speakers) and internal company meetings (two or more).

Transcripts generated from an ASR system are imperfect due to characteristics common to businesses, such as noisy environments, fast or quiet speakers, and poor-quality microphones. Recognition errors propagate to the final transcription, which can create difficulties in applying and evaluating the anonymization process.

3 Anonymization Process

Mindful of the ongoing discussion over the appropriate terminology for such processes (Garfinkey, 2015), we use the term "anonymization" herein because the intended outcome of our method is that no individual can be identified from the resulting text. Additionally, specifying anonymization distinguishes our method from *pseudonymization*, which appears superficially similar in that it includes replacing PI with tokens, e.g. *[PERSON_NAME_1]*.

dlp

The difference is that pseudonymization maintains a consistent mapping of the replacement token across conversations, potentially permitting later reidentification, whereas our process reuses these de-identified tokens across conversations, functionally eliminating the possibility of using them for re-identification purposes.

3.1 PI identification

There are several commercial offerings for PI identification and anonymization of text data. We surveyed services by Amazon,[2] Microsoft,[3] and Google.[4] We selected Google's Cloud Data Loss Prevention (DLP) service due to its broader coverage of PI categories. The DLP service defines a taxonomy of *information types*, or *infoTypes*; kinds of sensitive data such as names, email addresses, and telephone numbers.[5] An additional advantage of using the DLP service was the in-house access to data stored in BigQuery[6] and the ease of creating a configuration template to set up asynchronous jobs for large volumes of data, which was well suited for our use case.

In the PI identification process, we included most of the global infoTypes from the available taxonomy, as well as those infoTypes which are specific to the US and Canada (e.g. social security or social insurance numbers). A preliminary analysis suggested that the *ETHNIC_GROUP*, *GENDER*, *DATE*, and *TIME* infoTypes had a much higher rate of false positives (FPs) in our data sets, and so we excluded them. The taxonomy also includes categories for human names. The categories *FEMALE_NAME*, *MALE_NAME*, *FIRST_NAME*, and *LAST_NAME* are individually and collectively subsets of the *PERSON_NAME* infoType, and so we retain the latter while excluding all of the former.

We made the following modifications to DLP's PI identification to improve its performance on our data set:

1. **Exclusion List:** On the basis of the most frequent FPs seen in the masked transcripts we created an exclusion list for the *PERSON_NAME*, *ORGANIZATION_NAME*, and *LOCATION* infoTypes.

2. **Custom dictionary:** A custom dictionary was added to the PI detection configuration for the two infoTypes of *PERSON_NAME* and *ORGANIZATION_NAME* to reduce the number of false negatives (FNs) and increase the chance of correctly detecting names of organizations and people in the transcripts. Both of these resources were developed from a proprietary database of company and user names.

3. **Letters and digits**: After preliminary evaluation of the DLP API on our data, two additional infoTypes are created and added to the identification configurations:

    - *Spelled words:* Our transcription engine transcribes and formats letter sequences, for example verbally spelled-out words, with hyphens as separators e.g. A-L-P-H-A. The DLP API fails to detect and mask these instances, leaving potential PI in the anonymized data. A regular expression pattern to detect such groups in the transcript was added to the custom dictionary.
    - *Numbers:* Although our transcription engine can successfully decode and format digit sequences such as phone numbers, if a user repeats digits, or there is a transcription error such as "four" mistranscribed as "for", there is the potential for an unformatted sequence of digits to appear in the transcripts, which may not be detected by the DLP API. We therefore added a regular expression to detect numeric sequences of length 3, reducing the risk of missing potentially identifiable data due to mistranscription.

4. **Usernames:** Although they fall within the scope of DLP's built-in *GENERIC_ID* infoType, usernames such as *enigma52* or *Mrbigchef* were consistently not tagged as potential PI by the DLP service. We identified instances where these unmasked usernames were used across multiple social media platforms, or were some combination of multiple pieces of PI such as *first initial + last name*, *first name + last name* or *first name + birth*

[2] https://docs.aws.amazon.com/transcribe/latest/dg/pii-redaction.html

[3] https://learn.microsoft.com/en-us/azure/ai-services/language-service/personally-identifiable-information/how-to-call

[4] https://cloud.google.com/dlp/docs/sensitive-data-protection-overview

[5] For a complete list, see https://cloud.google.com/dlp/docs/infotypes-reference.

[6] https://cloud.google.com/bigquery

Original Transcript
Pam: This is Pam calling from Dunder Mifflin, may I speak to Jim?
Anonymized Transcript
[PERSON_NAME_1]: This is *[PERSON_NAME_1]* calling from *[ORGANIZATION_NAME_1]*, may I speak to *[PERSON_NAME_2]*?

Table 1: Example of context-aware anonymization

year, and in each of these instances could be used to identify the user.

The DLP service can detect domain or data-specific entities via the creation of a *hotword regex* (regular expression). We improved the detection accuracy of *GENERIC_ID* and *PERSON_NAME* in two ways. Firstly, we created a hotword regex for mentions of the word *user name* in our data, e.g. `(username|user name|Username|user ID)` and defined a context window of 100 characters around the hotword regex as an area of higher likelihood username detection. Secondly, we added a custom regex to the *GENERIC_ID* infoType to detect alphanumeric sequences of a certain length and commonly-used conditions for creating a username. Together, these approaches increased the hit rates for usernames up to 66% in our data set.

5. **Context-aware anonymization:** DLP does not offer means of differentiating tokens or instances of identified infoTypes, thus losing semantic information in the application of the anonymized text. In order to preserve context for later analysis, each masked span is assigned a unique numeric ID within the call. Multiple instances of the same masked information are assigned the same ID. See Table 1 for an example. [7]

4 Residual Risk Analysis

4.1 Identifying and annotating residual risks

Transcripts that were redacted using Google's DLP were subsequently annotated by humans to identify any residual PI that had not been detected, with a subset being subject to a second pass for verification.[8] Annotation of residual PI proved to be challenging, requiring multiple iterations of the guidelines with our annotators. Table 2 shows the output of post-anonymization annotation on a fictitious example.

Annotators did not tag instances of undetected PI that were not relevant to personal identification, even if there was an associated infoType. For example, DLP redacts generic ID numbers, but missed instances of these were only tagged if they could contribute to identifying an individual — for instance, organization-internal order numbers were not tagged, while a business registration license number would be. This choice was made because our goal was not to evaluate the accuracy of the PI tagging *per se*, but rather to quantify the risk of residual PI after anonymization. In Table 2, a transcription error results in partial detection, hence only partial anonymization, of the order number. It is not annotated, however, because the residual partial information of an internal order number is not usable for identifying the speaker.

Given the unstructured nature of transcript data and potential transcription errors, PI may be imperfectly formatted, so it may occur that only a portion of a span of PI is detected and tagged. To account for such cases, we associate with any given tag *[TAG]* a *TAG_PARTIAL* tag to be used by the annotators when only part of the PI is not anonymized. Table 2 demonstrates such cases; Person 1's last name and Person 2's email domain name are marked as *_PARTIAL*.

We found that the most common infoTypes missed by the de-identification process are *PRODUCT* and *ORGANIZATION*. There are two scenarios in which *PRODUCT* and *ORGANIZATION* are mentioned in a conversation: a common product or organization that can be used as a conversation topic, and the specific product or organization the speaker associates with. There is quite a difference between a person discussing using an iPhone from Apple and a person selling a product for their own company — the former does not provide much insight into identifying the speaker, but the latter does. However, DLP PI identification doesn't differentiate and doesn't have a consistent pattern in identifying the product and organization in the two scenarios. Therefore, in our evaluation, we only consider the missed product or organization to contain residual risk if they are closely related to the speaker. To illustrate, in Table 2, *Dunder Mifflin*

[7]Note that numeric IDs do not persist across calls, which would cross into pseudonymization and raise a reidentification risk.

[8]While we made some effort to mitigate false positives, this is not an issue that impacts our discussion here, which is concerned with preventing the leakage of PI.

Original Transcripts
Person 1: Dunder Mifflin, this is Rachel green speaking.
Person 2: Hi, this is mark from ABC Trust Fund, we just ordered a set of paper
and they have worse quality than staples. We would like to return and get refund.
Person 1: Okay, what is the order number?
Person 2: It's B. 231 C. for A. two.
Person 1: And the email for that order?
Person 2: It's M-K two one @abc.com
Anonymized Transcripts
Person 1: Dunder Mifflin, this is ***[PERSON_NAME_1]*** green speaking.
Person 2: Hi, this is ***[PERSON_NAME_2]*** from ***[ORGANIZATION_NAME_1]***,
we just ordered a set of paper and they have worse quality than staples.
We would like to return and get refund.
Person 1: Okay, what is the order number?
Person 2: It's B. ***[NUMERIC]*** C. for A. two.
Person 1: And the email for that order?
Person 2: It's M-K two one ***[EMAIL_1]***
Anonymized + Annotated Transcripts
Person 1: ***(Dunder Mifflin)[MISSED_ORGANIZATION_NAME_SPEAKER]***, this
is ***[PERSON_NAME_1] (Green)[MISSED_PERSON_NAME_PARTIAL]*** speaking.
Person 2: Hi, this is ***[PERSON_NAME_2]*** from ***[ORGANIZATION_NAME_1]***,
we just ordered a set of paper and they have worse quality than ***(staples)[MISSED_ORGANIZATION_NAME]***.
We would like to return and get refund.
Person 1: Okay, what is the order number?
Person 2: It's B. ***[NUMERIC]*** C. for A. two.
Person 1: And the email for that order?
Person 2: It's ***(M-K two one)[MISSED_EMAIL_PARTIAL] [EMAIL_1]***

Table 2: Example of post-anonymization annotation of residual PI. Missed PI is enclosed in parentheses and assigned a tag derived from the associated infoType.

was marked with the tag *_SPEAKER* to denote the risk associated with the missed PI, while *Staples* was not as it does not associate with any speakers in the conversation.

4.2 Quantifying residual risk

To assess residual risk for a conversation, we must first quantify the risk for each infoType. We begin by distinguishing *direct* and *indirect* identifiers, following Elliot et al. (2020):

- **Direct Identifier:** A variable or set of variables specific to an individual (e.g. name, address, phone number, bank account) that are explicitly or commonly used for the purpose of identification. These identifiers have a comparatively higher risk profile.
- **Indirect Identifier:** Information that in isolation does not enable identification (e.g. gender, nationality, city of residence), but may do so in combination with other indirect identifiers and/or background knowledge. These identifiers have a reduced but non-zero risk profile.

Residual risk is assigned an integer score ranging from 0 to 5. As stated above, for direct identifiers such as a person's name, credit card number, passport number, or social security/insurance number, we assign a maximal risk score of 5, to account for both the specificity of the identifier (a proxy for the likelihood of re-identification) and the impact of potential misuse. For indirect identifiers like company name or city of residence, we assign a risk score of 2 or 3. These risk categorizations for different infoTypes were developed in collaboration with privacy counsel. For the full list of categorizations and scores, see Table 6 in Appendix A.

For partially-redacted PI, tagged with the *_PARTIAL* annotation, the risk score of the associated tag is halved and rounded up or down to the next higher or lower integer, depending on the risk profile. For example, if the tag *[MISSED_EMAIL]* has a score of 3, then the score for *[MISSED_EMAIL_PARTIAL]* becomes $\lfloor 3/2 \rfloor = 1$. In the case of *[PERSON_NAME]*, which has a base score of 5, we round the score for *[MISSED_PERSON_NAME]* *up* to 3 to account for the wide variety of circumstances in which *[MISSED_PERSON_NAME_PARTIAL]* can occur. As noted above, we consider both first names and last names as *_PARTIAL* because the *[PERSON_NAME]* infoType is a superset of the other

[_NAME] infoTypes and using both created inconsistencies.

To calculate the residual risk score for an entire conversation, we sum the scores of the *[MISSED_]* tags, avoiding double-counting of multiple instances of a given token of missed PI. For example, in a conversation with four instances of *(Marc)([MISSED_PERSON_NAME_PARTIAL])*, the risk score contributed by this tag would be 3 rather than 12 ($= 4 \times 3$). Note that there can be variations in the spelling and formatting of a given token of PI due to ASR transcription error e.g. *Mark*, *Marc*, *M-A-R-K*. In this case, we consider them as a single piece of PI in three instances instead of different PIs if the annotators determine it is most likely a reference to the same entity.[9]

For the example in Table 2, the total residual risk is calculated as follows (tag names are shortened for consideration of space):

$$\begin{aligned} MISSED\_ORG\_NAME\_SPEAKER &= 2 \\ MISSED\_PERS\_NAME\_PARTIAL &= \lceil 5/2 \rceil = 3 \\ MISSED\_EMAIL\_PARTIAL &= \lfloor 3/2 \rfloor = 1 \\ \text{Total\_Risk\_Score} &= 2 + 3 + 1 = 6 \end{aligned} \tag{1}$$

The score assigned to $MISSED\_ORG\_NAME\_SPEAKER$ is 2 (see Appendix A, whereas the $PERSON$ and $EMAIL$ identifiers, being tagged $PARTIAL$ are halved and round up (down, resp), as discussed in Section 4.2. Note that the $MISSED\_ORGANIZATION\_NAME$ tag is not included in the calculation above as it is assigned a score of zero, because it does not represent a conversational participant, but is simply the name of a company.

4.3 Successful anonymization at the population level

We wish to know what proportion of a corpus of anonymized conversational transcripts carry an unacceptable residual risk profile. Pursuant to some preliminary data analysis, and in the absence of strong arguments to the contrary, we make the simplifying assumption that residual risks scores are well modeled by a normal distribution, $\mathcal{N} \sim (\mu, \sigma)$.

Given the previously-defined risk scores for each category, and our assumption of residual risk score normality, we define the following simple criterion as a measure of "successful" anonymization of a given conversational transcript:

$$\mu + \sigma < 5 \tag{2}$$

That is, we want the distribution of residual risk scores in our corpus of anonymized transcripts to be such that their mean plus one standard deviation is less than 5. We select 5 as our threshold of acceptability for the following reasons: (i) it is the risk score for a single occurrence of a direct identifier, which carries a maximal residual risk profile (high likelihood of re-identification and high impact of misuse), and (ii) it is equal to a combination of two complementary indirect identifiers such as company name + person's first name. Thus, 5 represents an easily-administerable target for assessing whether PI in the output of automated processes is sufficiently reduced to warrant more detailed review (see 4.5, below). We manually reviewed a set of high-scoring (above criterion) transcripts to ensure that this threshold met our needs.

Our assumption that residual risk is normally distributed implies that approximately 16% of our corpus of anonymized conversations carry a residual risk greater than 5.[10] Upon review of sample conversations, we find that anonymized transcripts with risk scores that are above the threshold—but do not have direct identifiers as part of the score—do not in practice enable re-identification. This is because as the indirect identifiers found in the masked text do not in general have a compounding effect. While we cannot *guarantee* the impossibility of re-identification in such, the risk after review was deemed acceptable. Table 3 provides an illustrative example: the total residual risk score is 6, with three independent instances of PI that do not combine to increase the risk of identification of any individual in the conversation.

We assessed the strength of our criterion manually, with anonymized call transcripts sampled from our corpora of business conversations in customer support, sales, videoconferencing, and direct call contexts. As shown in Table 4, after anonymization, human annotation of residual PI, and risk score assignment, none of the sampled corpora carried un-

[9]There is a potential difficulty here for conversations including multiple participants with the same name. We hope to address this in a future iteration of this work.

[10]Recall that one standard deviation to each side of the mean of a normal distribution accounts for approximately 68% of the probability mass. Since we are only worried about one tail of the distribution, i.e. the proportion with score greater than 5, we have one half of the tails' probability mass included in our coverage, for a total of 84%.

Person 1: Hi *[PERSON_NAME_2]*. This is *[PERSON_NAME_3]* calling back from *(XYZ lawyer)(MISSED_ORGANIZATION_NAME_SPEAKER)*.
Person 2: Oh, hi.
Person 1: I am calling regarding your request to change your business name on *(IRS dot gov)(MISSED_URL)* website.
Person 2: Oh, yes, I want it to be changed to *(ABC incorporated) (MISSED_ORGANIZATION_NAME_SPEAKER)*.

Table 3: Example conversation where residual risk score over-represents practical impact

acceptable risk profiles with our criterion (although several did so at $\mu + 2\sigma$).

We conclude that a target residual risk score of 5 represents a conservative but readily achievable level of assurance that the anonymization procedure is effective.

Context	Count	Mean	STD	P95	Max	$\mu + \sigma$
Customer Support 1	100	0.7	1.4	3.1	6	2.1
Customer Support 2	98	1.3	2.1	6.0	11	3.4
Meetings	99	1.2	3.1	6.1	20	4.3
Sales Calls	100	0.6	1.3	3.1	6	1.9
1-to-1 Phone Calls	100	1.0	1.7	5.0	8	2.7
Total	498	1.0	2.0	5.0	20	3.0

Table 4: Residual risk analysis

4.4 Results

We sampled 498 conversations across four business communication products to ensure the representation of different conversation contexts, such as video conferencing, customer support, and sales calls. Table 4 shows the residual risk statistics of the five data sets.

Conversations in the video conferencing data set tend to be longer than the other data sets, with word counts five to six times that in other data sets. [11] For the samples with high residual risks, the identified PIs are not compounding, i.e., they include multiple indirect identifiers that all refer to different people.

After the residual risk score passes the success criterion to demonstrate quantitatively that the anonymization process reliably reduces risk to an acceptable level, we conduct a red-team exercise to stress test the resulting output.

4.5 Red-Teaming

The term "red team" originates in the military context: a red team is a group that assumes the role of an adversary, simulating attacks to identify vulnerabilities so that they can be resolved before a real attacker can exploit them. In the context of anonymization, this means "attacking" the de-identified output using common internet resources (e.g. search engines) and creative thinking to attempt to re-identify participants. "Success" of the exercise in our context — PI protection — means that the adversary is unable to identify an individual based on remaining unmasked information in the data set.

The red team for this exercise consisted of data engineers, applied scientists, computational linguists, privacy counsel, and a security advisor.

We sampled 200 conversations across different conversation contexts for the red-teaming practice. The conversations were anonymized using the modified DLP method described above.[12] Our red team found that of 200 full conversations, 181 calls (90.5%) were fully anonymized (no PI identified by the red team) and 19 calls (9.5%) showed some residual PI. However, the team determined that even with creative research and inference, none of the remaining 19 calls contained enough PI to successfully identify any individual, meaning that the data set could be safely used to train an LLM with no risk of exposing identifiable PI in later generative tasks. The failure of the red team to achieve its goal is a strong indication of the success of our anonymization methods.

With the proposed anonymization workflow successfully passing both quantitative and qualitative evaluation, we conducted LLM fine-tuning experiments to demonstrate the usability of the anonymized data for downstream tasks.

5 Privacy-Preserving LLM Training

Given a successfully anonymized data set, it can be used in combination with training prompts to

[11] Meetings, the main source of video conferencing call data, are typically longer and have more speakers than audio-only calls.

[12] The conversations considered by the red team were not annotated with *MISSED_* labels, because this annotation step was only used during the calibration and quantitative evaluation of the automated de-identification method.

fine-tune an LLM. As the training prompts contain no PI either, the combined fine-tuning data set contains no PI. If the model remains suitably performant, this demonstrates the ability to benefit from highly relevant domain-specific (i.e. real-world) training data while substantially reducing or even eliminating the risk of leakage or extraction.

5.1 Model

We used the "Chat" version of the LLaMA-2 model (Touvron et al., 2023) with 7B parameters as our base model.[13] LLaMA-2 is an open-source LLM developed by Meta. We chose LLaMA-2-7B as it showed comparable performance to larger models with a reduced cost of deployment. This base model was fine-tuned with a Text-to-Text Transfer Transformer (Raffel et al., 2020) on 59000 external samples and 13000 in-domain conversations. In the following, we refer to our fine-tuned LLM as DialpadGPT.

5.2 Experiment

After the model was fine-tuned, we sampled 400 LLM outputs across four downstream tasks of interest (100 outputs per task), involving both generation and classification:

- **Action Item:** Generate a description of a well-defined task to be completed after the call conversation.
- **Summarization:** Generate a summary of the conversation.
- **Call Purpose:** Classify the call into one of a pre-defined group of broad conversational themes, and the speaker intention and/or attitude.
- **Call Outcome:** Classify the call into one of a pre-defined group of categories that specify the result of the call e.g. complaint resolved, callback requested.

The four tasks were included in the fine-tuning process. All inputs provided to the model to generate output samples were anonymized using the process described above (the process used on the fine-tuning data set).

5.3 Results

Human annotators manually reviewed the outputs for each task and found no instances of PI in any of the output samples — that is, each piece of PI remained anonymized in the output.

Model performance on the aforementioned test set is shown in Table 5, which compares ROUGE-1 scores (Lin, 2004) and F_1 scores of DialpadGPT to the following commercial LLMs:

- **GPT-3.5:** GPT-3.5 is the model behind OpenAI's[14] ChatGPT (Laskar et al., 2023). We use the *gpt-3.5-turbo-0613* model, which has a maximum context length of 4096 tokens.
- **GPT-4:** GPT-4 is the latest LLM released by OpenAI (OpenAI, 2023), which has a maximum context length of 8192 tokens. In this experiment, we evaluate two versions of the model: GPT-4 (*gpt-4-0613*) and GPT-4 Turbo (*gpt-4-1106-preview*).
- **PaLM-2:** PaLM-2 (Anil et al., 2023) is an LLM developed by Google. It leverages the mixture of objectives technique (Anil et al., 2023) and significantly outperforms the original PaLM (Chowdhery et al., 2023) model. We use the *text-bison@001 model*, which has an input context window length of 8192 tokens.[15]

Across two generative tasks and two classification tasks, DialpadGPT, fine-tuned with anonymized data, outperforms all four popular commercial models.

6 Conclusion

In this paper, we presented a method for improving data anonymization on transcripts of business conversations using a publicly available service. We proposed a framework for quantitative and qualitative criteria for anonymization (residual risk scoring plus red team review), and showed that an LLM fine-tuned with data anonymized by the proposed workflow on relevant tasks has superior performance compared to commercially available LLMs. This shows LLMs are still able to understand and leverage contextual information without access to those key entities. In practice, we found that having some key entities like user or company names is helpful for some downstream tasks. In future work we will assess the performance of LLMs

[13] `https://huggingface.co/meta-llama/Llama-2-7b`

[14] `https://platform.openai.com/docs/models/`

[15] Available via Google's *VertexAI* platform. `https://cloud.google.com/vertex-ai/docs/generative-ai/model-reference/text`

Models/Tasks	Summarization ROUGE-1	Action Items ROUGE-1	Call Purpose F_1	Call Outcome F_1
DialpadGPT	**0.6096**	**0.5532**	**0.6562**	**0.738**
GPT-3.5	0.4957	0.3918	0.5078	0.6638
GPT-4	0.5783	0.5483	0.5508	0.6114
GPT-4 Turbo	0.5243	0.4143	0.6289	0.6812
PaLM-2	0.4832	0.4629	0.4492	0.4803

Table 5: Comparison between LLMs on downstream tasks of interest.

fine-tuned on an augmented anonymized data set, with names substituted by gender-neutral names and companies substituted by synthetic companies.

7 Limitations

One limitation of relying on a commercial system for data anonymization is that it is not always clear how to improve the process when unexpected results are obtained. With the improvements we made to the system, person and company name are still the infoTypes most likely to have false negatives, especially in lexically ambiguous cases like the name *Mark*[16] or with uncommon or unusually formatted company names.

In addition, the use of proprietary data for evaluating the results of fine-tuning LLMs renders direct comparison to other organizations' models challenging. Despite the low residual risk and resulting high confidence in the anonymization of the data sets, privacy best practices nonetheless caution against publishing our resulting data sets (Narayanan and Shmatikov, 2007). That being said, the overall methodology described here is certainly replicable, using a publicly available anonymization API, with task or domain-specific modifications to the PI taxonomy, and with the residual risk threshold tuned appropriate to the use case.

Finally, in our evaluation we mainly focused on the recall/hit-rate of the PI tagging. The precision/recall trade-off in machine learning suggests that an anonymization system with very high recall, i.e. poor precision, will lose context and generate data that cannot be used in LLM training. In practice, however, we did not observe such cases and our experiment showed that LLMs are still able to capture enough context after the anonymization.

[16]The person's name *Mark* and verb *mark* are often confused in the formatting process in terms of casing and thus fail to be identified as PI in the anonymization process.

References

Rohan Anil, Andrew M Dai, Orhan Firat, Melvin Johnson, Dmitry Lepikhin, Alexandre Passos, Siamak Shakeri, Emanuel Taropa, Paige Bailey, Zhifeng Chen, et al. 2023. Palm 2 technical report. *arXiv preprint arXiv:2305.10403*.

Stella Biderman, USVSN Sai Prashanth, Lintang Sutawika, Hailey Schoelkopf, Quentin Anthony, Shivanshu Purohit, and Edward Raff. 2023. Emergent and predictable memorization in large language models.

Rishi Bommasani, Drew A. Hudson, Ehsan Adeli, Russ Altman, Simran Arora, Sydney von Arx, Michael S. Bernstein, Jeannette Bohg, Antoine Bosselut, Emma Brunskill, Erik Brynjolfsson, S. Buch, Dallas Card, Rodrigo Castellon, Niladri S. Chatterji, Annie S. Chen, Kathleen A. Creel, Jared Davis, Dora Demszky, Chris Donahue, Moussa Doumbouya, Esin Durmus, Stefano Ermon, John Etchemendy, Kawin Ethayarajh, Li Fei-Fei, Chelsea Finn, Trevor Gale, Lauren E. Gillespie, Karan Goel, Noah D. Goodman, Shelby Grossman, Neel Guha, Tatsunori Hashimoto, Peter Henderson, John Hewitt, Daniel E. Ho, Jenny Hong, Kyle Hsu, Jing Huang, Thomas F. Icard, Saahil Jain, Dan Jurafsky, Pratyusha Kalluri, Siddharth Karamcheti, Geoff Keeling, Fereshte Khani, O. Khattab, Pang Wei Koh, Mark S. Krass, Ranjay Krishna, Rohith Kuditipudi, Ananya Kumar, Faisal Ladhak, Mina Lee, Tony Lee, Jure Leskovec, Isabelle Levent, Xiang Lisa Li, Xuechen Li, Tengyu Ma, Ali Malik, Christopher D. Manning, Suvir P. Mirchandani, Eric Mitchell, Zanele Munyikwa, Suraj Nair, Avanika Narayan, Deepak Narayanan, Benjamin Newman, Allen Nie, Juan Carlos Niebles, Hamed Nilforoshan, J. F. Nyarko, Giray Ogut, Laurel Orr, Isabel Papadimitriou, Joon Sung Park, Chris Piech, Eva Portelance, Christopher Potts, Aditi Raghunathan, Robert Reich, Hongyu Ren, Frieda Rong, Yusuf H. Roohani, Camilo Ruiz, Jack Ryan, Christopher R'e, Dorsa Sadigh, Shiori Sagawa, Keshav Santhanam, Andy Shih, Krishna Parasuram Srinivasan, Alex Tamkin, Rohan Taori, Armin W. Thomas, Florian Tramèr, Rose E. Wang, William Wang, Bohan Wu, Jiajun Wu, Yuhuai Wu, Sang Michael Xie, Michihiro Yasunaga, Jiaxuan You, Matei A. Zaharia, Michael Zhang, Tianyi Zhang, Xikun Zhang, Yuhui Zhang, Lucia Zheng, Kaitlyn Zhou, and Percy Liang. 2021. On the opportunities and risks of foundation models. *ArXiv*.

Tom Brown, Benjamin Mann, Nick Ryder, Melanie Subbiah, Jared D Kaplan, Prafulla Dhariwal, Arvind Neelakantan, Pranav Shyam, Girish Sastry, Amanda Askell, Sandhini Agarwal, Ariel Herbert-Voss, Gretchen Krueger, Tom Henighan, Rewon Child, Aditya Ramesh, Daniel Ziegler, Jeffrey Wu, Clemens Winter, Chris Hesse, Mark Chen, Eric Sigler, Mateusz Litwin, Scott Gray, Benjamin Chess, Jack Clark, Christopher Berner, Sam McCandlish, Alec Radford, Ilya Sutskever, and Dario Amodei. 2020. Language models are few-shot learners. In *Advances in Neural Information Processing Systems*, volume 33, pages 1877–1901. Curran Associates, Inc.

Nicholas Carlini, Daphne Ippolito, Matthew Jagielski, Katherine Lee, Florian Tramer, and Chiyuan Zhang. 2023. Quantifying memorization across neural language models.

Aakanksha Chowdhery, Sharan Narang, Jacob Devlin, Maarten Bosma, Gaurav Mishra, Adam Roberts, Paul Barham, Hyung Won Chung, Charles Sutton, Sebastian Gehrmann, et al. 2023. Palm: Scaling language modeling with pathways. *Journal of Machine Learning Research*, 24(240):1–113.

Jacob Devlin, Ming-Wei Chang, Kenton Lee, and Kristina Toutanova. 2019. BERT: Pre-training of deep bidirectional transformers for language understanding. In *Proceedings of the 2019 Conference of the North American Chapter of the Association for Computational Linguistics: Human Language Technologies, Volume 1 (Long and Short Papers)*, pages 4171–4186, Minneapolis, Minnesota. Association for Computational Linguistics.

Mark Elliot, Elaine Mackey, and Kieron O'Hara. 2020. *The anonymisation decision-making framework, 2nd Edition: European practitioners' guide.* UK Anonymisation Network.

Simson L. Garfinkey. 2015. De-identification of personal information. Technical report, National Institute of Standards and Technology.

Alejandro Guerra-Manzanares, Leopoldo Julian Lechuga Lopez, Michail Maniatakos, and Farah Shamout. 2023. Privacy-preserving machine learning for healthcare: open challenges and future perspectives. In *ICLR 2023 Workshop on Trustworthy Machine Learning for Healthcare*.

Valentin Hartmann, Anshuman Suri, Vincent Bindschaedler, David Evans, Shruti Tople, and Robert West. 2023. Sok: Memorization in general-purpose large language models.

Fadi Hassan, David Sánchez, and Josep Domingo-Ferrer. 2023. Utility-preserving privacy protection of textual documents via word embeddings. *IEEE Transactions on Knowledge and Data Engineering*, 35(1):1058–1071.

Jordan Hoffmann, Sebastian Borgeaud, Arthur Mensch, Elena Buchatskaya, Trevor Cai, Eliza Rutherford, Diego de Las Casas, Lisa Anne Hendricks, Johannes Welbl, Aidan Clark, Tom Hennigan, Eric Noland, Katie Millican, George van den Driessche, Bogdan Damoc, Aurelia Guy, Simon Osindero, Karen Simonyan, Erich Elsen, Jack W. Rae, Oriol Vinyals, and Laurent Sifre. 2022. Training compute-optimal large language models.

Md Tahmid Rahman Laskar, M Saiful Bari, Mizanur Rahman, Md Amran Hossen Bhuiyan, Shafiq Joty, and Jimmy Xiangji Huang. 2023. A systematic study and comprehensive evaluation of chatgpt on benchmark datasets. *arXiv preprint arXiv:2305.18486*.

Haoran Li, Yulin Chen, Jinglong Luo, Yan Kang, Xiaojin Zhang, Qi Hu, Chunkit Chan, and Yangqiu Song. 2023. Privacy in large language models: Attacks, defenses and future directions.

Chin-Yew Lin. 2004. Rouge: A package for automatic evaluation of summaries. In *Text summarization branches out*, pages 74–81.

Pierre Lison, Ildikó Pilán, David Sanchez, Montserrat Batet, and Lilja Øvrelid. 2021. Anonymisation models for text data: State of the art, challenges and future directions. In *Proceedings of the 59th Annual Meeting of the Association for Computational Linguistics and the 11th International Joint Conference on Natural Language Processing (Volume 1: Long Papers)*, pages 4188–4203, Online. Association for Computational Linguistics.

Bernd Malle, Peter Kieseberg, and Andreas Holzinger. 2017. Do not disturb? classifier behavior on perturbed datasets. In *Machine Learning and Knowledge Extraction - First IFIP TC 5, WG 8.4, 8.9, 12.9 International Cross-Domain Conference, CD-MAKE 2017, Reggio di Calabria, Italy, August 29 - September 1, 2017, Proceedings*, volume 10410 of *Lecture Notes in Computer Science*, pages 155–173. Springer.

Bernd Malle, Peter Kieseberg, Edgar R. Weippl, and Andreas Holzinger. 2016. The right to be forgotten: Towards machine learning on perturbed knowledge bases. In *Availability, Reliability, and Security in Information Systems - IFIP WG 8.4, 8.9, TC 5 International Cross-Domain Conference, CD-ARES 2016, and Workshop on Privacy Aware Machine Learning for Health Data Science, PAML 2016, Salzburg, Austria, August 31 - September 2, 2016, Proceedings*, volume 9817 of *Lecture Notes in Computer Science*, pages 251–266. Springer.

Arvind Narayanan and Vitaly Shmatikov. 2007. How to break anonymity of the netflix prize dataset.

Milad Nasr, Nicholas Carlini, Jonathan Hayase, Matthew Jagielski, A. Feder Cooper, Daphne Ippolito, Christopher A. Choquette-Choo, Eric Wallace, Florian Tramèr, and Katherine Lee. 2023. Scalable extraction of training data from (production) language models.

OpenAI. 2023. Gpt-4 technical report.

Richard Plant, Valerio Giuffrida, and Dimitra Gkatzia. 2022. You are what you write: Preserving privacy in the era of large language models.

Colin Raffel, Noam Shazeer, Adam Roberts, Katherine Lee, Sharan Narang, Michael Matena, Yanqi Zhou, Wei Li, and Peter J Liu. 2020. Exploring the limits of transfer learning with a unified text-to-text transformer. *The Journal of Machine Learning Research*, 21(1):5485–5551.

Hugo Touvron, Louis Martin, Kevin Stone, Peter Albert, Amjad Almahairi, Yasmine Babaei, Nikolay Bashlykov, Soumya Batra, Prajjwal Bhargava, Shruti Bhosale, et al. 2023. Llama 2: Open foundation and fine-tuned chat models. *arXiv preprint arXiv:2307.09288*.

Runhua Xu, Nathalie Baracaldo, and James Joshi. 2021. Privacy-preserving machine learning: Methods, challenges and directions.

Ying Yin and Ivan Habernal. 2022. Privacy-preserving models for legal natural language processing. In *Proceedings of the Natural Legal Language Processing Workshop 2022*, pages 172–183, Abu Dhabi, United Arab Emirates (Hybrid). Association for Computational Linguistics.

Wayne Xin Zhao, Kun Zhou, Junyi Li, Tianyi Tang, Xiaolei Wang, Yupeng Hou, Yingqian Min, Beichen Zhang, Junjie Zhang, Zican Dong, Yifan Du, Chen Yang, Yushuo Chen, Zhipeng Chen, Jinhao Jiang, Ruiyang Ren, Yifan Li, Xinyu Tang, Zikang Liu, Peiyu Liu, Jian-Yun Nie, and Ji-Rong Wen. 2023. A survey of large language models.

A Residual Risk Categorization

Type	Missing Occurrence Tag	Google Tag	Score
Contact Info	(MISSED_EMAIL)	EMAIL_ADDRESS	4
	(MISSED_LOCATION)	LOCATION	2
	(MISSED_LOCATION_COORD)	LOCATION_COORDINATES	4
	(MISSED_US_STATE)	US_STATE	1
	(MISSED_PERSON_NAME)	PERSON_NAME	5
	(MISSED_PHONE)	PHONE_NUMBER	4
	(MISSED_ADDRESS)	STREET_ADDRESS	4
	(MISSED_USER_NAME)	USER_NAME	3
Entities	(MISSED_DOMAIN)	DOMAIN_NAME	1
	(MISSED_HTTP_COOKIE)	HTTP_COOKIE	1
	(MISSED_ORGANIZATION_NAME)	ORGANIZATION_NAME	0
	(MISSED_ORGANIZATION_NAME_SPEAKER)	ORGANIZATION_NAME	2
	(MISSED_PRODUCT)	PRODUCT	0
	(MISSED_PRODUCT_SPEAKER)	PRODUCT	2
	(MISSED_STORAGE_SIGNED_POLICY)	STORAGE_SIGNED_POLICY_DOCUMENT	2
	(MISSED_STORAGE_SIGNED_URL)	STORAGE_SIGNED_URL	3
	(MISSED_URL)	URL	2
Demographic	(MISSED_AGE)	AGE	1
Health Info	(MISSED_DATE_OF_BIRTH)	DATE_OF_BIRTH	3
	(MISSED_ICD9_CODE)	ICD9_CODE	2
	(MISSED_ICD10_CODE)	ICD10_CODE	2
	(MISSED_MEDICAL_RECORD_NUMBER)	MEDICAL_RECORD_NUMBER	5
	(MISSED_MEDICAL_TERM)	MEDICAL_TERM	1
ID number	(MISSED_ADVERTISING_ID)	ADVERTISING_ID	3
	(MISSED_GENERIC_ID)	GENERIC_ID	4
	(MISSED_ICCID_NUMBER)	ICCID_NUMBER	4
	(MISSED_IMEI_HARDWARE_ID)	IMEI_HARDWARE_ID	4
	(MISSED_IMSI_ID)	IMSI_ID	4
	(MISSED_IP_ADDRESS)	IP_ADDRESS	3
	(MISSED_MAC_ADDRESS)	MAC_ADDRESS	3
	(MISSED_MAC_ADDRESS_LOCAL)	MAC_ADDRESS_LOCAL	3
	(MISSED_PASSPORT)	PASSPORT	5
	(MISSED_VAT_NUMBER)	VAT_NUMBER	2
	(MISSED_VEHICLE_IDENTIFICATION_NUMBER)	VEHICLE_IDENTIFICATION_NUMBER	5
Payment Info	(MISSED_CREDIT_CARD_NUMBER)	CREDIT_CARD_NUMBER	5
	(MISSED_CREDIT_CARD_TRACK_NUMBER)	CREDIT_CARD_TRACK_NUMBER	5
	(MISSED_IBAN_CODE)	IBAN_CODE	5
	(MISSED_SWIFT_CODE)	SWIFT_CODE	1
	(MISSED_ROUTING_NUMBER)	ROUTING_NUMBER	3
	(MISSED_SSN)	SSN	5

Table 6: Residual risk scores assigned to infoTypes

When Is a Name Sensitive?
Eponyms in Clinical Text and Implications for De-Identification

Thomas Vakili, Tyr Hullmann, Aron Henriksson and Hercules Dalianis
Department of Computer and Systems Sciences
Stockholm University, Kista, Sweden
{thomas.vakili, aronhen, hercules}@dsv.su.se
tyrhullmann@gmail.com

Abstract

Clinical data, in the form of electronic health records, are rich resources that can be tapped using natural language processing. At the same time, they contain very sensitive information that must be protected. One strategy is to remove or obscure data using automatic de-identification. However, the detection of sensitive data can yield false positives. This is especially true for tokens that are similar in form to sensitive entities, such as eponyms. These names tend to refer to medical procedures or diagnoses rather than specific persons. Previous research has shown that automatic de-identification systems often misclassify eponyms as names, leading to a loss of valuable medical information. In this study, we estimate the prevalence of eponyms in a real Swedish clinical corpus. Furthermore, we demonstrate that modern transformer-based de-identification systems are more accurate in distinguishing between names and eponyms than previous approaches.

1 Introduction

De-identification of data invariably reduces information content by either removing, concealing, or replacing sensitive text with pseudonyms. Pseudonymization of data based on automatic identification and replacement of personally identifiable information (PII) may also introduce misleading information if tokens or text spans are erroneously misclassified as PII. Tokens are more likely to be misclassified as PII if they share common features with PII of a certain class. Such situations often arise in clinical texts, which often contain *eponyms* (Kucharz, 2020). These medical terms are named after a researcher or clinician, typically somebody involved in the discovery or invention or discovery of the phenomenon bearing their name. Sometimes, it can also be the name of a patient affected by a disorder. Since eponyms refer to medical phenomena rather than persons, they should not be considered sensitive.

It is believed that there are over 8,000 medical eponyms. As discussed by Kucharz (2020), eponyms can refer not only to diseases but to a wide range of categories including tests, surgical procedures and anatomical structures. These eponyms can cause difficulty when trying to automatically detect PII. In one study, it was shown that while only 0.81% of clinical entities were misclassified as PII, this was substantially higher for eponyms, where between 10 and 49% of eponyms were misclassified as PII (Meystre et al., 2014).

The following example highlights the problem: *Dr. Sjögren suspects the patient has Sjögren's syndrome*. In this example, *Sjögren's syndrome* is an eponymous disorder which is being treated by a physician who happens to have the same name. When de-identifying the sentence, *Sjögren* should be concealed in *Dr. Sjögren* but not in *Sjögren's syndrome*. Concealing the eponymous name of the syndrome removes clinical information which could potentially be very important for the intended users of the data. However, it is not clear how prevalent eponyms are in clinical text and to what extent transformer-based named entity recognition (NER) systems trained to identify PII can distinguish between eponyms and sensitive names.

In this study, we estimate the prevalence of eponyms in a large corpus of Swedish clinical text. We also create a manually annotated corpus of clinical notes containing one or more eponyms and use this corpus to study the extent to which classifications of names overlap with eponyms. To that end, we employ a NER system trained to detect sensitive entities (e.g., names). In other words, we seek to understand how eponyms affect these models' ability to distinguish between actual names and eponyms. The main contributions of this study are summarized below:

Proceedings of the Workshop on Computational Approaches to Language Data Pseudonymization
CALD-pseudo 2024, pages 76–80
March 21, 2024

- We estimate that around 0.04% of tokens in clinical notes are eponyms and that these have a slight tendency to cluster in the same notes.
- We show that modern NER systems based on BERT are less likely to misclassify eponyms than older systems evaluated in previous studies.
- We discuss the implications of eponyms for automatic de-identification of clinical text and data utility.
- We create a clinical corpus annotated with eponyms that we plan to de-identify and make available to researchers.

2 Related Research

Research looking specifically at eponyms is scarce. The studies that are available often focus on the intersection of the de-identification of clinical texts and the detection of disorders. Berg et al. (2020) performed de-identification experiments and observed that rare eponyms in the training data tended to be misclassified as last or first names to a very high degree, but there were also cases where eponyms in the training data were misclassified as last or first names. Meystre et al. (2014) compare five de-identification systems and their flaws in erroneously detecting eponyms as protected health information (PHI)[1] in American clinical text. Three systems (MIT, MIST and HIDE) misclassify approximately 10% of all eponyms as PHI, and the other two systems (HMS and MEDs) misclassify as many as 40% of all eponyms as PHI.

Berg et al. (2020) created an eponym lexicon by using a NER model for clinical entities, i.e., a system to identify *Findings*, *Disorder*, *Body Parts* and *Drugs* in a Swedish clinical text. Then, they investigated whether these were based on the name of a person, in which case it was marked up as an eponym and added to the eponym lexicon. Finally, the created lexicon was manually reviewed to ensure correctness. The resulting eponym lexicon contains 275 eponyms.

Several studies have examined the impact of de-identification on data utility for machine learning. Results are highly contingent on an appropriate sanitization algorithm and a sufficiently strong NER model for detecting sensitive data (Berg et al., 2020; Lothritz et al., 2023). However, there are several examples of studies showing that data utility can be maintained for both fine-tuning, pre-training, and combined scenarios (Vakili and Dalianis, 2022; Verkijk and Vossen, 2022; Vakili et al., 2023). These studies examine the impact of de-identification by evaluating models trained to perform downstream tasks. A shared limitation is that these studies study the impact on downstream task performance overall. As such, these studies cannot conclusively rule out that there may be other scenarios where de-identification could still have a disparate impact on data utility. For instance, misclassifying and removing information contained in eponyms could be harmful in many scenarios, and examining this specific risk provides deeper insights into possible pitfalls in de-identifying clinical data.

3 Data and Experiments

In this study, we estimate the prevalence of eponyms in a large sample of Swedish clinical texts by using an eponym lexicon to automatically identify mentions of eponyms in clinical notes. We use this to create an eponym corpus by randomly sampling 1,000 clinical notes with at least one detected eponym mention. These notes are then manually reviewed and corrected while we also calculate inter-annotator agreement among four annotators. Finally, we fine-tune a Swedish clinical BERT model to identify PII and calculate to what extent eponyms are misclassified.

3.1 Creating an Eponym Corpus

The data used in this study was the Stockholm Eponym Corpus[2]. This is a subset extracted from the research infrastructure Health Bank[3] (Dalianis et al., 2015), which contains over 2 million patient records from the years 2007-2014 from over 500 clinical units. The data originates from the Karolinska University Hospital in Stockholm, Sweden. The eponym lexicon created by Berg et al. (2020) was used to find eponyms in the clinical text.

The total number of detected tokens and eponyms can be seen in Table 1. In the corpora, approximately 0.04% of all tokens are eponyms. For scale, this can be compared with the prevalence of

[1]PHI are a form of PII specified by the American HIPAA regulation.

[2]This research has been approved by the Swedish Ethical Review Authority under permission no. 2019-05679.

[3]Health Bank, `https://www.dsv.su.se/healthbank`

Corpora	Tokens	Flagged eponyms	Estimated eponyms
Health Bank Subset (1%)	27,837,617	12,066	11,016
Entire Health Bank	~2,800,000,000	N/A	~1,108,000

Table 1: The number of flagged eponyms (based on the matching algorithm) and the estimated minimum number of real eponyms (based on the precision of the algorithm).

Term	Occurrences
Babinski(s)	1869
Romberg(s)	1777
Grasset(s)	1325
Crohn(s,'s)	944
Parkinson(s,'s)	738
Alzheimer(s,'s)	490
Sjögren(s)	475
Donder(s)	351
Valsalva	322
Lasegue(s,é)	295
Graves('s)	290
Akilles	256
Raynaud(s,'s)	217
Bechterew(s)	216
Whipple(s)	173
Willebrand(s)	169
Wegener(s)	162
Waldenström(s)	176
Robin(s)	179
Dix	154

Table 2: Top 20 highest occurrences of the eponyms from the Stockholm Eponym Corpus, including spelling variants.

PII which has been estimated as being two to four times more common (Dalianis, 2018).

Due to computational constraints, one percent of the Health Bank corpus was randomly extracted for the experiments. This subcorpus consists of 1,402,782 notes containing 27,837,617 tokens and was tagged for eponyms using exact matching with the eponym lexicon. In total, 9,795 notes were flagged as containing eponyms, and 12,066 matching eponyms were found, as shown in Table 1.

Out of the 9,795 notes with eponyms, 1,000 notes containing the eponym tag were randomly extracted for manual annotation. The order of the notes was randomized before being split into five subsets of 200 notes. These notes were manually annotated by four annotators. Each annotator was assigned 400 notes, 200 of which were unique and 200 that were shared. The resulting 1,000 notes corpora is called the Stockholm Eponym Corpus. The inter-annotator agreement (IAA) was determined using the Krippendorff's alpha (Krippendorff, 1970) and was calculated as 0.97 for the 200 samples annotated by all four annotators.

These 200 shared samples were then used to estimate the precision of the eponym lexicon. After resolving the disagreements between the annotators, the precision was determined as 0.913. No attempts were made to estimate the recall of the matching algorithm, as the annotated samples were only selected from the subset in which the algorithm had found eponyms. Based on the precision of the matching algorithm, a lower bound for the total number of eponyms in the Health Bank was estimated and listed in Table 1.

During the manual annotation, new eponyms were discovered, annotated, and added to the lexicon. This process led to extending the eponym lexicon from 275 eponyms to 317 eponyms. The updated eponym lexicon was used for the final matching presented in Table 1 and 2, respectively.

3.2 Evaluating Misclassification of Eponyms

Previous studies have shown that NER systems for classifying PII tend to have lower precision for tokens that are eponyms. To study this, a BERT-based NER model was trained using the Stockholm EPR PHI Corpus (Dalianis and Velupillai, 2010). This corpus covers a range of PII classes and consists of 380,000 tokens, of which 4,800 are PII. Crucially, it covers both first and last names – entity types that are commonly associated with eponyms. A Swedish clinical BERT model called SweDeClin-BERT (Vakili et al., 2022) was used as the base model. The fine-tuned NER model was then used to tag the corpus described in Section 3.1, creating a version containing both tags for PII and eponyms.

The new version of the corpus, which contained parallel tags for eponyms and PII, was examined to determine how often eponyms were misclassified as PII. A total of 82 tokens out of the 1,319 tokens annotated as eponyms were classified as PII. In other words, approximately 6.2% of eponyms were misclassified. Interestingly, the NER tagger did not only confuse eponyms with names but also with locations and organizations. Statistics for the misclassifications are shown in Table 3.

PII tag	Misclassified Eponyms	Non-Eponym Classifications
Last Name	72	227
First Name	7	254
Organization	2	14
Location	1	58

Table 3: Many PII were predicted in the Eponym Corpus. Some of these were eponyms. Eponyms were misclassified mainly as names and, in a few cases, as locations or organizations.

4 Discussion and Conclusions

4.1 Observations During Annotation

One observation during the annotation process was that eponyms were rarely present in the same context or sentence as PHI. In other words, the scenario showcased in the example in the introduction was uncommon. Eponyms often occur in bursts in the text, in discussions of possible disorders, or in descriptions of tests that had been conducted. This phenomenon is illustrated in Figure 1.

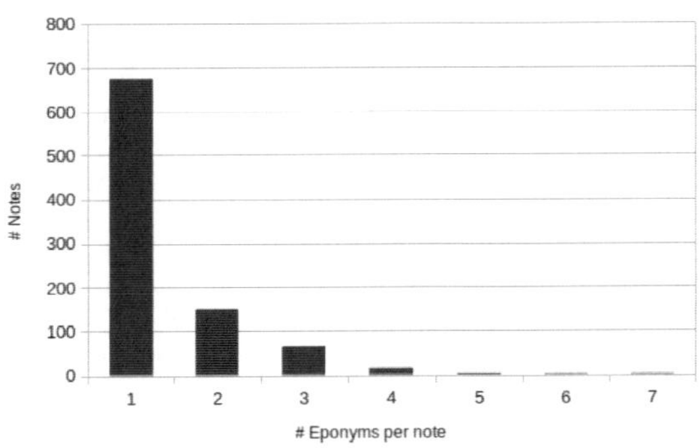

Figure 1: Although the majority of notes contain just one eponym, nearly half of all detected eponyms occurred in notes containing at least one additional eponym.

There were some examples where either the clinician's name or the patient's name coincided with the eponym. *Robin* was present in the eponym lexicon to catch references to Robin's syndrome, but these mentions were more often misclassified as eponyms since Robin is a common Swedish name.

Many names are also non-eponymous words. For example, *Still* was in the eponym lexicon but was also a common non-eponymous word (with the same meaning as in English e.g., *to sit still*).

4.2 Improvements Over Previous Research

The results highlighted in Section 3.2 indicate that the problem of eponyms being misclassified as PII is less prevalent in our study compared to previous research. In particular, the outcome can be contrasted to the results of Berg et al. (2020), who also used data from the Health Bank. It is difficult to confidently conclude what these differences are caused by. One hypothesis is that transformer-based models better capture the context surrounding a token. This could allow them to better distinguish when a name is used as a name and when it is used as an eponym. Indeed, these uses are grammatically distinct and are often obvious to a human observer. Further experiments would be needed to conclusively ascribe the differences in results to this capability or determine if they are due to other factors.

4.3 Conclusions

Protecting privacy is crucial in the clinical domain but also comes with domain-specific challenges. Eponyms contain valuable clinical information and we estimate, based on our results, that at least 0.04% of all tokens in clinical notes are eponyms. Previous research has found that automatic de-identification systems can struggle to distinguish between eponyms and actual private names that need to be sanitized. Our results show that modern transformer-based NER models, such as those based on BERT, are more effective in separating these two forms of names. This study also presents a new annotated corpus containing a wide range of eponyms. We plan to release a de-identified version of this resource once the necessary ethical permissions have been obtained.

5 Limitations

While three of the four annotators had prior experience working with clinical text, none were trained medical professionals but computer scientists. Some eponyms may have been missed during the annotation process, and others may have been erroneously annotated. In cases where the annotators needed clarification, they searched online for sources indicating whether or not a name was an eponym. The high IAA indicates that the annotations are reliable, but the lack of medical expertise limits the extent to which the annotations can be trusted.

A related issue is that the eponym corpus is not a random sample of the entire Health Bank. Instead, it is a consciously chosen subset that was deemed highly likely to contain eponyms based on the matching algorithm described in Section 3.1. Starting from a purely random subset of the Health Bank could have led to more robust results and would have allowed us to calculate the recall for the matching algorithm. This was not deemed feasible due to the very low prevalence of eponyms in the overall corpus. Starting from a random sample would have required far more annotators than were available for this project.

The risk of misclassifying eponyms was only examined for the SweDeClin-BERT model. It is possible that other architectures and models trained on other datasets may perform better or worse. Further research could benefit from including a more diverse range of models, including generative models. Nevertheless, the results of this study show that transformer-based models can be less affected by the misclassification risks than models described in earlier studies. Determining the mechanism behind this greater resilience is an interesting topic for future research.

Acknowledgement

We want to thank Hanna Berg for providing details about the eponym lexicon. We are also grateful for the helpful comments and suggestions from the reviewers. Finally, we want to thank the DataLEASH project and Digital Futures for funding this research.

References

Hanna Berg, Aron Henriksson, and Hercules Dalianis. 2020. The Impact of De-identification on Downstream Named Entity Recognition in Clinical Text. In *Proceedings of the 11th International Workshop on Health Text Mining and Information Analysis*, pages 1–11, Online. Association for Computational Linguistics.

Hercules Dalianis. 2018. *Clinical text mining: Secondary use of electronic patient records*. Springer Nature.

Hercules Dalianis, Aron Henriksson, Maria Kvist, Sumithra Velupillai, and Rebecka Weegar. 2015. HEALTH BANK- A Workbench for Data Science Applications in Healthcare. In *Proceedings of the CAiSE-2015 Industry Track co-located with 27th Conference on Advanced Information Systems Engineering (CAiSE 2015)*, pages 34–44. CEUR Workshop Proceedings.

Hercules Dalianis and Sumithra Velupillai. 2010. De-identifying Swedish clinical text - refinement of a gold standard and experiments with Conditional random fields. *Journal of Biomedical Semantics*, 1(1):6.

Klaus Krippendorff. 1970. Bivariate Agreement Coefficients for Reliability of Data. *Sociological Methodology*, 2:139–150. Publisher: [American Sociological Association, Wiley, Sage Publications, Inc.].

Eugeniusz Józï Kucharz. 2020. Medical eponyms from linguistic and historical points of view. *Reumatologia*, 58(4):258–260.

Cedric Lothritz, Bertrand Lebichot, Kevin Allix, Saad Ezzini, Tegawendé Bissyandé, Jacques Klein, Andrey Boytsov, Clément Lefebvre, and Anne Goujon. 2023. Evaluating the Impact of Text De-Identification on Downstream NLP Tasks. In *Proceedings of the 24th Nordic Conference on Computational Linguistics (NoDaLiDa)*, pages 10–16, Tórshavn, Faroe Islands. University of Tartu Library.

Stéphane M Meystre, Oscar Ferrández, F Jeffrey Friedlin, Brett R South, Shuying Shen, and Matthew H Samore. 2014. Text de-identification for privacy protection: a study of its impact on clinical text information content. *Journal of biomedical informatics*, 50:142–150.

Thomas Vakili and Hercules Dalianis. 2022. Utility Preservation of Clinical Text After De-Identification. In *Proceedings of the 21st Workshop on Biomedical Language Processing*, pages 383–388, Dublin, Ireland. Association for Computational Linguistics.

Thomas Vakili, Aron Henriksson, and Hercules Dalianis. 2023. End-to-End Pseudonymization of Fine-Tuned Clinical BERT Models.

Thomas Vakili, Anastasios Lamproudis, Aron Henriksson, and Hercules Dalianis. 2022. Downstream Task Performance of BERT Models Pre-Trained Using Automatically De-Identified Clinical Data. In *Proceedings of the Thirteenth Language Resources and Evaluation Conference*, pages 4245–4252.

Stella Verkijk and Piek Vossen. 2022. Efficiently and Thoroughly Anonymizing a Transformer Language Model for Dutch Electronic Health Records: a Two-Step Method. In *Proceedings of the Thirteenth Language Resources and Evaluation Conference*, pages 1098–1103, Marseille, France. European Language Resources Association.

Did the Names I Used within My Essay Affect My Score? Diagnosing Name Biases in Automated Essay Scoring

Ricardo Muñoz Sánchez[†], **Simon Dobnik**[‡], **Maria Irena Szawerna**[†], **Therese Lindström Tiedemann**[§], **Elena Volodina**[†]

[†] Språkbanken Text, University of Gothenburg, Sweden
[‡] CLASP, FLoV, University of Gothenburg, Sweden
[§] Department of Finnish, Finnougrian and Scandinavian Studies, University of Helsinki, Finland
`mormor.karl@svenska.gu.se`
[†][‡]`{ricardo.munoz.sanchez,simon.dobnik,maria.szawerna,elena.volodina}@gu.se`
[§]`therese.lindstromtiedemann@helsinki.fi`

Abstract

Automated essay scoring (AES) of second-language learner essays is a high-stakes task as it can affect the job and educational opportunities a student may have access to. Thus, it becomes imperative to make sure that the essays are graded based on the students' language proficiency as opposed to other reasons, such as personal names used in the text of the essay. Moreover, most of the research data for AES tends to contain personal identifiable information. Because of that, pseudonymization becomes an important tool to make sure that this data can be freely shared. Thus, our systems should not grade students based on which given names were used in the text of the essay, both for fairness and for privacy reasons. In this paper we explore how given names affect the CEFR level classification of essays of second language learners of Swedish. We use essays containing just one personal name and substitute it for names from lists of given names from four different ethnic origins, namely Swedish, Finnish, Anglo-American, and Arabic. We find that changing the names within the essays has no apparent effect on the classification task, regardless of whether a feature-based or a transformer-based model is used.

1 Introduction

Artificial intelligence is being deployed in high-stakes situations, such as automated grading of second language essays in proficiency assessment. While AI can improve the opportunities students have in education, the job market, etc., such systems often display human-like biases (Blodgett et al., 2020). Aldrin (2017) notes that human graders have a slight bias based on names appearing in essay texts. In this paper we aim to identify whether the same pattern holds in automated systems.

The broad question for our study is: are there any implicit biases that models have learnt from the training data that can influence automated essay scoring in a negative way? In particular, we are interested in uncovering potential biases that can be associated with use of names representing different ethnic groups – and how this can be reflected in the domain of automatic essay scoring (AES).

For the purposes of this work, we say that there is bias in AES when an essay is scored not only by its contents but also by the assumed demographic characteristics of its author. We use this definition as we are looking for biases in a downstream application (i.e. extrinsic biases) as opposed to biases either in the training data or in any intermediate representations (i.e. intrinsic biases). Even though we know that biases in deep learning models cannot be removed in absolute terms (Gonen and Goldberg, 2019), we can attempt to minimize their impact.

Because of this, we have set out to create a novel paradigm of diagnostic benchmarks for identifying hidden biases in AES models as a safety gatekeeping before they are approved for use in real-life scenarios. In such a dataset each essay is duplicated (several times), artificially altering given names appearing in the text to identify if such perturbation affects how an essay is scored. Since the essays are identical as far as linguistics, language complexity, and content are concerned, we expect them to be graded similarly. Thus, we would say that our model for this task presents bias if it systemically assigns lower grades when using versions of the essays with names coming from specific ethnicities.

Our research questions are the following:

- Does changing given names inside a second language learner essay affect the way the text is graded when using automated essay scoring?
- How much does this differ between feature-based machine learning and deep learning?

For this, we use a de-anonymized (i.e. origi-

Proceedings of the Workshop on Computational Approaches to Language Data Pseudonymization
CALD-pseudo 2024, pages 81–91

nal) version of the SweLL-pilot corpus of second language Swedish learner essays (Volodina et al., 2016a), which consists of 502 essays annotated with CEFR levels[1] (Council of Europe, 2001), as our source data.

First, we compile four lists of given names inspired by those in Aldrin (2017): traditional Swedish names; modern Swedish names of Anglo-American origin; Finnish names (due both to the close sociocultural links between Finland and Sweden and to Swedish being an official language of Finland being learnt by the population that does not speak it as their first language); and names of Arabic origin (the most prominent group of learners in the corpus).

Second, we create a diagnostic dataset to identify biases in the classification task. We select SweLL-pilot essays in which a given name appears only once. Then, we generate an essay version for each name on the lists by substituting the name in the original text with one from the list. All of the essays chosen have the names in their base form.

Third, we fine-tune a BERT (Devlin et al., 2019) model on the original SweLL-pilot data to predict the CEFR level of a given essay and compare it to an existing feature-based model (Pilán et al., 2016).

Finally, we test the two models and compare the equality of opportunity between the different given name groups on the diagnostic dataset, as described by Hardt et al. (2016).

As mentioned previously, we would expect an unbiased or a fair model (in terms of given names) to not show systemic misclassification for the ethnic groups considered. It does not mean that it will be unbiased towards names from other ethnic groups or that different names would not elicit unexpected responses from our model (Antoniak and Mimno, 2021). It is important to note that a model being fair for a downstream application does not mean that the model itself, the data, or the annotation lack biases (and vice versa). Social biases are a very complex phenomenon and they can be embedded in a variety of ways, as illustrated by Suresh and Guttag (2021). Moreover, Goldfarb-Tarrant et al. (2023) note that the presence or absence or intrinsic biases (e.g. in language models) does not necessarily correlate with the presence or absence of extrinsic biases (e.g. in downstream applications). Because of this, it is important to monitor and to audit AES models regularly regardless of whether they are fair. And, given that this is a high-stakes task, it is essential to always have a human-in-the-loop approach.

The rest of the paper is structured as follows: Section 2 reviews some of the related work both in terms of automated essay assessment and of bias and fairness in NLP. Section 3 presents our methodology, the models and data we used, as well as how they were evaluated. In Section 4 we show and discuss the results from our experiments, while in Section 5 we present some ideas for future work.

2 Related Work

Language assessment and subsequent documented language proficiency, be it for citizenship, university admission or a job application, are extremely influential, if not life-changing, both on the individual, societal and political levels (Roever and McNamara, 2006). Assessment should therefore be guaranteed to be fair and unbiased, and assessors should be kept accountable for the results, i.e. be able to motivate the assigned scores (e.g. ASLHA, 2023; ALTE, 2020). This is a non-trivial requirement even for human assessors, and is clearly a much greater challenge for automated language assessment.

2.1 Biases in Humans

People carry a multitude of implicit associations which have been acquired through previous experiences, for example, an association between '`day and ...`' (`night`, supposedly) or '`commit a ...`' (`crime`, most probably). These associations are called *implicit biases*, which can be neutral, positive or negative in nature. Implicit associations (or biases) do not necessarily have an impact on the life around us, but in certain cases they do – and then they can risk jeopardizing our ideals of fairness and equality, for example when it comes to racial or gender discrimination (Greenwald et al., 2015). Especially important are the associations that are triggered in ambiguous and confusing contexts, when our brain falls back on the associations stored in our memory from earlier experiences, especially those that are stored repeatedly (Greenwald and Krieger, 2006).

For example, Foster (2008) has suggested that there may be a correlation between ethnicity and (lower) results at a university, but that this is un-

[1] CEFR stands for Common European Framework of Reference for Languages. It is a framework to evaluate foreign language learning and assigns one of six reference levels to determine the proficiency level of a second language speaker.

likely to be directly due to ethnically marked names at that stage of education. Aldrin (2017) took it further and investigated whether there was an influence from stereotypically marked given names in first language Swedish essays by letting 113 human assessors mark one text where she inserted, in quite a discrete place, one of three names: a traditional Swedish name, an ethnically marked name or an Anglo-American name with certain socio-economical associations. The results showed a certain influence on the assessment of language proficiency, "stylistic precision" and "writing technique", but nothing statistically significant. She believed the fact that the results were not as clear as in previous international work (e.g. Anderson-Clark et al., 2008; Figlio, 2003) could be due to the fact that (1) the name was discreetly placed, and (2) several of the teachers worked in schools with students of heterogeneous background and were therefore less likely to have a bias, or (3) that the names picked were not found to be stereotypical in the way they were thought to be.

2.2 Biases in Machine Learning Systems

Similar to humans, language models, including Large Language Models (LLMs), store associations between various linguistic and non-linguistic information types that they meet during the training stage. These models do this by looking at large amounts of data, finding patterns and repeating them. An important issue here is that social biases are also reflected in the data that we, humans, produce (Marchiori Manerba et al., 2022), leading to models that parrot sexist (e.g. Zhao et al., 2018), racist (e.g. Sap et al., 2019), or xenophobic (e.g. Narayanan Venkit et al., 2023) ideas.

Following Blodgett et al. (2020), we claim that any work on biases in NLP and AI-based systems should be well-grounded in the domain where biases need to be uncovered, since (negative) biases in one domain are not necessarily negative in another. For example, absence of Past Simple in an essay is an indication of a lower grade. However, it might not be a negative feature when applied to filtering application letters for appropriate job candidates. Therefore studying biases in a vacuum can be misleading for a particular domain.

Some previous papers have studied biases regarding names in NLP. Several of the word embedding association tests (WEAT, Caliskan et al., 2017) compare lists of Anglo-American and Afro-American given names and lists of stereotypical characteristics associated with each. Meanwhile, several studies have found that the appearance of names in text can affect how it is translated (e.g. Wang et al., 2022; Sandoval et al., 2023). Furthermore, some studies have seen how nationalities and names of countries are related to the text that auto-decoders generate (e.g. Narayanan Venkit et al., 2023).

2.3 Biases in Automated Essay Scoring

Concerns about risks of introducing biases into automatic assessment scores have also been raised. Some studies criticize automatic essay scoring algorithms for flawed grading of high-stakes exams pointing out bias against certain demographic groups[2] (e.g. Madnani et al., 2017; Loukina et al., 2019) due to data imbalance or rater bias reflected in the data. Despite the criticism, the technology has been embraced and has shaped life stories of thousands of people.

Kane (2001) views validity and fairness in language assessment as closely related ways of looking at the same question. That is, whether the proposed interpretations and uses of test scores are appropriate for a population over some range of contexts. The traditional definition of fairness in the field of educational measurement is when a test does not unduly advantage or disadvantage any groups (Kane, 2001). The concept of fairness is also closely connected to bias, or the lack thereof. Bias is when the validity of a given test score is different for subgroups of test-takers. For example, this may happen if a set of items would favor a particular group in a given test. Test scores would then not reflect the participants' true ability.

To overcome the technological biases, Madnani et al. (2017) suggest a scheme to detect demographic and construct-irrelevant biases (such as rater biases, data-imbalance, machine-learning biases) applying model validation based on psychometric and statistical checks using an open-source tool RSMTool.[3] They also suggest reducing susceptibility to construct-irrelevant factors by design, among others by using feature review by experts and combining features into several models by feature type instead of mixing all features in one model. However, more advanced machine learning and neural network algorithms and LLMs are not

[2] https://www.vice.com/en/article/pa7dj9/flawed-algorithms-are-grading-millions-of-students-essays

[3] https://rsmtool.readthedocs.io/

as easily interpretable (Alishahi et al., 2020), which requires other approaches and solutions.

3 Experiment Setup, Materials and Methods

Our major question for the experiment is whether algorithms for essay classification are sensitive to names (or pseudonyms) used in essays. If we need to pseudonymize research data on a constant basis to protect writer identities, which is a GDPR requirement (EU Commission, 2016), we should find ways to do so that do not affect students. This means that it is our responsibility to check the effect the replacement candidates may have on the data and its downstream tasks and research applications. In this experiment we study the effects that replacing given names in learner essays might have on essay assessment in terms of CEFR[4] level, as described in the Introduction (section 1). The CEFR levels are a six-level scale to gauge the proficiency of an individual on a foreign language (i.e. not their first language or languages) and they range from A1 to C2, with A1 being the lowest.

3.1 Dataset

For our experiments we use SweLL-pilot (Volodina et al., 2016a; Volodina, 2024), a corpus of essays written by learners of Swedish as a second language (L2 Swedish). It contains 502 essays labeled with CEFR levels, distributed as shown in Table 1. Given the specifics of learner essays, many of them touch on personal stories, mostly in response to topics like 'The best day of my life', 'My school', 'My best friend', etc., which, of course, elicits a lot of private or sensitive information, starting with personal names, place names and other information that can reveal the writer's identity either in a direct or in an indirect way. This is natural, given that some of the CEFR levels expect the student to be able to describe topics about the personal lives.

To select essays for purposes of identifying biases based on given names, a few guidelines were applied:

- there should be, optimally, only one personal name used in its base form in each essay;
- if possible, no geographical context of the country of origin should be present;
- two essays per level are included.

[4]CEFR stands for Common European Framework of Reference for Languages.

		# of diagnostic essays	
Level	**# essays**	**original**	**pseudonymized**
A1	59	2	160
A2	143	2	160
B1	86	2	160
B2	105	1	80
C1	96	0	0
C2	7	0	0
Total	497	7	560

Table 1: Number of essays in the SweLL-pilot corpus per CEFR level, and statistics over the diagnostic dataset.

These guidelines aim to modify as little as possible in the text of the essays. This should allow for more controlled experimentation, leading in turn to a better way to ascertain the presence or absence of biases.

The selection proved to be more challenging than expected. First of all, in essays where personal information was elicited through a topic, usually more than one name were used, e.g. 'I have five brothers: name1, name2, name3, ...'. Second, the higher levels in the corpus (B2, C1 and C2) contain practically no essays where personal information is provided. This is due to the topics present in the dataset being of a non-personal nature at higher levels of proficiency, e.g. book reviews, argumentative essays and the like. We have, therefore, limited the diagnostic dataset to levels A1, A2, B1 and B2, with only one original essay for B2. No essays were found to meet our requirements at levels C1 and C2.

The IDs of the selected essays can be found in Appendix A and we call the resulting dataset with substituted names the diagnostic dataset.

3.2 Name Selection

The names used to check for biases were inspired by those chosen by (Aldrin, 2017). The idea behind this is to allow for better comparison in terms of the kinds of social biases we expect to find. In general, the idea is to compare how the model perceives stereotypical Swedish given names in the essays in comparison to those that are not usually associated with people with a Swedish background, particularly those that people in Sweden may be familiar with through their social contact.

We balance the different name lists by (binary)

gender[5] and by name group. Thus, we got 10 names for each combination of gender + name group, 20 names for each group and 80 names in total. The full lists of names can be found in Appendix B.

As mentioned in Section 1, we have chosen the following four name groups:

- Swedish names, taken from lists containing the top 100 given names normally used by men and by women[6]. These lists were obtained from Statistics Sweden, an official government website dedicated to publishing statistics about the country. This group was chosen as we are dealing with essays written in Swedish in Sweden. Furthermore, we made sure that none of the names chosen for the three originally non-Swedish given names appeared in other two lists.

- Finnish names, taken from lists of the top 10 first names throughout different decades[7]. This list was obtained from the Digital and Population Data Services Agency in Finland. This group was chosen due to Finland's and Sweden's close historical and cultural proximity and because Swedish is also one of the official languages in Finland, which means that it is not uncommon that students have to take exams in that language. As with all of the other groups other than the Swedish name, particular care was put into looking for names that are used as given names in Sweden, while checking that they do not overlap with common Swedish names.

- Anglo-American names, taken from the list of the top 100 names over the last 100 years in the United States[8]. This list was obtained from the Social Security Administration of the United States. This group was chosen as popular culture from the United States has permeated different countries in different ways. On top of that, these names can have different socio-cultural connotations in non-English speaking countries, including Sweden (Malm and Zetterström, 2007).

- Arabic names, taken from lists of commonly used Moroccan names used in the Netherlands (Gerritzen, 2007) and of commonly used Syrian names in Sweden (Gustafsson, 2021). These lists were later cross-referenced with information from Statistics Sweden[9] to verify that they are indeed commonly used given names in Sweden without being traditional Swedish names.

It is important to note that we combined different spellings of these names and kept just the one that is the most common in a Swedish context. This was necessary both to ensure that all of the lists contain the same amount of names and to keep the lists with as little overlap as possible (e.g. not including Sarah in the Anglo-American list as Sara was already in the Swedish list).

3.3 Models

We compare biases on the automated essay scoring task on two models, one feature-based and the other using a transformer architecture. The idea being that a feature-based system that does not explicitly use proper names should not exhibit name-based biases, while a model based on distributional semantics might pick up unwanted biases during its pre-training along all of the useful semantic information.

The feature-based approach we follow is that of Pilán et al. (2016) and Volodina et al. (2016b). They extract length-based, lexical, morphological, syntactic, and semantic features. Then they use an SVM as a classifier as well as feature selection and found that lexical features work best for classification. Even though they did not use any features that directly relate to proper names, there are some that are based on token length and some names that are also common nouns might appear in frequency-based lists (for example Hope in English).

The dataset used originally was SweLL-pilot (Volodina et al., 2016a) and they used adjacent accuracy to evaluate the model. What is, they treat the classes as an ordinal scale and consider that an answer was correct if it was either the correct class or the immediate one either before or after. That is under the intuition that misclassifying an A2 essay

[5]Finding common gender-neutral names proved to be a challenge as both the papers and the government agencies we consulted only listed male and female names.

[6]https://www.scb.se/en/finding-statistics/statistics-by-subject-area/population/general-statistics/name-statistics/

[7]https://verkkopalvelu.vrk.fi/nimipalvelu/default.asp?L=3

[8]https://www.ssa.gov/OACT/babynames/decades/century.html

[9]https://www.scb.se/en/finding-statistics/sverige-i-siffror/namesearch/

as B1 is a smaller mistake than misclassifying is as a B2 or C1 essay. Do note that we do not use this metric for this work, we report regular accuracy instead. This is, to the best of our knowledge, the current state of the art regarding CEFR level assessment in Swedish.

We also use a transformer-based model for our experiments to see whether their contextual behavior leads to biases in AES. This is a Swedish version of BERT trained by KBLab[10] (Malmsten et al., 2020), the NLP research group at the National Library of Sweden. It was trained on slightly less than 3.5 million tokens, with text coming from digitized newspapers, official reports from the Swedish government, legal resources, social media, and Wikipedia in Swedish. They used the same code and hyperparameters as the original BERT (Devlin et al., 2019) model did.

The specific implementation that we are using is the one released on KBLab's HuggingFace repository.[11] Furthermore, we use the BERT for classification class from HuggingFace. It adds a linear layer on top of the base model, with an output for each of the classes. The whole model is then fine-tuned on the training data.

3.4 Evaluation

To measure the biases within the classification task, we use equality of opportunity (Hardt et al., 2016). Equality of opportunity is achieved when the recall between a given class and the rest of the population is equal. This metric is used to minimize false negatives, thus measuring whether any of the groups gets a systemic unfair disadvantage.

In more mathematical terms, if we have the name group A, the recall on its respective diagnostic essays RC_A, and the recall for the rest of the essays on the diagnostic set RC_{-A}, then we can define equality of opportunity for group A as follows:

$$Eq.of Opp.(A) = RC_A - RC_{-A}$$

A negative value in the metric means that using names from group A in the text of the essay increases the possibility of an unfair disadvantage, while a positive value means that names from that group are less likely to be disadvantaged.

Do note that Hardt et al. (2016) also propose another metric called equalized odds, where we expect both recall and precision to be the same. However, they argue that it is a much stronger requirement and prove that predictors in general cannot be balanced post-hoc to achieve this definition of fairness.

4 Results and Discussion

We can notice from Table 2 that the transformer-based model performs much better than the feature-based model across all evaluation metrics. On top of that, we realized both during training and during inference that BERT was much faster than the feature-based model due to the API calls required to obtain said features.

When looking at the performance on the diagnostic set in Tables 3 and 4, we noticed that changing the names in the text of the essays yielded no change in performance with either of the models. That is, the equality of opportunity of the different groups and subgroups is zero, indicating that the model is not unfair under this metric. Testing with a wider array of names yielded no differences either in terms of class assigned. On a similar note, when checking for biases regarding whether the names were male or female we found no difference in performance.

As mentioned in Section 3.3, we did not expect the feature-based model to show much bias, if at all. This is due to it not using features directly related to the vocabulary.

On the other hand, we expected the transformer-based model to display some sort of bias considering the previous literature on name biases in NLP (see Section 2). This means that ultimately neither the distribution of the demographics in the training set nor the biases in the base BERT model (i.e. intrinsic biases) had any effect on the fairness of the model (i.e. extrinsic bias). A possible direction on which this study could be expanded to would be a thorough analysis of given names present in the vocabulary of the BERT model and seeing whether there is any correlation between how the model behaves for each of these.

These results are consistent with what we would expect from a fair model for AES for second language assessment. That is, we expect it to score the students in terms of their linguistic skills and proficiencies as opposed to other unrelated things.

One of the possible issues that we could have run into were the essays used for the diagnostics dataset. While they represent different CEFR lev-

[10] https://www.kb.se/in-english/research-collaboration/kblab.html

[11] https://huggingface.co/KBLab/bert-base-swedish-cased

Model	Accuracy	F1 Macro	F1 Weighted
Feature-Based	0.25	0.08	0.1
BERT	0.66	0.65	0.65

Table 2: Performance of the models on the test set. Note that the transformer-based architecture fares much better than the feature-base one. Also note that the test set contains unaltered essays, as opposed to the diagnostic set.

	Feature-Based		BERT	
Name Groups	Accuracy	Recall	Accuracy	Recall
Swedish	0.14	0.20	0.86	0.60
Finnish	0.14	0.20	0.86	0.60
Anglo-American	0.14	0.20	0.86	0.60
Arabic	0.14	0.20	0.86	0.60

Table 3: Performance of the models on the diagnostics set. Note that both the accuracy and the recall are the same for all ethnic groups. Also note that the diagnostic set contains the essays with the substituted names, as opposed to the test set.

Name Groups	Feature-Based	BERT
Swedish	0.0	0.0
Finnish	0.0	0.0
Anglo-American	0.0	0.0
Arabic	0.0	0.0

Table 4: Equality of opportunity results for the different name groups chosen. Note that the values are zero for all, meaning that the models do not discriminate based on these names for the essays in the diagnostic set.

els, text genres, and who the name refers to, we still had a small amount of essays to work with. Antoniak and Mimno (2021) note that the choice of seeds for measuring bias can affect the results of such measurements. Thus, using more essays would be good way to verify that our results indeed generalize. However, none of the essays in SweLL-pilot are fit for the criteria we mentioned in Section 3.1 so this would require either gathering new data or generating synthetic data. It is also important to take into account that the size of the diagnostic dataset scales quickly, as it gets 80 new datapoints for each new essay we add.

It is important to note that these results do not mean that neither the base model nor the training data contain biases. They just mean that we did not find biases when using them for the AES task. It has been noted before that intrinsic and extrinsic biases do not necessarily correlate with each other (Goldfarb-Tarrant et al., 2021). That is, just because we did not find biases on our specific task, that does not mean that one can assume that neither Swedish BERT nor the SweLL-pilot are bias-free. That is, we cannot use them for other tasks or applications without worrying about bias or fairness.

5 Conclusions and Future Work

In this work we examined how changing given names within the text of second language learner essays of Swedish affects the CEFR level they are assigned to by the models. We found that changing the names did not change the performance of the model in any noticeable way across four different name groups with twenty names each.

This points to our models learning to differentiate the level of an essay based on linguistic characteristics, as opposed to the kind of personal identifiable information found within the essays, such as given names. Because of this, we think that pseudonymization should be considered as a viable method to allow for research data to be used and shared.

However, it is important to note that these results could vary from language to language and from dataset to dataset. There is no silver bullet to solve the bias issue in NLP, as it is deeply ingrained within human perception and the data we generate, which can lead to unexpected results (Wang et al., 2019-10). Moreover, it is possible that the chosen given names and ehtnic groups could have had an impact on our results, as argued by Antoniak and Mimno (2021). This would be particularly important when considering people coming from regions under-represented in our data, as they are the most at risk of being the most affected by discrimination, be it from humans or from machines.

There are several directions in which our work could be expanded to. One would be to use more essays for the diagnostic dataset. As mentioned in Section 4, this would require either acquiring new essays or generating synthetic data, both of which can be challenging tasks.

Another possible direction to expand our work to would be to do an in-depth analysis of the given names appearing both in different corpora as well as in the training data of the different models. This would allow us to verify that the lack of perceptible bias we found was not due to the names not appearing on the data.

Both of these could be used as a paving stone to create guidelines on how to generate diagnostic datasets to identify biases in automated essay scoring of second language learner essays. It would be particularly interesting to analyze whether the same patterns hold for different kinds of personal identifiable information, such as other kinds of personal names and places. Moreover, it would be good to check whether this apparent lack of bias is maintained when dealing with several pieces of private information at the same time.

Ethics Statement

Different kinds of data are more likely to contain personal information. This impacts how the data can be used in an ethical way for research. Written consent was obtained during the collection process of the essays from the SweLL-pilot corpus and the data was processed in accordance to the GDPR. The original, non-anonymized data is used strictly within the project, with the real names of the authors of the essays never being disclosed. At the moment in which the data was originally gathered and released, there was no requirement of ethical review.

Special care was put when selecting both the ethnic groups to include and the names belonging to these, as noted in Section 3.2. As mentioned, both of these were chosen to represent some of the most commonly ocurring names in which we would expect AES for second language assessment to occur. While this would showcase any systemic biases that could occur at scale, it ignores under-represented minorities which tend to be the most affected by these kind of things. Thus, it is of utmost importance that if any such system were to be put to use on any potentially life-changing situation, care should be taken to show that even these minorities are assessed in a fair and unbiased manner.

Even though our study strongly points to a lack of biases regarding given names appearing in the text of the essays, any such systems should be continuously monitored to avoid biases appearing seemingly out of nowhere. The use of different datasets and of different methodologies could lead to different results, especially considering how these things might drift over time. Moreover, any high-stakes applications should still have a human-in-the-loop approach so as to ensure that test-takers have access to their rights of explanation and of revision.

Acknowledgements

This work has been possible thanks to the funding of two grants from the Swedish Research Council.

The project *Grandma Karl is 27 years old: Automatic pseudonymization of research data* has funding number 2022-02311 for the years 2023-2029.

The Swedish national research infrastructure *Nationella Språkbanken* is funded jointly by contract number 2017-00626 for the years 2018-2024, as well 10 participating partner institutions.

References

Emilia Aldrin. 2017. Assessing Names? Effects of Name-Based Stereotypes on Teachers' Evaluations of Pupils' Texts. *Names*, 65(1):3–14.

Afra Alishahi, Yonatan Belinkov, Grzegorz Chrupała, Dieuwke Hupkes, Yuval Pinter, and Hassan Sajjad, editors. 2020. *Proceedings of the Third BlackboxNLP Workshop on Analyzing and Interpreting Neural Networks for NLP*. Association for Computational Linguistics, Online.

Association of Language Testers in Europe ALTE. 2020. ALTE Principles of Good Practice.

Tracy N Anderson-Clark, Raymond J Green, and Tracy B Henley. 2008. The relationship between first names and teacher expectations for achievement motivation. *Journal of Language and Social Psychology*, 27(1):94–99.

Maria Antoniak and David Mimno. 2021. Bad seeds: Evaluating lexical methods for bias measurement. In *Proceedings of the 59th Annual Meeting of the Association for Computational Linguistics and the 11th International Joint Conference on Natural Language Processing (Volume 1: Long Papers)*, pages

1889–1904, Online. Association for Computational Linguistics.

American Speech-Language-Hearing Association ASLHA. 2023. Rights and Responsibilities of Test Takers: Guidelines and Expectations.

Su Lin Blodgett, Solon Barocas, Hal Daumé III, and Hanna Wallach. 2020. Language (technology) is power: A critical survey of "bias" in NLP. In *Proceedings of the 58th Annual Meeting of the Association for Computational Linguistics*, pages 5454–5476, Online. Association for Computational Linguistics.

Aylin Caliskan, Joanna J. Bryson, and Arvind Narayanan. 2017. Semantics derived automatically from language corpora contain human-like biases. *Science*, 356(6334):183–186. Publisher: American Association for the Advancement of Science Section: Reports.

COE Council of Europe. 2001. *Common European Framework of Reference for languages: Learning, teaching, assessment*. Cambridge University Press.

Jacob Devlin, Ming-Wei Chang, Kenton Lee, and Kristina Toutanova. 2019. BERT: Pre-training of deep bidirectional transformers for language understanding. In *Proceedings of the 2019 Conference of the North American Chapter of the Association for Computational Linguistics: Human Language Technologies, Volume 1 (Long and Short Papers)*, pages 4171–4186, Minneapolis, Minnesota. Association for Computational Linguistics.

EU EU Commission. 2016. *General data protection regulation*. Official Journal of the European Union, 59, 1-88.

David N Figlio. 2003. Names, expectations and black children's achievement. *Unpublished manuscript*.

Gigi Foster. 2008. Names will never hurt me: Racially distinct names and identity in the undergraduate classroom. *Social science research*, 37(3):934–952.

Doreen Gerritzen. 2007. First names of moroccan and turkish immigrants in the netherlands. In Eva Brylla and Mats Wahlberg, editors, *Proceedings of the International Congress of Onomastic Sciences 21, Uppsala August 2002*, pages 120–130. SOFI (Språk- och folkminnesinstitutet, Institute for Dialectology, Onomastics and Folklore Research).

Seraphina Goldfarb-Tarrant, Adam Lopez, Roi Blanco, and Diego Marcheggiani. 2023. Bias beyond English: Counterfactual tests for bias in sentiment analysis in four languages. In *Findings of the Association for Computational Linguistics: ACL 2023*, pages 4458–4468, Toronto, Canada. Association for Computational Linguistics.

Seraphina Goldfarb-Tarrant, Rebecca Marchant, Ricardo Muñoz Sánchez, Mugdha Pandya, and Adam Lopez. 2021. Intrinsic bias metrics do not correlate with application bias. In *Proceedings of the 59th Annual Meeting of the Association for Computational Linguistics and the 11th International Joint Conference on Natural Language Processing (Volume 1: Long Papers)*, pages 1926–1940, Online. Association for Computational Linguistics.

Hila Gonen and Yoav Goldberg. 2019. Lipstick on a pig: Debiasing methods cover up systematic gender biases in word embeddings but do not remove them. In *Proceedings of the 2019 Conference of the North American Chapter of the Association for Computational Linguistics: Human Language Technologies, Volume 1 (Long and Short Papers)*, pages 609–614, Minneapolis, Minnesota. Association for Computational Linguistics.

Anthony G Greenwald, Mahzarin R Banaji, and Brian A Nosek. 2015. Statistically small effects of the Implicit Association Test can have societally large effects. *American Psychological Association*.

Anthony G Greenwald and Linda Hamilton Krieger. 2006. Implicit bias: Scientific foundations. *California law review*, 94(4):945–967.

Linnea Gustafsson. 2021. Syriska förnamn i sverige. en första kartläggning. In *Navn på minoritetsspråk i muntlige og skriftlige sammenhenger*, volume 99, pages 55–68. Sámi allaskuvla / Sámi University of Applied Sciences, NORNA-förlaget. Conference Name: 49th NORNA-symposium: Minority Names in Oral and Written Contexts in a Multi-Cultural World, Guovdageaidnu (Kautokeino), Norway, 24–25 april, 2019 Publisher: Sámi allaskuvla Accepted: 2022-02-22T08:18:55Z ISSN: 0332-7779 Journal Abbreviation: Minoritehtagielaid namat njálmmálaš ja čálalaš oktavuođain Publication Title: 276.

Moritz Hardt, Eric Price, and Nathan Srebro. 2016. Equality of opportunity in supervised learning. In *Proceedings of the 30th International Conference on Neural Information Processing Systems*, NIPS'16, pages 3323–3331. Curran Associates Inc.

Michael T Kane. 2001. Current concerns in validity theory. *Journal of educational Measurement*, 38(4):319–342.

Anastassia Loukina, Nitin Madnani, and Klaus Zechner. 2019. The many dimensions of algorithmic fairness in educational applications. In *Proceedings of the Fourteenth Workshop on Innovative Use of NLP for Building Educational Applications*, pages 1–10.

Nitin Madnani, Anastassia Loukina, Alina Von Davier, Jill Burstein, and Aoife Cahill. 2017. Building better open-source tools to support fairness in automated scoring. In *Proceedings of the first ACL workshop on ethics in natural language processing*, pages 41–52.

Ylva Malm and Pontus Zetterström. 2007. *Kevins konnotationer - skillnader i högstadielärares associationer till tio olika förnamn*. Örebro University.

Martin Malmsten, Love Börjeson, and Chris Haffenden. 2020. Playing with words at the national library of sweden – making a swedish bert.

Marta Marchiori Manerba, Riccardo Guidotti, Lucia Passaro, and Salvatore Ruggieri. 2022. Bias discovery within human raters: A case study of the jigsaw dataset. In *Proceedings of the 1st Workshop on Perspectivist Approaches to NLP @LREC2022*, pages 26–31, Marseille, France. European Language Resources Association.

Pranav Narayanan Venkit, Sanjana Gautam, Ruchi Panchanadikar, Ting-Hao Huang, and Shomir Wilson. 2023. Nationality bias in text generation. In *Proceedings of the 17th Conference of the European Chapter of the Association for Computational Linguistics*, pages 116–122, Dubrovnik, Croatia. Association for Computational Linguistics.

Ildikó Pilán, Elena Volodina, and Torsten Zesch. 2016. Predicting proficiency levels in learner writings by transferring a linguistic complexity model from expert-written coursebooks. In *Proceedings of COLING 2016, the 26th International Conference on Computational Linguistics: Technical Papers*, pages 2101–2111, Osaka, Japan. The COLING 2016 Organizing Committee.

Carsten Roever and Tim McNamara. 2006. Language testing: The social dimension. *International Journal of Applied Linguistics*, 16(2):242–258.

Sandra Sandoval, Jieyu Zhao, Marine Carpuat, and Hal Daumé III. 2023. A rose by any other name would not smell as sweet: Social bias in names mistranslation. In *Proceedings of the 2023 Conference on Empirical Methods in Natural Language Processing*, pages 3933–3945, Singapore. Association for Computational Linguistics.

Maarten Sap, Dallas Card, Saadia Gabriel, Yejin Choi, and Noah A. Smith. 2019. The risk of racial bias in hate speech detection. In *Proceedings of the 57th Annual Meeting of the Association for Computational Linguistics*, pages 1668–1678, Florence, Italy. Association for Computational Linguistics.

Harini Suresh and John Guttag. 2021. A framework for understanding sources of harm throughout the machine learning life cycle. In *Proceedings of the 1st ACM Conference on Equity and Access in Algorithms, Mechanisms, and Optimization*, EAAMO '21, New York, NY, USA. Association for Computing Machinery.

Elena Volodina. 2024. On two SweLL learner corpora – SweLL-pilot and SweLL-gold. *Huminfra Conference*, pages 83–94.

Elena Volodina, Ildikó Pilán, Ingegerd Enström, Lorena Llozhi, Peter Lundkvist, Gunlög Sundberg, and Monica Sandell. 2016a. SweLL on the rise: Swedish learner language corpus for European reference level studies. In *Proceedings of the Tenth International Conference on Language Resources and Evaluation (LREC'16)*, pages 206–212, Portorož, Slovenia. European Language Resources Association (ELRA).

Elena Volodina, Ildikó Pilán, and David Alfter. 2016b. Classification of Swedish learner essays by CEFR levels. In *CALL communities and culture – short papers from EUROCALL 2016*, pages 456–461. Research-publishing.net.

Jun Wang, Benjamin Rubinstein, and Trevor Cohn. 2022. Measuring and mitigating name biases in neural machine translation. In *Proceedings of the 60th Annual Meeting of the Association for Computational Linguistics (Volume 1: Long Papers)*, pages 2576–2590, Dublin, Ireland. Association for Computational Linguistics.

Tianlu Wang, Jieyu Zhao, Mark Yatskar, Kai-Wei Chang, and Vicente Ordonez. 2019-10. Balanced datasets are not enough: Estimating and mitigating gender bias in deep image representations. In *2019 IEEE/CVF International Conference on Computer Vision (ICCV)*, pages 5309–5318. ISSN: 2380-7504.

Jieyu Zhao, Tianlu Wang, Mark Yatskar, Vicente Ordonez, and Kai-Wei Chang. 2018. Gender bias in coreference resolution: Evaluation and debiasing methods. In *Proceedings of the 2018 Conference of the North American Chapter of the Association for Computational Linguistics: Human Language Technologies, Volume 2 (Short Papers)*, pages 15–20, New Orleans, Louisiana. Association for Computational Linguistics.

A Essays Used for Diagnostics Purposes

The following are the IDs for the essays chosen for diagnostic purposes:

- S143ST18
- S147ST18
- S42ST9
- S53ST12
- W13WT2
- W53WT5
- W2WT2

B Lists of Names Used

This appendix contains Tables 5, 6, 7, and 8. These four tables show the names used for each group in this study.

Female	Male
Anna	Lars
Eva	Mikael
Maria	Anders
Karin	Johan
Sara	Erik
Christina	Karl
Lena	Per
Emma	Olof
Kerstin	Nils
Marie	Jan

Table 5: List with the Swedish names chosen for this study, as specified in Section 3.2.

Female	Male
Hannele	Juhani
Marjatta	Eino
Maarit	Olavi
Annikki	Antero
Aurora	Tapani
Aino	Kalevi
Helmi	Tapio
Ilona	Matti
Minna	Ilmari
Sari	Onni

Table 6: List with the Finnish names chosen for this study, as specified in Section 3.2.

Female	Male
Mary	Kevin
Patricia	James
Jennifer	Charles
Nancy	John
Betty	Matthew
Barbara	Anthony
Susan	William
Jessica	Donald
Ashley	Steven
Karen	Brian

Table 7: List with the Anglo-American names chosen for this study, as specified in Section 3.2.

Female	Male
Fatima	Muhammad
Hala	Ali
Amal	Ahmed
Mariam	Ibrahim
Hiba	Hassan
Huda	Mahmoud
Khadija	Omar
Mirna	Abdullah
Samira	Ismail
Fatemeh	Hamza

Table 8: List with the Arabic names chosen for this study, as specified in Section 3.2.

Author Index

Altuna, Begoña, 18
Aramaki, Eiji, 8
Azizi, Masha, 64

Budrionis, Andrius, 37

Cabrera-Diego, Luis Adrián, 25
Chomutare, Taridzo, 37

Dalianis, Hercules, 37, 76
Dobnik, Simon, 54, 81

Gardiner, Shayna, 64
Gheewala, Akshita, 25
Gonzalez-Agirre, Aitor, 44
Gonzalez-Dios, Itziar, 18

Habib, Tania, 64
Henriksson, Aron, 76
Hullmann, Tyr, 76
Humphreys, Kevin, 64

Lindström Tiedemann, Therese, 54, 81

Mailhot, Frederic, 64
Mina, Mario, 44
Muñoz Sánchez, Ricardo, 54, 81

Ngo, Phuong, 37
Nishiyama, Tomohiro, 8

Olsen Svenning, Therese, 37

Paling, Anne, 64

Raithel, Lisa, 8
Rodríguez, Carlos, 44
Roller, Roland, 8

Sierro, Maria, 18
Simancek, Dalton, 1
Szawerna, Maria Irena, 54, 81

Tejedor, Miguel, 37
Thomas, Preston, 64

Vakili, Thomas, 76
Villegas, Marta, 44
Volodina, Elena, 54, 81
Vydiswaran, VG Vinod, 1

Zhang, Nathan, 64
Zweigenbaum, Pierre, 8

Association for Computational Linguistics
209 N. Eighth Street
Stroudsburg, Pennsylvania 18360

ISBN 978-1-7138-9448-3

CURRAN ASSOCIATES INC.
proceedings.com